Carthage
fact and myth

edited by

Roald Docter
Ridha Boussoffara
Pieter ter Keurs

COLOPHON

Graphic Design
Atelier Lukes, Leiden

Cover Design
Atelier Lukes & Sidestone Press, Leiden. Cover design based on Carthage campaign designed by DoubleMatured, Leiden

Photography cover (front)
Anneke de Kemp and Peter Jan Bomhof (Dutch National Museum of Antiquities): Statue Goddess with lion head;
Canonman29 | dreamstime.com: Ruins of Roman Carthage, Baths of Antoninus Pius

Photography (book)
Anneke de Kemp and Peter Jan Bomhof (Dutch National Museum of Antiquities), unless otherwise stated

English Translation
Beverley Jackson

Printed by
HRG, Czech Republic

Coördination in Tunesia
Ridha Boussoffara

Transport
Tunis Air

Text credits
The text of chapter 2 is largely based on previous publications by Docter 2002/2003; 2005b; 2009; 2013; the text of chapter 9 is based on an article about Hannibal published in Lampas (Docter 2005c)

Project leader
Tanja van der Zon

Project assistent
Inge den Oudsten

The exhibition contained objects on loan from
Musée National du Bardo, Musée National de Carthage, the Louvre, the British Museum, the Soprintendenza del Mare, Palermo, the Nederlandsche Bank (Dutch National Bank), the Rijksmuseum in Amsterdam, Leiden University, the Allard Pierson Museum, the Eye Film Museum, the Koninklijke Bibliotheek (Royal Library), the Groninger Museum (Veenkoloniaal Museum Veendam), the Koninklijk Oudheidkundig Genootschap, Museum Boymans van Beuningen and a private collection (Leuven)

© 2015 Roald Docter, Ridha Boussoffara and Pieter ter Keurs

Published by Sidestone Press, Leiden
www.sidestone.com

ISBN 978-90-8890-311-3

CONTENTS

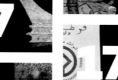

NS AGO

Roman Carthage from 146 BC

After the destruction of Carthage in 146 BC at first the intention was to never rebuild the city again. After some time this changed. Under emperor Augustus the new Roman Carthage quickly grew into a metropole. Again the city became the pivot of an extended trading network. In the Christian era, Carthage remained a city of importance.

PREFACE

In March 1796, the Dutch military engineer Jean-Émile Humbert (1771-1839) arrived in Tunis. He had been hired by Hamouda Pasha, the Bey van Tunis, to modernise the city and large sections of the fortifications. When not busy with his official activities, Humbert pursued an interest in archaeology, particularly in relation to Ancient Carthage. His long stay in what is now called Tunisia would eventually produce spectacular results.

Humbert would become known as the man who rediscovered Punic Carthage, collecting large numbers of Punic and Roman antiquities for the National Museum of Antiquities in Leiden. These included large statues of Roman emperors, which Humbert shipped via Utica to Leiden with the Bey's permission. The Punic stelae he discovered, which made it possible to pinpoint the location of Ancient Carthage, also found their way to Leiden.

In the partnership between the Institut National du Patrimoine in Tunis and the National Museum of Antiquities in Leiden, the long-standing ties between Tunisia and the Netherlands play an important role. Historical ties alone cannot sustain a partnership in the 21st century, however. Both partners are well aware of this, and are constantly searching for vibrant and inspiring modes of cooperation. The exhibition on Carthage at the museum in Leiden is one result – a visible testimony to this relationship. In 2015 a sequel to this exhibition will open at the Musée National de Carthage, in the form of an exhibition on Jean-Émile Humbert.

Every country attaches importance to the fascinating details of the history in which it is rooted. For Tunisia, where great political changes are taking place at the moment, the past is an essential part of the present. Our partnership plays an important role in this. We are proud of this role, and look forward to setting up many more activities in the future.

In 1963 a collaborative venture between the National Museum of Antiquities and the Musée National du Bardo produced an exhibition on mosaics. The current event is the first exhibition about Carthage ever to be held in the Netherlands.

Most of the items on display as part of the Leiden exhibition, aside from the National Museum of Antiquities' own collection, come from the collections of the Musée National du Bardo and the Musée National de Carthage. In addition, objects were provided on loan by the Louvre, the British Museum, Soprintendenza del mare, Palermo, De Nederlandse Bank, the Rijksmuseum, Amsterdam, the University of Leiden, the Allard Pierson Museum, Eye Film Institute, the National Library of the Netherlands (Koninklijke Bibliotheek), the Royal Antiquarian Society, Groningen, Museum (Veenkoloniaal Museum, Veendam), Museum Boymans van Beuningen, and a private collection in Leuven. We should like to thank all lenders for their generosity in making parts of their collection available for this exhibition.

Nabil Kallala
Institut National du Patrimoine
Tunis

Wim Weijland
National Museum of Antiquities
Leiden

The exhibition 'Carthago' in the Dutch National Museum of Antiquities in Leiden, was open to the public from 27 November 2014 to 10 May 2015. It consisted of three parts. The first room presented the story of Punic Carthage from its founding in the ninth century B.C. to the end of the Second Punic War in 201 B.C. The second room started with Cato's campaign for the destruction of Carthage and mainly dealt with the Roman period. Separately, there was a presentation on the history of archaeological research in Carthage, from the rediscovery by Jean-Émile Humbert (1817) to the work of archaeologists from the University of Amsterdam in 2000/2001.

The exhibition was made possible by the support of the Institut National du Patrimoine in Tunis. Many important loans came from the Musée National du Bardo and the Musée National de Carthage.

Punic and Roman ruins on Byrsa Hill. In the background we can just make out the cathedral that the French Missionaries for Africa had built on the hill. Today, the cathedral's spire is the highest point of the Byrsa.

1

CARTHAGE: FACT AND MYTH

Pieter ter Keurs

ANCIENT CARTHAGE PLAYED AN IMPORTANT PART IN THE CULTURAL HISTORY OF THE MEDITERRANEAN REGION AND OF EUROPE. ITS IMPORTANCE WAS NOT LIMITED TO THE CITY–STATE'S LONG HEYDAY, FROM APPROXIMATELY THE FIFTH TO THE SECOND CENTURY BC; CARTHAGINIAN CULTURE REMAINED IMPORTANT LONG AFTER THAT, EXERCISING A STRONG APPEAL TO THE IMAGINATION. EUROPEAN RULERS AND MILITARY LEADERS DREW INSPIRATION FROM ITS HISTORY. OVER THE CENTURIES, ARTISTS PRODUCED PRINTS, MUSIC, FILMS AND NOVELS THAT KEPT THE CITY–STATE'S FASCINATING PAST ALIVE, FREQUENTLY INFUSED WITH CONTEMPORARY MORALISTIC MESSAGES.

The city of Carthage, on the north coast of present–day Tunisia, is said to have been founded in the ninth century BC by Phoenician merchants from Tyre (now in Lebanon). There are several versions of the myth describing the city's origin. In all these versions, the Lebanese Phoenician Elissa (whom the Romans called Dido) plays a key role. Forced to flee from Tyre for political reasons, along with a few followers, Elissa journeyed by way of Cyprus to the West. The small company eventually disembarked on the coast of North Africa, where Elissa negotiated with the local ruler to acquire a piece of land. By means of a clever trick (see chapter 3), Elissa obtained far more land than had been intended, but the local population accepted it and Carthage was founded. By a few hundred years later, the city had become one of the wealthiest and most prosperous of the Mediterranean. Its strategic location gave Carthage the opportunity to become the nexus of a range of commercial networks, in frequent competition with others, such as the Greeks, but also in harmony with groups such as African merchants from the south and Etruscans to the north.

Although the myth described above contains many elements that bear little relation to reality, the core of the story appears to be correct. For centuries the Carthaginians undertook annual trade missions to Tyre, partly to offer sacrifices to the city's gods, in a clear recognition of Tyre as the 'mother city'. In North Africa itself, it must have been clear for a very long time that the Carthaginians were immigrants. After all, until the fifth century BC they paid rent to the local population for the land on which they lived. They only stopped doing so once they considered themselves strong enough to be able to resist any local opposition to the cessation of payments. It should be noted that the inscriptions on steles in graveyards – even as late as in Roman times – continued to be written in Phoenician script, and contained references to Phoenician gods. This is another clear reference to the origins of the population of Carthage.

Even so, Carthaginian culture is frequently referred to not as Phoenician but as Punic. Possibly the very word 'Punic' had a derogatory meaning. However, Carthage had a hybrid culture that consisted not only of Phoenician elements. It included influences from Africa, from Greece, from the Etruscans, and from Spain. This wide range of external influences left their imprint on everyday life and religious practices in Carthage from a very early stage: Egyptian gods were depicted and worshipped, and Carthaginian products reflect Greek influences and features of cultural expressions from the Eastern Mediterranean region, such as Cyprus. In truth, the hybrid culture of Carthage merits a particular name of its own, but archaeologists generally opt to call it Punic.

The importance of trade made Carthage a vibrant multicultural centre. People flocked to this prosperous city–state both from the African hinterland and from overseas trade regions. It is difficult to estimate the precise size of its population, but some 300,000 to 400,000 people are believed to have lived in Carthage during the various peaks in its prosperity. It was a huge metropolis, in the heart of which were houses with several storeys,

Goddess with lion's head; Tinissut; 1st century AD; Musée National du Bardo.

Some researchers have identified this goddess as Tanit. This seems improbable, since Tanit is generally depicted far more abstractly. The figure might be an expression of Egyptian influence. Many of its features recall those of the goddess Sekhmet. In the Roman period, such figures were seen as personifications of Africa.

> *'Hannibal's district'.
Part of the ruins of
Carthage, with a
view of the suburbs
of Tunis. This part of
Punic Carthage was
built in the time when
the city was ruled by
Hannibal.*

∨ *Signet ring, woman
with bird; Carthage,
necropolis in the
vicinity of Sainte–
Monique; 3rd century
BC; Musée National de
Carthage.*

arts and crafts aplenty, and a flourishing religious life with particular attention for the gods venerated in Tyre. Carthage was protected by robust walls, and from the second century BC it possessed a characteristic harbour, composed of a rectangular commercial and a circular military harbour, which are still visible in the landscape today.

The Carthaginian fleet was invincible in the Mediterranean until the First Punic War. On the Italian mainland, however, Rome was a power that could not be ignored. The Romans' interest in Sicily brought them into conflict with the Carthaginians, who included the entire western part of the island within their sphere of influence. In 264 BC the tension exploded into open conflict in the First Punic War, with Rome largely prevailing on land and Carthage at sea. The crushing defeat of the Carthaginian fleet off the coast of Sicily was therefore utterly unexpected (see chapter 7). Rome had become unassailable, and the power of Carthage would gradually decline.

Then, during the Second Punic War (218-201 BC), the most famous Carthaginian of all time appeared on the scene: Hannibal. Born in 247 or 246 BC as the son of the general Hamilcar, Hannibal was more or less predestined for a military career. While still young he followed his father to Spain and witnessed the successful campaigns that consolidated the Carthaginian presence on the Iberian peninsula. The Carthaginians had had trade settlements in southern Spain for centuries, but under Hamilcar came a great wave of territorial expansion. After Hamilcar's death, Hannibal's brother initially took over as commander of the armies, but when he was killed in battle, Hannibal – though still a young man – became the unchallenged leader of the Carthaginian armies in Spain (see chapter 9).

Hannibal's military expedition through Spain to northern Europe, first crossing the Rhône and then marching over the Alps to northern Italy, took the Romans completely by surprise. They had already tried to halt Hannibal's army in Spain and France, but after this they had 'lost track of it'. When the army suddenly appeared in northern Italy, complete with a herd of elephants, the Romans suffered a severe psychological shock. Hannibal dealt a series of defeats to Roman forces and threatened Rome itself, but was unable to clinch victory.

With the counter–attack through Spain to North Africa, the Romans finally turned the tables on the Carthaginians. The Roman general Scipio Africanus defeated Hannibal in 202 BC at Zama, to the southwest of Carthage.

At the end of the Third Punic War, in 146 BC, Carthage was laid waste by the Roman troops. The glorious era of this proud city–state was over, never to revive.

Since few written sources from Punic Carthage have been preserved, there are many gaps in the existing historiography. While archaeolog-

ical research can fill in parts of Carthaginian history in greater detail, the picture remains fragmentary, leaving many questions unanswered. Partly because of this, the reality is often obscured by the mythical past. Sometimes the picture painted is dominated by aggression, violence and child sacrifices (for instance in the work of the French novelist Gustave Flaubert), while at other times Carthage is glorified. Some writers discuss the democratic nature of the city–state's governance, or the fact that the first agricultural treatise is said to have been written there (by Mago, a manuscript of which only fragments have survived, in Latin translation rather than the Punic original).

While it is true that Carthage had a range of administrative bodies within which affairs of state could be debated at length, decisions were mainly the prerogative of the wealthiest families. Later on there was a kind of representative body that was able to enforce its will in certain issues, for instance regarding the appointment of military leaders, but there was probably no democratic governance with voting rights for the population.

Slave bracelet; Bulla Regia; 4th century AD; Musée National du Bardo.

The Carthaginians imported large numbers of slaves from regions such as Central Africa for domestic and agricultural work.

As for Mago's treatise on agriculture, it should not be seen solely in the context of an idealisation of the land and rural life. On the one hand, it was a practical manual on agriculture, and on the other hand, it reflected the custom of Carthage's wealthy elite to build mansions in the countryside, while administering and deriving profit from the surrounding estates. The land was fertile and hence yielded a welcome supplementary income, frequently achieved by the deployment of numerous slaves. Carthage long had a reputation as the granary of the Roman Empire.

Carthage would endure for a long time. After the devastation the city was rebuilt by the Romans and enjoyed a new period of great prosperity. Later in the Byzantine period, too, Carthage remained important. After that, however, Tunis would emerge as the major city in this part of North Africa. Many houses and other buildings would be constructed using stones from Carthage, which gradually slipped into decline as a result. By the end of the eighteenth century, when the Dutchmen Jean–Émile Humbert was hired as a civil engineer by the Bey of Tunis, Hammouda Pacha, the location of the ancient Punic city of Carthage was no longer known. It appeared to have vanished from the face of the earth (see chapter 14).

In the course of the nineteenth century, however, Dutch, Danish, French and British archaeologists discovered more and more about the city's past. Even today, we are still steadily expanding our stock of knowledge of the location, infrastructure and material culture of Carthage. Much work remains to be done, and we may not be able to fill in every blank. Still, however rudimentary our understanding of Carthaginian material culture, we should bear in mind that Carthage never disappeared entirely. It endures in the collective memory of the local population, and in the European imagination it indeed plays a leading role. In prints produced in the sixteenth to eighteenth centuries we find a wealth of images representing Carthaginian mythical themes, generally with some moralistic import. Great rulers and military leaders identified with generals from the Punic wars. Charles V, who was eager to conquer parts of North Africa, modelled his ambitions on Scipio Africanus. Napoleon saw himself as marching in the footsteps of Hannibal, in his expedition across the Alps. Carthage still appeals to the popular imagination to this day. The history of this city–state and its position in the Mediterranean region is evidently a living legend.

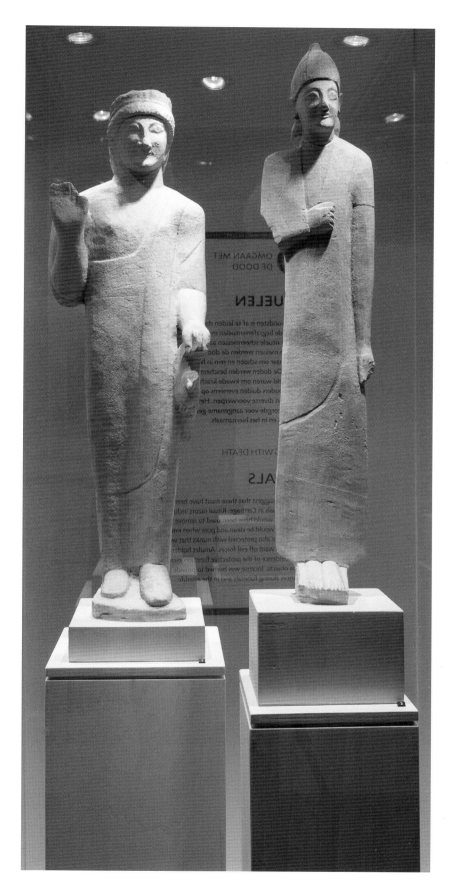

Statues from Idalion, Cyprus. Collection British Museum, London (photo: E. van den Bandt).

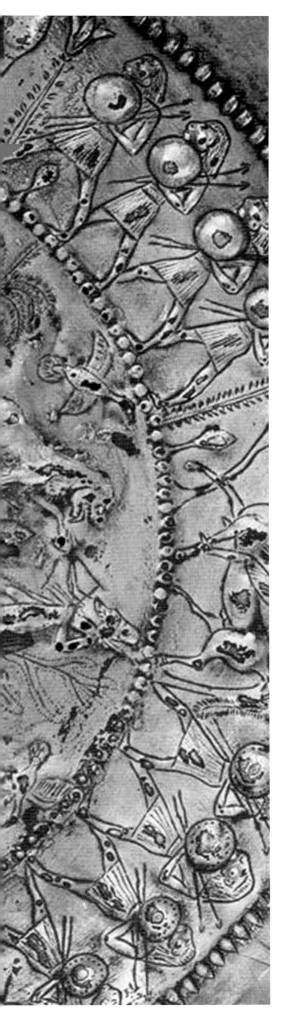

*Phoenician silver–gilt
dish. c. 700-675 BC.
National Museum of
Antiquities, Leiden.*

2

PHOENICIA: FROM PLACE OF TRANSIT TO TRADING NATION

....

Lucas P. Petit

ACCORDING TO THE GREEKS, THE BOATS THAT OCCASIONALLY PUT IN ALONG THEIR SHORES CAME FROM PHOENICIA, THE REGION THAT ROUGHLY CORRESPONDS TO PRESENT–DAY LEBANON. THEY WERE MANNED BY GIFTED MERCHANTS, THE PHOENICIANS. IN SPITE OF THEIR LIMITED TERRITORY, WITH JUST A HANDFUL OF MAJOR CITIES, THEY CONTROLLED THE MEDITERRANEAN SEA FROM THE TENTH CENTURY BC ONWARDS AND FOUNDED NUMEROUS NEW CITIES, AMONG THEM THE POWERFUL PORT OF CARTHAGE. THE STORY OF A SMALL NATION THAT PLACED ITS STAMP ON THE HISTORY OF THE MEDITERRANEAN IS ONE THAT TRULY FIRES THE IMAGINATION.

Canaan and Lebanon

From archaeological research and very early texts, we know that Phoenicia was a strategic location in the ancient Near East as far back as the third millennium BC. The coastal region was a narrow fertile corridor through which everything and everyone – most notably merchants – had to pass on the way to Anatolia, Mesopotamia and Egypt. On clay tablets found in Ebla in present–day Syria, this coastal strip is called *Ganane* (Canaan) or *Labanaan* (Lebanon), and its biggest city was Gubla. This city is better known by its Greek name of Byblos/Βύβλος. It has been said that this was an Egyptian settlement, but it may have merely been a place of transit for cedarwood and lapis lazuli. Archaeological remains prove that there were in any case close and frequent ties with Egypt in this period. Other major settlements around this time were those of Sidon and Tyre. This means that over a thousand years before the first references in the sources to Phoenician merchants, their ancestors were already playing a key role in the economy of the ancient Near East. Around 2200 BC these coastal cities sank into a malaise and were abandoned. Like other cities, they were unable to respond adequately to the severe regional crisis that was caused, among other things, by deteriorating climate conditions. This led to major economic and political tensions in the region, partly caused by waves of migration.

An Egyptian Place of Transit

At the beginning of the second millennium BC, most of the cities in the coastal region experienced a revival. Byblos still proved to be of great strategic importance to Egypt. Sumptuous graves filled with gold and silver have been found in the city, and the Egyptian–inspired Obelisk Temple, where the city–goddess Ba'alat–Gubla was worshipped, dates from the second millennium BC. Much of our information about this period comes from the Egyptian correspondence archives at El–Amarna. These archives are a vast storehouse of diplomatic correspondence on clay tablets between Egyptian and foreign officials, including inhabitants of the cities of Tyre and Byblos, and provide a unique picture of the economic life of the fourteenth century BC. We learn from these texts that cities in Phoenicia were crucial partners and trading centres for the Egyptian Pharaoh.

Sarcophagus of Ahiram, with decorations and inscriptions honouring the memory of Ahiram, King of Byblos.

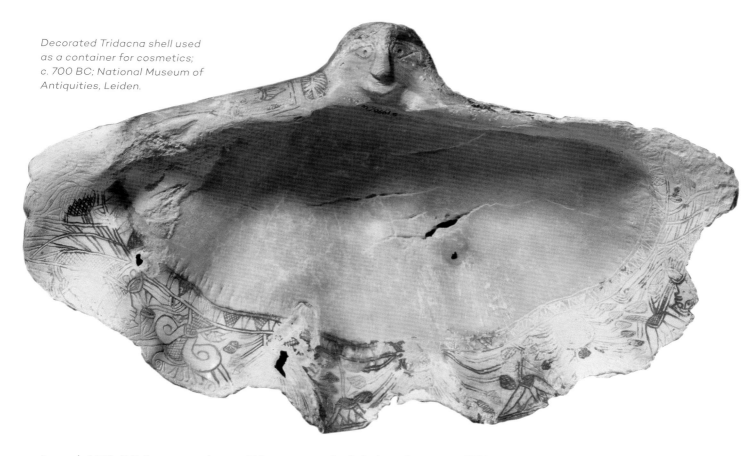

Decorated Tridacna shell used as a container for cosmetics; c. 700 BC; National Museum of Antiquities, Leiden.

Around 1200 BC began an almost 200–year period of decline during which many of the important cities of the Near East crumbled into ruins. The explanation for the turbulence may lie, perhaps, in the diverse regional changes: the Egyptian Empire had collapsed, the Israelites were strengthening their power base in the Southern Levant, the Philistines and other maritime peoples settled in the coastal region, and the Arameans conquered large swathes of what had been Canaan. While many other settlements, especially those within the Philistines' direct sphere of influence, were abandoned, the Phoenician cities withstood the pressures of the times. They certainly suffered from the tense situation in the eastern Mediterranean, but Phoenician society did not collapse. There are some indications that trade continued in this period, not only with the interior, but also with the islands and coastal regions in the Mediterranean. Nonetheless, there was certainly a shift in the balance of power: Sidon had taken over from Byblos as the most important city in Phoenicia. It was in this period that the Phoenician language and script developed and became disseminated.

A Very Early Alphabet

Phoenician is a Semitic language, which strongly resembles the (later) Aramaic and biblical Hebrew. Of particular interest was its use of an alphabetical script consisting of twenty–two letters. There was a kind of alphabet in Ugarit as far back as the fifteenth century, which used cuneiform script, but most linguists assume that Phoenician script derives from the Proto–Sinaitic of the Middle and Late Bronze Age

TYPICAL PHOENICIAN CRAFTS

The Phoenicians were not just successful merchants; they were also highly skilled in glassmaking, ivory carving, and metalworking. They created a hybrid culture, which spread through their large trade network, permeating the entire Mediterranean region by about 700 BC. Their silver–gilt dishes have been found in graves from Italy to Mesopotamia. These Phoenician works of art display a mixture of styles: Egyptian charioteers driving Hittite chariots, a hovering bird of prey depicted in Egyptian style above a Mesopotamian hill, and Assyrians sporting long beards alongside clean–shaven Egyptian soldiers.
– Lucas Petit

Tyre. Ruins of Roman Palaestra, with columns made of Egyptian granite. (© Ddkg | dreamstime.com)

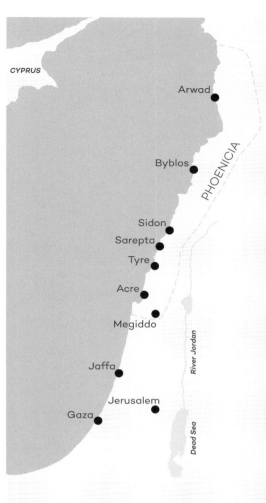

Map of Phoenicia.

THE WORD 'PHOENICIAN'

The Phoenicians did not refer to themselves by that name. They were *can'ani* or Canaanites. It was the Greeks who thought up the name *phoinix* for the inhabitants of present–day Lebanon. The word's etymology remains unclear. It may refer to the crimson dye of the colourful cloths for which the Phoenicians were known. Alternatively, it may derive from the name of the hero Phoenix, the Phoenicians' primogenitor. The Romans, basing themselves on Greek literature, used the terms *poenus* and *phoenix*. The former, from which the English word Punic derives, refers to the Phoenicians' North African descendants.

– *Lucas Petit*

(c. 2000-1200 BC). The oldest known Phoenician inscription is the Ahiram epitaph, an inscription on a royal sarcophagus dating from c. 1200 BC. It would appear that the language and script were not fully adopted by society, however, until the eleventh century BC. The script was written entirely without vowels, in contrast to Aramaic and biblical Hebrew.

Thanks to the city–state's commercial network, the Phoenician language spread throughout the Mediterranean region from the ninth century BC onwards, a process that was naturally assisted by the fact that this alphabetical system, unlike cuneiform script and Egyptian hieroglyphics, was not only easy to learn but could also be used in other languages. Both the Greek and Latin alphabets are based on the original Phoenician script. As the various colonies acquired greater independence, the script changed. For instance, around the third century BC the script in Carthage, also known as Punic, was cursive (see chapter 4).

A Trading Nation

Trade flourished, and the explosive population growth in the Phoenician coastal region meant that many were compelled to migrate west. What happened in their home country over the next two centuries is partly veiled in obscurity. It is striking that we know more about the Phoenicians' western commercial relations and colonies than we do about Phoenicia itself. This is mainly because very few original texts have been found in the mother country. Most of the information we possess about Phoenicia comes from Assyrian annals, biblical texts and later Greek works. Partly for this reason, we do not find any references to important cities such as Tyre until a relatively late period, whereas we know that they had played an important part long before that. It can be assumed that Tyre was the most powerful city in the coastal region from the tenth century BC onwards, having overtaken Byblos and Sidon. It was situated on an island just off the coast and possessed a satellite city on the mainland. In addition to two large harbours, a market and a palace, Tyre also possessed several temples that were dedicated to the city's most prominent deities: Melqart, Astarte and Ba'al–Shamem.

The Phoenician Deities

The Phoenicians' gods were closely linked to the pantheon of other Levantine cultures. Chief among them were the mother goddess Astarte – also known as Ishtar – and Asherah, the fertility goddess, who was frequently depicted with a tree of life. As the Phoenician world gained in importance, we see a growth in the number of male gods. Thus, Asherah acquired a husband named El, and other gods too appeared on the stage, such as Adonis (the god of bread), Yam (the god of the sea) and Reshef (the god of lightning and plagues). Each of the major Phoenician cities had its own city–god, who was worshipped in one of the main temples. While Adonis was of great importance in Byblos, and somewhat later also on Cyprus, it was Melqart, the god of the sea and the underworld, who prevailed in Tyre and Carthage.

Temple of the obelisks in Byblos.

Kition. In the Phoenician period, Kition, like Carthage, was known as the 'New City'. Phoenician temple of Astarte, Temeros.

From East to West

Phoenician silver–gilt dish. c. 700-675 BC. National Museum of Antiquities, Leiden.

The colonisation process in the Mediterranean to which the Phoenicians owe their fame appears to have been initiated primarily by the city of Tyre. It was there, in the tenth century BC, that King Hiram I acquired a trade monopoly, giving rise to an expansion that made the city the most important Phoenician port in the eastern Mediterranean. He started by focusing on trade with the interior and the Red Sea. But written sources show that Hiram also exercised control on Cyprus. Still, the island was not a real colony at this point. It was not until the mid–ninth century BC, under his successor, that the first settlement was built on Cyprus: Kition. The presence of copper on the island was a major attraction at first. But Cyprus was also used as

a transit port and later as a place for the growing population to live. Besides being skilled in commerce, the Phoenicians were also known for their excellent craftsmanship, producing products that were much in demand, many of which were soon reaching Cyprus. Not only Cyprus: from the eighth century BC, Phoenician products were turning up everywhere: carved ivory in Megiddo, silver dishes in Mesopotamia and Italy, decorated Tridacna shells in Palestine, and glass in Egypt.

From Cyprus, the Phoenicians sailed along to Crete, Sardinia and even Spain, probably motivated more than anything else by a desire to obtain raw materials, especially metals. Because of the rapid growth of Tyre and other cities, there was a growing need for food for the homeland, and soon the trade expanded to include grain, olive oil and other vegetable products. This diversity of merchandise led to the enormous Phoenician trade network in the Mediterranean and numerous settlements with a Phoenician presence, extending as far as Spain and Northwest Africa. The question of precisely when the Phoenicians started colonising territories still provokes debate to this day. Some scholars believe that the process was already under way before 1000 BC, but no convincing evidence has been presented so far. A careful review of the data cannot place the colonisation process any earlier than the late tenth century BC, a hypothesis that seems to be confirmed by recent archaeological research in the

southern Spanish city of Huelva. With the explosive growth of Phoenicia's population, and under pressure from the Assyrians, the Phoenicians were compelled to turn westward. In consequence, the Phoenicians acquired control of territories they already knew. The many contacts they had built up in trade during the twelfth and eleventh centuries BC undoubtedly guided their choices for certain colonies rather than others.

The End of the Phoenician Mother Country

In the first half of the first millennium BC, the Phoenician coastal cities benefited from their Mediterranean trade contacts. Partly by concluding shrewd agreements, their inhabitants could operate with a fair degree of autonomy; something that scarcely changed with the rise of the Neo–Assyrian Empire in the eighth and seventh centuries BC. Though they were obliged to fend off a number of attacks, and had to pay tribute, the people of Phoenicia had a fairly peaceful existence. Still, Phoenicia's influence in the Mediterranean gradually declined. In the west, Carthage was in the ascendancy. Towards the end of the sixth century BC, the Persians conquered the coastal region. They would control the cities and their immediate Mediterranean trade contacts until the advent of Alexander the Great in 332 BC. Finally, the plundering of these cities by the Greeks signalled the real demise of the once so powerful Phoenician Empire.

The Mediterranean region in the Phoenician-Punic period.

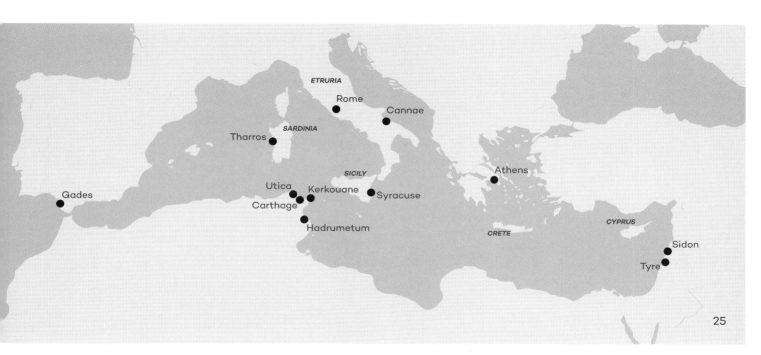

3

PUNIC CARTHAGE

....

Roald Docter

ACCORDING TO LEGEND, THE PUNIC METROPOLIS OF CARTHAGE WAS FOUNDED WITH THE AID OF A CRAFTY TRICK AND AN OX HIDE. THE EARLIEST VERSION OF THE STORY IS TOLD BY TIMAEUS OF TAUROMENIUM (TAORMINA), A GREEK WRITER FROM THE LATTER HALF OF THE FOURTH CENTURY BC. AFTER A STRUGGLE FOR POWER AMONG THE NOBLES OF TYRE (IN PRESENT–DAY LEBANON), PRINCESS ELISSA (DIDO) AND A GROUP OF ARISTOCRATIC COMPANIONS BOARDED SEVERAL SHIPS AND SAILED WESTWARDS TOWARDS THE COAST OF NORTH AFRICA, WHICH WAS KNOWN IN ANTIQUITY AS LIBYA.

APHRODITE [VENUS] DRAPED, WEARING OLIVE WREATH AND HOLDING DOVE

[262] C118 DALI [IDALIUM]

They planned to found a new capital city there, a new Tyre. On the way to Africa, the refugees dropped anchor at the island of Cyprus, where they took on board the High Priest of Astarte and eighty girls who were involved in temple prostitution. After all, the successful expansion of a colony requires women as well as men.

Timaeus relates that the company arrived on the coast of Libya (present–day Tunisia) in the thirty–eighth year before the first Olympiad, that is, in 814/13 BC. There, they entered into negotiations with the local population, who agreed to sell them a piece of land as large as could be covered by an ox hide. With devious cunning, however, the newcomers cut an ox hide into tiny strips, laying them down so as to encircle the hill of Byrsa, a far larger area than the Libyans had intended. This should almost certainly be regarded as an apocryphal story, invented because Byrsa sounds similar to the Greek word βυρσα for ox hide. Even so, the story contains elements that chime perfectly with the negative image of the Phoenicians in antique sources – right back to Homer, who describes the Phoenicians as a crafty and mendacious people who will seize every opportunity to make a profit wherever they go, and who will not scruple, for instance, to combine abductions with slave trade. Even the reference to an ox as part of the foundation of an ancient city may contain a grain of truth. Among the Greeks and the Romans, and probably the Phoenicians, the boundaries of a future city were marked out in a ritual ceremony with the aid of a plough drawn by a bull and a cow.

The current name of Carthage derives from the Phoenician Qrt–hdšt (Kart–Hadasht), meaning 'new city' – a parallel to Νεάπολις (Naples) among the Greeks. In this context it is certainly not unimportant that Carthage is the only city in the Phoenician–Punic world of which we possess an elaborate legend about its foundation. This ancient tradition clearly contains elements, added primarily to create a non–Greek and non–Roman representation of Carthage in the later Greek and Latin sources. Even so, the story also contains elements that are so typically Oriental and non–classical that they are very unlikely to come from Greek or Roman historians. The 'monarchic' explanation underlying the colony's foundation in this myth is certainly atypical in this regard, but possesses a certain logic – particularly for a settlement named 'New City'. Earlier Phoenician colonies in the central and western Mediterranean had been founded for commercial reasons, for instance because of the proximity of ore–mining areas. Real agricultural colonies, such as those so often encountered in Greek colonisation, were quite uncommon in the Phoenician world. Carthage moved into the ascendancy among the Punic colonies, certainly from the end of the sixth century BC onwards; before then, it had been obliged to share this preeminent position with other great colonial settlements mentioned in ancient sources: Cádiz in Spain, Utica in Tunisia, and Lixus in Morocco.

Not so long ago, the early date of the city's foundation, as suggested by the ancient sources, could not be corroborated by archaeological finds. Traces of the oldest city could not be dated any earlier than the second quarter of the eighth century BC, on the basis of meticulous studies of Greek ceramic sherds. Quite recently, however, animal bones from the earliest layers of the settlement have been dated, using radiocarbon dating technology, to the end of the ninth century BC, which would be compatible with the city's foundation in 814/813 BC.

Urban Development and Living Culture

With the benefit of some two centuries of archaeological research (since Humbert), we are fairly well informed on what the Punic city looked like and how it developed. Since the 1970s in particular, there has been an upsurge in research on the structure of the ancient city. It is striking that the earliest city was not built on the peak of the later central hill of Byrsa, but on the hill's southeast and eastern slopes, facing the sea. The earliest traces of human presence have been found here in layers as deep as six metres below the current ground level. This early settlement area lies on a peninsula extending into the Gulf of Tunis, a highly strategic position that duplicated the characteristic model of Phoenician coastal cities of the Levant, especially the mother city of Tyre, with its two landing areas for ships – one to the south, the other to the north. These were probably also the areas where the peripheral parts of the settlement were located, with all the diverse functions that are typical of harbours: warehouses, shipyards, houses for sailors and merchants, inns and brothels. Unfortunately, it has not yet been possible to examine these parts of the city, which may be called, by analogy with the Levantine examples, the 'Lower City' (or perhaps 'Lower Cities'). A marketplace (*maqom*) in the vicinity of these harbours can also be reconstructed, by analogy with the famous Eurychoros in Tyre.

Finds from excavations enable us to estimate the surface area of Carthage in its earliest phase at approximately 25 hectares. This urban region

Glass beads, Carthage; 4th -3rd century BC; Musée National de Carthage. Pendants like this, made from glass paste, were found in graves.

*The 'sarcophage of
the priestess of Isis',
as it is known. Found
in a shaft tomb, 12
metres deep; Musée
National de Carthage.*

would have had a population of 5,000 to 8,000 in the seventh century BC, which is very large in the context of ancient civilisations. By the second century BC this figure had grown to at least 50,000, if not 100,000, and even 300,000 is mentioned. From at least the seventh century BC onwards, the 'Upper City' was surrounded by city walls with gates and bastions. In the fifth century BC, these walls were renewed and expanded to enclose a larger surface area. As was customary in the ancient world, the burial grounds and some of the artisans' quarters lay beyond the city walls (*extra muros*). The Tophet of Carthage was also initially *extra muros*. On this sacred site, the cremated remains of tens of thousands of infants were laid to rest in urns: child sacrifices or – as some believe – the graves of children who were too young to be regarded as members of society (see also chapter 5). Not far from the Tophet, an artificial canal, 15 to 20 metres wide and two metres deep, ran parallel to the coast. Since this was built before the mid–fourth century BC, this canal too must have been within the later city wall. It was filled in after c. 350 BC and replaced by a double harbour southeast of its course. The final version of this double harbour is described in ancient literature (by Appian) and can be dated archaeologically to just before the outbreak of the Third Punic War. A small canal connects the rectangular commercial harbour to a circular naval harbour and sheds that could accommodate 170 to 180 warships (triremes). This number is quite close to the 220 ships mentioned by Appian as the harbour's capacity.

All this suggests that the city was built from the outset according to a well–defined structural design, with rectangular houses sharing their outer walls and arranged in blocks (*insulae*) surrounded by streets. It appears that the first colonists had already divided up the urban area according to a rational design based on a radial, fan–shaped built–up area with streets leading to the slopes of the Byrsa. An orthogonal pattern of building is also found in the lower–lying coastal plain. From the earliest years, the streets of Carthage were paved with stone chips and had irregular, open drainage conduits. Towards the last quarter of the fifth century BC, at least some of the streets were reconstructed in a strikingly monumental form, with large limestone plates and central drainage conduits. The final renovation of the streets, at the beginning of the second century BC, even included drainage conduits consisting of limestone plates with carefully–carved channels. Monumental street paving of this kind could last for generations and put an end to the unregulated periodic raising of the road surface that had been customary before then, using sherds and other waste materials from the settlement. Since there was no longer any reason to fear the constant raising of the street level, which caused rainwater to run into the houses, we also see a halt in the rapid succession of floor levels in the houses. Instead of the tamped–down limestone floors that had been customary until then, people started investing in more expensive lime mortar and tessellated (mosaic) floors, the 'Pavimenta Punica', which would likewise endure for several generations. An essential condition for maintaining a permanent street level was the organisation of a garbage collection service. Dung and garbage collection services are familiar from written sources relating to ancient Greek cities such as Athens: the workers who provided this service were known as *koprologoi*. It is no coincidence that the remains of toilets that have been found in diverse parts of the city date from this period. The collected dung was probably used in the irrigated horticultural area to the west of the city, in Megara. Whether urine was also collected separately and used in tanneries, as was common in Roman times, is not known but highly probable.

Left: Mask, Demeter or Medusa; Carthage; 3rd-2nd century BC; Musée National de Carthage.

Right: Mask; Carthage, necropolis of Dermech; late 6th century BC; Musée National du Bardo. Masks of this kind were found in graves. They were probably intended to ward off evil spirits.

THE BLACKSMITH'S SECRET

Excavations carried out by the University of Amsterdam in Carthage revealed the remains of a large industrial site dating from the 7th to 5th century BC. A wealth of iron objects were produced here in small forges. The Amsterdam metallurgist Hans Koens analysed the waste from this site (e.g. of terracotta bellows pipes), and discovered that all the samples were rich in organic limestone – that is, calcium. Similar iron waste from this period in Syria and Etruria, and on Elba and Ischia, contains only sporadic traces of calcium. This is the pattern still found in the mediaeval Netherlands, and in England even until the early nineteenth century. These small quantities reflect natural impurities in the ore or the material from which the forges were made.

Many types of iron ore contain sulphur in their natural state. The presence of sulphur, however small the quantity, leads to a brittle end product. Even minor stresses produce cracks that weaken the iron object. Until the mid-19th century, sulphur was removed by heating the sulphurous iron ore in the presence of air in roasting furnaces until it was red-hot, but without melting it.

The first patent for the production of high-quality steel from raw iron, in one uninterrupted process, was granted to Henry Bessemer on 17 October 1855. Importantly, this patent was later expanded to include a method to neutralise sulphur during production by adding calcium, thus removing at a stroke the need for the roasting process, saving both time and fuel. The Amsterdam research project shows that the Carthaginian forges had already mastered this 'secret' procedure. This was confirmed by the findings of Koens's earlier analyses of iron objects from Punic Carthage, which also turned up high percentages of calcium. The excavations revealed that this calcium probably derived from the crushed shells of Murex sea snails. All the evidence suggests that the early Carthaginians could produce iron of high or indeed superior quality, and that they did so on a large scale. With the Roman conquest, this knowledge was lost.
– *Roald Docter*

The water supply of the urban population initially came from deep wells dug out of the virgin soil. Certainly by the mid-fourth century BC, these wells had been replaced by cisterns. Such was the technical perfection of these Punic cisterns and the hydraulic mortars needed to operate them that the Romans continued to use them for many centuries after the fall of the city. In the final years of Carthage, in the first half of the second century BC, every house had at least one cistern.

The floor plans of the Carthaginian houses largely followed the customary design in the 'mother cities' of the Levant, certainly in the first few centuries after the city's foundation. House designs that are known to us include the courtyard house and – from the second quarter of the seventh century onwards – the four-room house. Not until the late fourth century BC does the architecture start to incorporate Greek, Hellenistic elements such as the larger open courtyard known as a peristyle and the

Baal-Hammon; sanctuary of ancient Thinissut; 1st century AD; Musée National du Bardo.

Baal-Hammon was one of Carthage's most important gods. The worship of this deity was imported from Tyre.

wall decorations in the so–called 'Constructive Style' (in the Vesuvius cities better known as the First Pompeian Style). This type of decorative work makes ample, exuberant use of Greek mouldings in stucco relief. In Carthage and in other Punic cities in North Africa, the continuing popularity of the Doric order is particularly striking. But we also see Egyptian influences in the wall decorations, especially in the mouldings. Notwithstanding these international influences, in essence the floor plans remained typically Punic, largely because of the long connecting corridors between rooms (giving rise to the name 'Corridor houses'). To Greek and Roman visitors, the city must have presented an Oriental aspect, because of the sea of flat roofs that was so unlike the urban landscape in other parts of the Greek and Roman world; indeed, people lived part of their lives on the roof. Scarcely any roof tiles have been found during the excavations of the Punic city, making it extremely unlikely that there were any gable or saddle roofs. From at least the latter half of the eighth century BC, the houses were several storeys high. Appian's account of the siege and capture of the city in the Third Punic War states that some of the houses were six storeys high. This may not be true: possibly the Romans were confused by a certain optical distortion. Looking at the city from a great distance, they saw houses built in terraced form against the side of the hill; in reality, each may have been only two or three storeys high.

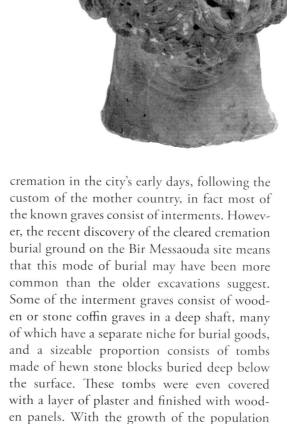

Incense burner, Baal–Hammon; Carthage, from the Tophet; mid–2nd century BC; Musée National de Carthage.

The Kingdom of the Dead

Many studies have been made of the Carthaginian necropolises since the nineteenth century, although not all are based on solid scholarship. In the earliest known phase, the grounds extended around the city in an arc: in the west on the Byrsa, and in the north and northeast on the Juno and Dermech hills. Recently a joint Tunisian–Belgian team working on the Bir Messaouda site discovered the remains of an eighth–century necropolis, which appears to close the circle around the city in the south. This burial ground was already being cleared to make way for a large industrial site in the seventh century BC. Although one might assume that the local population would have preferred

cremation in the city's early days, following the custom of the mother country, in fact most of the known graves consist of interments. However, the recent discovery of the cleared cremation burial ground on the Bir Messaouda site means that this mode of burial may have been more common than the older excavations suggest. Some of the interment graves consist of wooden or stone coffin graves in a deep shaft, many of which have a separate niche for burial goods, and a sizeable proportion consists of tombs made of hewn stone blocks buried deep below the surface. These tombs were even covered with a layer of plaster and finished with wooden panels. With the growth of the population

The Tophet, in the south of the city.

35

> *The 'sarcophage of the priestess of Isis', as it is known. Found in a shaft tomb, 12 metres deep; Musée National de Carthage.*

Oenochoe, wine jug with female figure; Henchir Beni Nafa; example of Greek influence on Punic ceramics, 3rd century BC; Musée National du Bardo.

and the city's expansion, the necropolises shifted further north, to the hill of Sainte Monique and the plateau of Borj Jedid. From the fifth century BC onwards, cremation became the rule, possibly because of a lack of space; in the fourth to third centuries, the cremated remains were frequently buried in a small limestone box with a lid shaped like a saddle roof. This most probably reflects the influence of the Greek world, as certainly applies in the case of the Necropolis of the Rabs, where the graves of high–ranking administrative officials and religious leaders lay in Hellenistic Carthage. Grave gifts tend to be highly standardised and traditional, but differ in quality and number according to the status of the deceased. The strong link with the mother country is reflected in the city's burial rituals. For instance, the custom of smashing plates at the grave after the funeral meal as well as funerary inscriptions point to burial rites intended to preserve the deceased's memory among the living.

Land Use, Trade and Food Supply

An extensive archaeological survey in a radius of thirty kilometres around Carthage has shown that small settlements and farms did not appear in the rural hinterland until the mid–sixth century BC, and even then they were few in number. This picture appears to derive confirmation from several ecological studies at Dutch universities. Research on the animal bone material originating from Carthage reveals that bird hunting played a major role in the earliest period. In addition, the importance of cattle and horses in this period gives an impression of the immediate hinterland, since these are large mammals that need considerable grazing space. What is more, studies of incinerated wood residues in Tophet urns prove that the interior was still covered with wild vegetation well into the sixth century BC; it was only later that prunings from olive trees started to predominate. In other words, it seems that Carthage initially made little use of its immediate hinterland, relying instead on the sea and on overseas territories such as Spain, Sicily, and Sardinia. So in its earliest period at least, the city fits the 'scattered hinterlands' model that is so typical of the Mediterranean region from antiquity until early modern times.

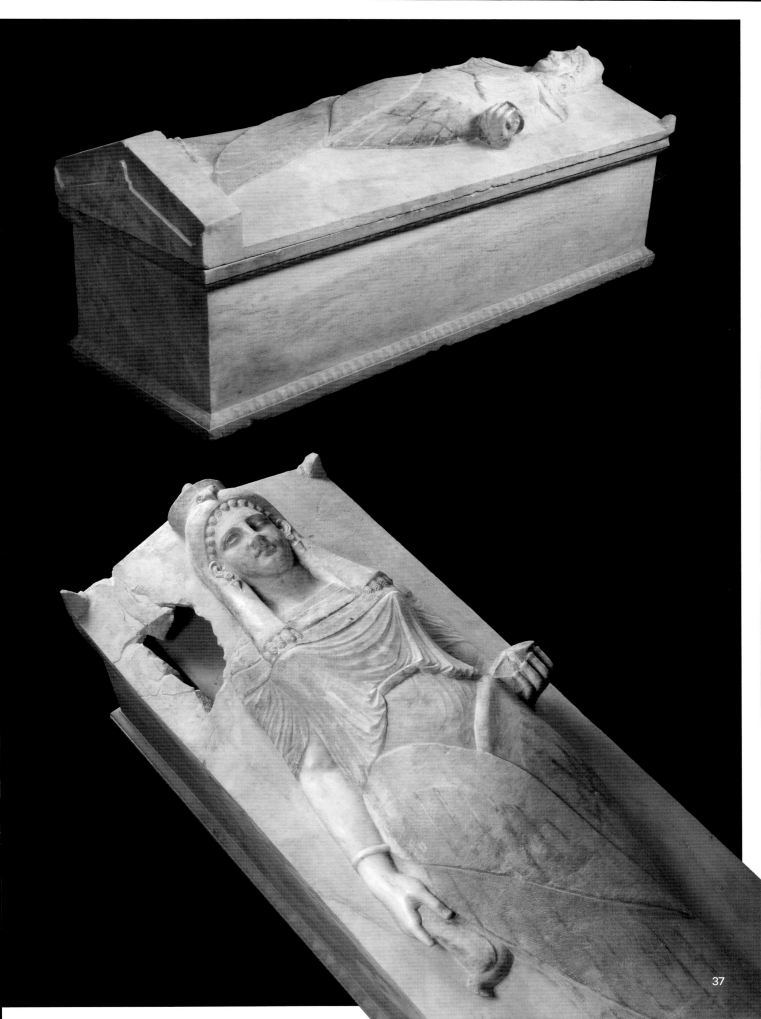

Analyses of transport amphorae, the most common food containers in ancient times, largely confirm this picture. In the earliest layers of Carthage, a majority of amphorae come from Nuragic Sardinia, Central Italy and the Phoenician region of southern Spain. In the subsequent period (c. 675-530 BC), Carthage's immediate hinterland was already providing half of the transport amphorae, a shift that has been recorded with a slight delay in the major survey mentioned above. The trend towards growing self–sufficiency continued in the following century, in which 80–85% of the amphorae were made locally or regionally. A relative rise to c. 30% of imported transport amphorae between c. 430 and 300 BC can be explained by imports of specialised produce (especially wine) from southern Italy (Calabria and Lucania), the Ionian–Adriatic region (Apulia, Corfu and Albania), Sicily, Sardinia, and the Northern Aegean. The third century BC is poorly documented in Carthage, but in the final period (from 200 to 146 BC) we

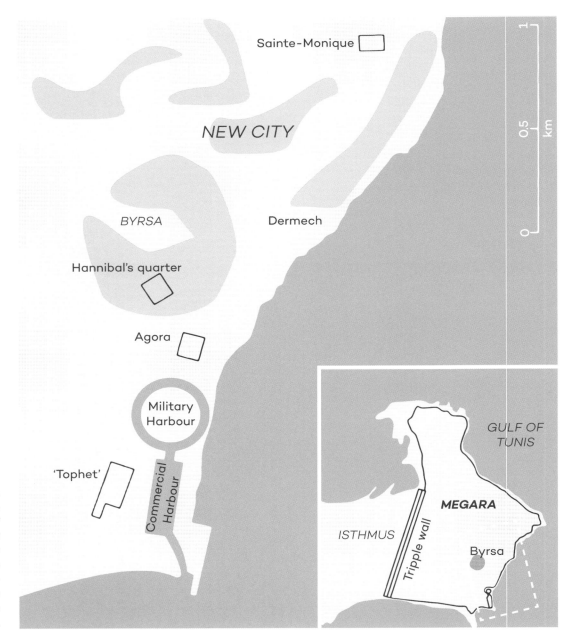

The Byrsa was the centre of ancient Carthage. South of the hill the commercial and military harbour were located. The Tophet is the place where many urns were found with remains from young children.

Religion and Society

again see a preponderance of local and regional produce (c. 85%). With the definite loss of its overseas territories after the Second Punic War, Carthage was compelled to greatly expand its rural settlements in the interior of North Africa. The archaeological survey mentioned above has provided convincing evidence of this.

It is therefore fair to ask what Carthage had to offer in exchange for the imports of such large quantities of food produce. In part, Carthage paid for these goods with tribute collected from dependent regions, but this cannot possibly be the whole explanation, certainly not in the earliest period. Inscriptions on gravestones and votive stelae, classical sources and archaeological remains all give a clear picture of an urban society that relied heavily on craftsmanship and the processing of primary raw materials into high–quality products. Recent research has supplied important evidence of ivory carving and textile working combined with purple extraction and the making of very high–quality iron products.

'King of the City' Melqart – whom the Greeks identified with Heracles – was the tutelary god of Tyre and its monarchy. He was also the pivotal divinity that linked Carthage to its mother city. Well into the Hellenistic period, the great temple dedicated to Melqart in Tyre received annual tributary gifts from Carthage and other colonies. In Carthage too, there was a clear connection with the local monarchy, and Melqart's role remained important, even after the end of the fourth century BC, when Carthage adopted a more 'democratic' polity.

The Punic pantheon included numerous other gods besides Melqart, which can likewise be identified (with varying degrees of confidence) with Greek gods and mythical beings: Eshmoun (Aesculapius), Astarte (Aphrodite, Hera?), Baal Hammon (Zeus), Tanit (*daimon* of the Carthaginians), Baal Shamin ('Lord of the Heavens' – Zeus?), Baal Magonim ('Lord of the Shields' – Ares?), Baal Haddad (Ares), Baal Malage (Triton), Baal Saphon (Poseidon),

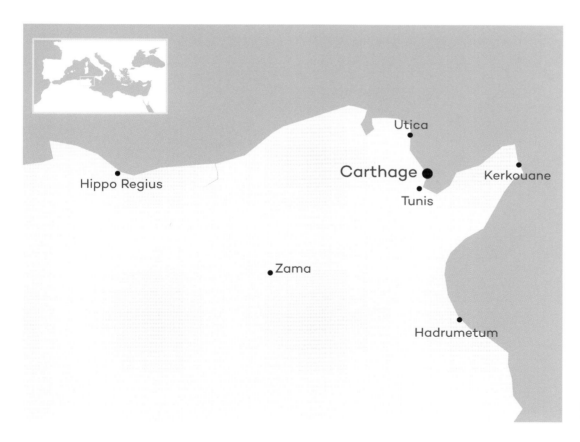

Map of northern Tunisia.

Sid (Iolaus), and Reshef (Apollo, who is not documented in Carthage, however, aside from the temple dedicated to him that is mentioned by Appian).

The earliest images of the Phoenician–Punic gods were generally non–figurative or aniconic. The gods were worshipped in the form of sacred stones called *baetyli* and stone pillars (stelae); later in the form of abstract symbols. Fine examples have been found in the floor of a small sanctuary in the town, dating from the end of the fifth century BC in the excavations carried out by the University of Hamburg. Three of the primary divinities are depicted here using their respective symbols: the stylised small female figure with outstretched arms (Tanit), the sun disk (Baal Hammon) and the star (Astarte).

From the fourth century BC onwards, the Punic pantheon underwent a marked assimilation with the world of the Greek gods, certainly in terms of iconography. In 396 BC, the cult of Demeter and Kore (Persephone) was imported into Carthage from Sicily, to atone for the sacrilege committed by Carthaginians in the Greek sanctuaries of Agrigentum and Syracuse and the calamities it had brought down on them. Characteristic of the newly–introduced cult are the terracotta incense burners in the shape of Demeter as a *kernophoros*, one who bears a sacrificial bowl or *kernos*. A terracotta figurine found during the excavations of the German Archaeological Institute in a large Carthaginian sanctuary has an engraved Tanit symbol on the back, which suggests an amalgamation or syncretism of the two goddesses. However, this same sanctuary is known primarily in relation to the discovery of over 3,600 clay seals, which were burnt to terracotta in the devastating fire of 146 BC. These were the seals of rolled/folded papyrus documents in the temple's archives. In all cases, the papyrus structure and the imprint of the binding string are preserved on the backs of the clay seals. About half of the scenes are printed in the wet clay with stone seals or scarabs with the name of the Egyptian Pharaoh Mencheper–Re. This is Thutmosis III, who reigned in the fifteenth century BC, but was extremely popular in the age of the Saite Pharaohs in the seventh and sixth centuries BC. The name is sometimes interpreted cryptographically as Ammon–Re, which may possibly denote the cult of the sun god (in Carthage this is Baal Hammon). These Egyptian Mencheper–Re seals most probably belonged to the temple and were used by the priests to seal contracts. The other half of the scenes on the seals are extremely diverse (no two are identical) and are probably the stamps of specific private individuals, who used their own signet rings to validate contracts. They include Punic, Egyptian, Greek and Etruscan seals.

The priesthood in Carthage was reserved for males of the aristocracy and was hereditary. The chief of the priests or *rab kohanim*, besides his important religious role, also exercised great influence over the workings of the State and economic life. The extent to which religion and society were intertwined is also clear from the remarkable number of theophoric names, certainly in comparison to other ancient cultures. Two examples will suffice here: Hasdrubal ('he who has Baal's help') and Hannibal

Markings of a grave at the Tophet. Stylised image of the goddess Tanit with sun disk and crescent moon.

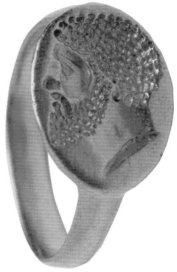

Signet ring with man's head; Carthage, necropolis in the vicinity of Sainte–Monique; 3rd century BC; Musée National de Carthage.

‹ *Statue of Demeter. The cult of Demeter and Kore was imported into Carthage from Sicily. Collection: Musée National de Carthage (photo: E. van den Bandt).*

Large mask; Carthage, from the Tophet; 3rd -2nd century BC; Musée National de Carthage.

('he who enjoys Baal's favour'), names that occur with great frequency, also among the most prominent ruling families.

We owe our knowledge of the Carthaginian constitution largely to Greek and Latin sources (e.g. Aristotle and Polybius), but the labels they use for the various functions and organs of State cannot always be linked unambiguously to the reality of Punic governance. The supreme executive magistrates or suffetes performed the most important tasks. The Greeks saw the suffete, who also commanded the army, as the 'King' (βασιλεύς), while the Romans referred to him as *rex* or *princeps*. Although the monarchy was certainly not hereditary, the most important po-

sitions were reserved for the members of certain families, which had the effect of creating dynasties. The religious changes made in 396 BC, with the introduction of the cult of Demeter and Kore cult, were a direct consequence of the disastrous course of the campaign on Sicily and the suicide of the Carthaginian general, King Himilco, ending the Magonid dynasty. After this, Carthage appears to have developed into an aristocratic republic in the fourth century, with existing institutions acquiring a clear role: in addition to the 'Kings', the city–state was governed by a Council of Elders (*adirim*, comparable to the Greek gerousia/γερουσία or the Roman Senate), the 'Tribunal of 104', and a parliamentary assembly or *ham*, comparable to the Greek demos/δῆμος). From the late fourth century BC onwards, Carthage was governed by two annually–elected suffetes, similar to Roman consuls, and the parliamentary assembly also appears to have increased in importance.

The End of the City

The city's wealth and luxury in both the public and private domains, which is so obvious from its archaeological remains, was a thorn in the side of the Romans. When a committee of the Roman Senate, including Cato the Elder, visited Carthage in 157 or 153 BC, this opulence made a great impression on him. Even though Carthage had been defeated in the Second Punic War, forced to pay enormous sums in war indemnities for almost half a century, it did not seem reduced to sackcloth and ashes; quite the contrary. With the end of the fifty–year treaty between Roma and Carthage looming, at which point the payments would cease, the Romans feared the worst. The expansion or reconstruction of the great harbour complex with a separate circular naval harbour in this period will have exacerbated these fears. In this context, Cato's immortal, oft–repeated phrase 'ceterum censeo Carthaginem esse delendam' – 'Moreover, I consider that Carthage must be destroyed' – is easy to understand. Although this version, with its threefold alliteration, was not reconstructed until 1821, by the German historian Franz Fiedler, it is true to the spirit of Cato's words. Plutarch wrote that Cato had said 'Δοκεῖ δέ μοι καὶ Καρχηδόνα μὴ εἶναι', 'I believe that Carthage must not continue to exist'.

After a three–year siege, Roman troops finally seized the city and completely destroyed it. The Roman general Scipio then had salt scattered around the whole area and the ground ploughed up, symbolising a curse on the city's renewed inhabitation. An entire metropolis and its cosmopolitan culture ceased to exist for all time, living on only as a memory.

Statue of a Kore, a young woman. This statue was found in the 'Maison de la Cachette' in Carthage. It was probably hidden in early Christian times, to prevent it from being destroyed by fanatic Christian sects. Collection: Musée National de Carthage.

44

Detail of a Punic stela discovered by Jean-Émile Humbert (see chapter 14); Carthage; 3rd -2nd century BC; National Museum of Antiquities; inv. no. H 1 (photo: E. van den Bandt).

4

THE PUNIC WRITING SYSTEM

··

Ahmed Ferjaoui

THE PUNIC WRITING SYSTEM IS ALPHABETICAL, AS IS THE PHOENICIAN 'MOTHER SYSTEM' THAT FORMS THE BASIS FOR ALL THE ALPHABETICAL SYSTEMS THAT ARE USED IN THE WORLD TODAY. AS THEY EXPANDED THEIR POSSESSIONS AROUND THE MEDITERRANEAN REGION, THE PHOENICIANS DISSEMINATED ALL THE VEHICLES AND EXPRESSIONS OF THEIR CULTURE, SUCH AS THEIR LANGUAGE AND SCRIPT, THROUGH THEIR TRADE SETTLEMENTS. AT SOME POINT THIS SCRIPT CAME TO BE DESCRIBED IN THE WEST AS 'PUNIC'.

We may recall that the word 'alphabet' is made up of the first two letters of the Semitic alphabet (*aleph* and *bet*). It is appropriate to start by giving a brief overview of the origins of this alphabet in its original surroundings, and of the historical and cultural conditions that fostered this invention.

The earliest evidence dates from the first half of the second millennium BC and comes from Syria–Palestine and Egypt. The peoples inhabiting the former, such as the Hebrews, the Phoenicians and the Arameans, spoke languages related to the Semitic family of languages from the West, such as Ugaritic and Canaanite. It was from these that Hebrew and Phoenician developed in the first millennium BC, with a Punic variant in the western Mediterranean region. The eastern Semitic branch (Akkadian) which was spoken in Mesopotamia (present–day Iraq), and the southwestern Semitic branch (Ancient and Classical Arabic with its dialects, South Arabian and the Ethiopian languages) existed alongside them.

In the second millennium BC, the northwestern region of the Middle East, that is, the Mediterranean region that was bounded by Anatolia and Egypt, was dominated by the political and cultural influence of the two major regional powers: Mesopotamia on one side and Egypt on the other. However, Akkadian was the prevailing language in the Middle East, particularly in diplomatic circles. Akkadian had many similarities to other languages in the region, with a syllabic, cuneiform script – notwithstanding the large number of characters – that was more accessible than Egyptian hieroglyphics. Hieroglyphics were not only more complicated, but they did not belong to the Semitic group.

It was in this political and cultural context that alphabetical script was invented in the first half of the second millennium BC. There are too few surviving documents to date the invention more precisely. The new script was consonantal: that is, with a specific grapheme or letter for each consonant. This is perfectly suited to the consonantal structure of Semitic languages.

The consonants are grouped in threes, producing a three–letter root that expresses a word's fundamental meaning. Consonants attached to the root as prefixes and suffixes convey derived meanings, moods (i.e. active/passive/subjunctive) and grammatical forms. The vocalisation of words took place in a natural way, and the meaning of each word was immediately clear. This consonantal structure of the Semitic languages provided the basis for the invention of the alphabet. The phonemes (sounds) of each word are indicated by the consonants. By isolating these, and by writing down each one as a separate character or letter, it became possible to convey a word by using the letters that represented the consonants – in other words, in script. This writing is termed alphabetical since the vowel signs were only added later.

Origins of the early alphabet

According to documents that are available to us today, the oldest full consonantal alphabet was used in the fourteenth century BC in Ugarit, the ancient kingdom whose remains can be found at Ras Shamra, close to the city of Latakia in the north of present–day Syria. With its thirty cuneiform characters, which are simpler in shape than those of Akkadian, this alphabet represents the consonants of Ugaritic, which belongs to the Northwest Semitic family of languages. Hundreds of mythical, legal, diplomatic, and religious texts that are drawn up in this script show that the inhabitants of the region had a good command of it and that its invention dated from an earlier age. Certain similarities suggest that the inventors adapted the Western alphabetical system to the cuneiform technique. The Ugaritic *'ayin*, for instance, resembles the Phoenician *'ayin*. In addition, the letters in the Ugaritic and Phoenician alphabets appear in a similar order. Clearly, then, Ugaritic did not provide the basis for Phoenician script.

Similarly, we exclude the scripts which are not yet deciphered and in which are written some so–called proto–Canaanite texts. These date from the mid second millennium BC. Then there is another script, which uses a limited number of characters, some in the form of schematic pictograms and others more geometrical. This script can be dated to no later than the fifteenth century BC, on the basis of thirty–one inscriptions found in the southwestern Sinai, on the plateau of Serabit el–Khadim, in a mine from which the Egyptians extracted turquoise. These inscriptions were engraved like hieroglyphic texts on the walls of mine galleries and on sandstone plaques and statues, but written in a different script. This script is believed to be alphabetical, based on the theories put forward by Flinders Petrie and most notably Gardiner; it uses a limited number of characters that represent consonants, which can be assumed to derive from hieroglyphics. The deciphered sequences reveal that this script is an expression of a western Semitic language. We do not know who wrote these inscriptions. They may have been Semitic workers in the service of the Pharaohs, or high–ranking officials who supervised these workers or who belonged to an expedition led by a prince from a region on the eastern coast of the Mediterranean. Two other inscriptions, which were recently found at Luxor in the vicinity of the Nile, make it clear that this script did not originate from the Sinai, where the natural environment was not suited to the development of urban and cultural life.

This script uses pictograms to render the consonants in written form. Each consonant is represented by an abstracted drawing of an object whose name begins with this consonant. The letter *aleph*, for instance, is represented by the head of an ox, which is called *aleph* in this western Semitic language. This is known as an 'acrophonic' system, and is different from the hieroglyphics system. In the latter, the signs representing consonants were used to transcribe foreign names, and particularly as phonetic supplements to ideograms.

From these inscriptions we can infer that an alphabetical system was developed and used in and around the region of Syria–Palestine at some point in the latter half of the second millennium BC. This probably took place just before the time in which the Proto–Sinaitic inscriptions were made, the shapes of whose letters still greatly resembled pictograms. This develop-

ment is very clear from the first Phoenician inscriptions which date from the eleventh century BC at the earliest, and which reveal that the Phoenicians had long been using an alphabet.

This alphabet consists of twenty–two letters, whose shapes continued to develop over the years, both in the east and west of the Phoenician territories. As the Phoenicians expanded towards the west – according to Greek and Roman literary sources, explorers from Tyre embarked on this westward expansion in the twelfth century BC – they took their writing system with them.

According to the inscription on a grave dating from the ninth century BC, they initially settled on Cyprus, which forms the first step in this expansion. Other epigraphs reveal that the script was used on Crete and Sardinia in the ninth century. There are a great many inscriptions dating from the eighth and especially the seventh century BC, which prove that the script was very common in the western Phoenician world.

The largest number of inscriptions, however, were found in Carthage. Over six thousand inscriptions were found in the Tanit and Baal Hammon sanctuary or Tophet (see Chapter 5). A large literary oeuvre was produced in this script, but it has sadly perished almost without trace, leaving only echoes in the writers of the antique world.

From the seventh century BC onwards, these inscriptions and other cultural expressions of the western Phoenician world are classified as 'Punic' on the basis of certain distinctive features. Studies of these epigraphs reveal that it was in the seventh century that Punic script started to display a number of characteristic details in certain letters (*aleph*, *yod*, and *kaf*). In the latter half of the sixth century BC, these changes also influenced the shapes of other letters, such as *gimel*, *zayin*, *lamed*, *mêm*, *nun*, *samek* and

qoph. This phenomenon continued in the following centuries, with the shapes of these letters gradually becoming more flexible, with a tendency towards lengthening and elegance.

Under the influence of cursive script, the shapes of certain letters in some inscriptions were simplified towards the end of the third century BC. After the destruction of Carthage, this development spread around North Africa. The trend towards more schematic shapes became so universal that the script of these texts is classified as neo–Punic. Some letters, such as *bet*, *daleth* and *resh*, were indicated only by small dashes, making inscriptions confusing to read.

In addition, the phonetic system started to disintegrate. The guttural sounds were frequently omitted or used interchangeably. This indicates that their role in pronunciation was declining. At the same time confusion arose with other phonemes, such as sibilants and hissing consonants.

Further research indicates that these guttural sounds had another function. They denoted vowels as well as consonants. The vowel /o/ is rendered by an *aleph*, the /a/ by one of the consonants *'ayin*, *het* and *hé*. These gutturals were therefore not real vowels; rather, they facilitated pronunciation and reading, indicating vowels as what are known as *matres lectionis*.

The creation of this vocalisation system in neo–Punic undoubtedly took place under the influence of Latin. However, it was known well before this. The Arameans started using the semi–consonants *waw* and *yod* to indicate vowels at the beginning of the first millennium. The neo–Punic script continued to be used in North Africa until at least the third century AD. It was because of this that the Phoenician alphabet, which had long become extinct in the East, was able to survive here.

5
THE TOPHET OF CARTHAGE

Imed Ben Jerbania

THE TOPHET OF CARTHAGE, WHICH GUSTAVE FLAUBERT IMMORTALISED IN HIS NOVEL *SALAMMBÔ* (1862), WAS SPIRITED INTO TOPICALITY IN 1921 WHEN FRANÇOIS ICARD, A POLICE INSPECTOR IN TUNIS, AND THE LOCAL MUNICIPAL OFFICIAL PAUL GIELLY DISCOVERED A PIECE OF LAND THAT WAS STUDDED WITH *CIPPI,* AND EPIGRAPHIC AND ANEPIGRAPHIC STELAE, AND CINERARY URNS WHICH CONTAINED INFANT AND ANIMAL BONES FOR THE *MLK* SACRIFICE.

51

This discovery made it possible to locate the site that was known from ancient literature. The existence of this Tophet with its thousands of memorials and urns was already well known in the mid–nineteenth century, since several parts of it had been uncovered during clandestine excavations. The discovery of the famous stela with priest and child, which is now in the Bardo Museum, prompted Gielly to conduct his own research, and he purchased the piece of land on which the object had been found. This purchase marks the start of regular excavations in the Tophet.

Mask, 4th century BC; Musée National du Bardo.

Since then, several projects have been carried out on the adjacent plots of land, which had been acquired earlier. Between the first excavations under the supervision of Icard in 1922 and the last ones conducted by Lawrence Stager in 1972 as part

of the international campaign for the preservation of Carthage, several others were carried out: those of Byron Khun de Prorok, Jean–Baptiste Chabot, Francis Willey Kelsey, Donald Harden, G.G. Lapeyre, and finally Pierre Cintas. The results prove that this sacred site was important from the Archaic period until the destruction of Carthage in 146 BC. The Tophet has been the primary focus of attention in the research conducted on the Phoenician and Punic world. The close connection between this site and the child sacrifices that are described in the Bible and in several literary sources has generated a debate on the significance of the ritual practices that once took place here, a debate that continues to this day. Fuelled by the numerous excavations on the site, recent researchers have set out to gain a better understanding of the different forms of worship that took place on this sacred site.

We should begin by noting clearly that modern authors have linked the term 'Tophet' to passages in the Old Testament referring to the Valley of Ben–Hinnôm, near Jerusalem, as a place where boys and girls were slaughtered as sacrifices (Jeremiah 7:30–31). It is therefore curious that these sacred sites should have been discovered instead in the western Mediterranean region, most notably in Carthage. Archaeologists define the term 'tophet' as an enclosed sacred place in the open air, or a plot of land that is separated from the secular world by a particular configuration of the terrain. In the Punic metropolis of Carthage, this place occupied the southern periphery of the city from the Archaic period onwards. Not until the late Punic period, when the circular and rectangular harbours were built, was the Tophet enclosed within the built–up fabric of the city. From then on, it also lay within the city walls.

It seems that since its earliest days, the Tophet in Carthage possessed a key role in shaping the city's identity. It was first and foremost a burial ground for urns containing the cremated bones of children or animals (mainly sheep, although the remains of fowls and other small creatures have also been found), and sometimes of both together. These urns, which were sealed and protected by clay bungs or placed inside other earthenware vases, also contained small objects such as amulets or pieces of jewellery. The cremated remains that were buried in this way were frequently marked by monuments erected on top, but in the earliest phase of the Tophet this was done only in select cases. These markers, which are found in the deepest layers, are monoliths, large river stones or *cippi* (columns). The stelae, some of them bearing inscriptions, start appearing frequently in the fourth century BC. They are decorated with ritual images (emblems and divine attributes, idols, and occasionally sacrificial scenes) and votive inscriptions intended to preserve the memory of the sacrifice to the gods Baal Hammon and his consort Tanit. The wording of the prayers and thanks to these divinities, which are often preceded by genealogies of the dedicant, are highly standardised and repetitive. The relationship between the stelae and the urns is variable, and it would be wrong to assume that every urn must have had a memorial stone of some kind. Indeed, the excavations have brought to light a variety of combinations: one or more urns beneath or beside a memorial stone, one or more urns without any memorial stone at all, and memorial stones with or without one or more urns. What is more, efforts to establish the direct stratigraphical relations between these important elements of the tophet have not yet succeeded. The inscribed and in some cases sculpted motifs that are visible on the *cippi* and stelae generally possess a symbolic and/or decorative function. The most common emblems are the sign of Tanit and the so-called 'bottle idol'. They were usually placed in a shrine on the altar. Determining the place of these iconographical scenes in Punic religious symbolism is not always simple, and their significance is more obscure still.

The various excavations that have been conducted on the sacred site reveal that each level, or layer, contains certain fixed types of depositions. In other words, different types of urns, *cippi* and stelae have been found in successive layers with different dates. The oldest layer dates from the eighth century BC. The urns that occur most frequently in this layer are pots based on Oriental examples. They are egg–shaped or spherical, and have two symmetrically–placed handles on the shoulders. They have a ring–shaped base and are decorated with geometrical motifs. The presence

An Urn in Leiden and the Excavations of Kelsey and Khun De Prorok

The National Museum of Antiquities in Leiden possesses a number of cremation urns from the Tophet of Carthage. One of them, according to its label, comes from the excavations conducted by Francis W. Kelsey in 1925, which were financed by the flamboyant self–styled 'Count' Khun De Prorok, an American of Hungarian descent and a typical exponent of the 'Roaring Twenties'. He had purchased the land on which François Icard and Paul Gielly conducted their first excavations in the Tophet in 1922. The urn bears Kelsey's inventory number S1466. According to the numbering in the Journal with Inventory of Objects Found that is preserved in Harvard, it was one of 74 urns excavated on 15 April 1925. Three numbers are missing from the list in Harvard, including S1466, which is now in Leiden. How did the urn end up here? The likeliest explanation is that it was given or sold to a visitor, during or shortly after the excavation. In fact we probably know that visitor's identity. For the collection of Tophet vases to which this urn belongs was purchased by the museum on 20 February 1952 from Mr G.A.H. Bisseling, who was curator of the Dutch Museum of Education (the precursor of Museon). According to the information recorded at the time of the sale to the National Museum of Antiquities, he had acquired the items himself in Carthage. The British Museum in London and the Ashmolean Museum in Oxford also possess urns from these excavations. The label also refers to a location number, 316, which showed where the urn was buried in relation to those excavated just before and just after it. Unfortunately this contextual information can no longer be reconstructed.

The urn can be dated to the sixth or fifth century BC and contains the cremated remains of a newborn baby and a lamb.
– *Roald Docter*

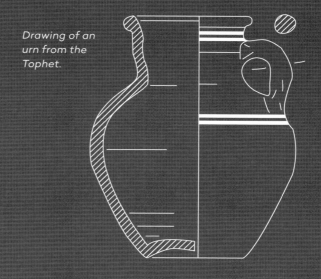

Drawing of an urn from the Tophet.

of these jars is sometimes marked by simple stones or L–shaped sandstone *cippi*. But the items of pottery that are generally regarded as the most important from this early period of the Tophet are those found in the shrine known as the 'Chapelle Cintas'. Recent studies suggest that these miniature vases may have been produced locally. The city's expansion and development appears to have greatly reduced the available space for the deposition of offerings. Several excavations in the Tophet of Carthage have demonstrated that the ground was regularly worked and raised. Whenever there was a lack of space, the ground was raised to the level desired, to make room for the deposition of new urns and the placing of monuments, separated by paths. The urns on the upper levels are less and less elegant. They are increasingly slender, and their decorations are largely rudimentary, in many cases confined to a few painted or scored lines. It is on the basis of this ceramic material that D.B. Harden proposed a classification of the Tophet into three major phases (Tanit I, II and II), which some authors accept as a broad chronological framework.

The question of the significance to be attached to the rituals that were enacted at the Tophet for almost seven centuries still fuels debate to this day. Should we accept that child sacrifices were offered to the gods in Carthage, or reject this explanation as a myth? The subject still divides opinion in the community of experts on the Semitic world.

Many ancient and Christian historians adopted a polemic approach to the subject. Today, some authors search for evidence in the literature that may support the hypothesis of child sacrifices. It should be borne in mind, however, that contemporary historians such as Thucydides and Polybius never mentioned this subject. Furthermore, archaeology has not yet provided any convincing evidence to corroborate the 'literary evidence' that children were sacrificed to the bronze statue of Cronos. One source relates that Carthaginian children were laid in the statue's arms, and would slide down onto a bed of glowing coals below. There have always been two camps. On the one side are the revisionists, who believe that the Tophet was simply a burial ground for children who were stillborn or who died in infancy, on the other side a group of scholars who insist that children were sacrificed. Nowadays a third group has arisen, a group that adopts something of an intermediate position. These are scholars who posit that the Tophet was a sacred necropolis, which may contain some sporadic remains of sacrifices, but that it was essentially a cemetery for children who died from natural causes.

Whatever the case may be, the authors do not believe that discussions of the Tophet should be limited to a controversy about whether or not it was used for sacrifices, leading to research such as a recent study based on osteological analyses of the human and animal bone remains. To gain more insight into the beliefs and the religious outlook of the Carthaginians, it may be of greater importance to focus on the Tophet's archaeology (i.e. its stratigraphy, its component parts, and its topography), to analyse the urns, and to study the Tophet's visual culture, especially the iconography of the stelae and their inscriptions.

Stela with elephant; Carthage; 3rd -2nd century BC; Musée National de Carthage.

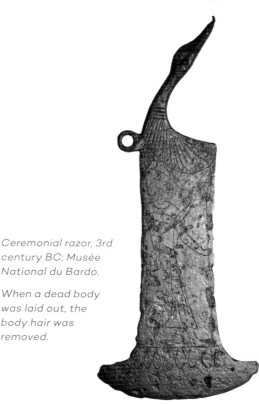

Ceremonial razor, 3rd century BC; Musée National du Bardo.

When a dead body was laid out, the body hair was removed.

Terracotta statue of
a sphinx; 7th century
BC; Musée National
de Carthage (photo: E.
van den Bandt).

6
EGYPTIAN INFLUENCE IN CARTHAGE

Taoufik Redissi

THE PAST THIRTY YEARS HAVE SEEN A GROWING INTEREST IN RESEARCH ON THE INFLUENCE OF EGYPTIAN CULTURE ON OTHER REGIONS AROUND THE MEDITERRANEAN SEA. OF ALL THE PLACES IN THE WESTERN MEDITERRANEAN REGION, IT IS IN CARTHAGE THAT THE LARGEST NUMBER OF AMULETS, SCARABS AND SCARABOIDS HAVE BEEN FOUND. THE PAST THIRTY YEARS HAVE SEEN A GROWING INTEREST IN RESEARCH ON THE INFLUENCE OF EGYPTIAN CULTURE ON OTHER REGIONS AROUND THE MEDITERRANEAN SEA. OF ALL THE PLACES IN THE WESTERN MEDITERRANEAN REGION, IT IS IN CARTHAGE THAT THE LARGEST NUMBER OF AMULETS, SCARABS AND SCARABOIDS HAVE BEEN FOUND.

Ivory plaque from Carthage; 900-700 BC; British Museum (photo: E. van den Bandt).

The findings and conclusions of recent research now place us on firmer ground in discussing the diverse categories of objects from Carthage reflecting Egyptian influence. These Egyptian–style artefacts or *Aegyptiaca* circulated around the Mediterranean in the first millennium BC. Objects found in Carthage that are either Egyptian or produced under Egyptian influence occur mainly in graves and sometimes in the Tophet, and most are amulets and seals.

They illustrate the role that the Punic metropolis played in the dissemination of Egyptian culture. This took place not only in the territory of present–day Tunisia, but also much further afield, by way of Phoenician and Punic settlements in the western Mediterranean region.

The use of amulets in Carthage demonstrates the influence of Egyptian religion and magic. These items were mainly used to protect individuals, whether dead or alive, from evil forces. While many of the amulets found in Carthage came from Egypt, others originated from the coastal regions of the ancient Near East. Comparative studies enable us to identify similarities with amulets found in Carthage and archaeological finds from the Nile Delta, the coast of Phoenicia–Palestine, and Cyprus.

Most of the amulets originating from Egypt and the Orient date from the early Iron Age III (600-333 BC). From the mid–seventh century to the fourth century BC, amulets of this kind were found in Carthage primarily in funereal contexts. In general, the Egyptian or Eastern prototypes, made in quartz–bearing paste from the sixth century BC, served as an inspiration for Punic imitations in soapstone, and remained popular until the end of the third century BC. The first amulets produced by Carthaginian and Punic artisans were also initially made from quartz–bearing paste. These date from the end of the fifth century BC, but were found more frequently from the early fourth century BC onwards. In contrast to the Egyptian amulets and the rare specimens from the Near East, the Punic imitations are characterised by a more rudimentary mode of execution, which is easy to identify from the highly stylised and distorted facial features displayed on them.

The use of scarabs in Carthage derives from Ancient Egypt. The scarab symbolises the afterlife, and is used especially in funerary contexts. Administrative bodies also used it on seals to authenticate written documents. The scenes carved into the seals are either Egyptian or based on Egyptian examples: they depict gods, the names of the pharaohs, and legends or symbols. This is suggestive of the ritual use of Egyptian magic. According to the relative chronology of the graves, the scarabs and scaraboids made of quartz–bearing paste or soapstone found in Carthage date from the seventh and sixth centuries BC. The seal imprints of the classical Egyptian type, which are copied after iconographic models dating from the second millennium BC, are rare in Carthage. However, an impressive number of seal imprints in clay from Carthage bear the first name of Thutmose III (Mn–hpr–Rc) and that of the Hyksos king (M3c–ib–Rc). This proves that seals made after Egyptian examples were used from at least the fifth century BC onwards.

The presence of different kinds of seals, either classical Egyptian or produced under Egyptian influence, in the first millennium BC on the Phoenician coast and on Cyprus, Crete, Rhodes,

Malta and in other parts of the central and western Mediterranean region, lends support to the hypothesis that shipping routes between islands played a key role in the movements of Aegyptiaca during the first millennium BC. Carthage was an important centre for the import and distribution of seals made in the workshops of the Nile Delta, on the coast of Syria–Phoenicia, and on Cyprus. Yet the diverse classical Egyptian, Phoenician, Greek and Oriental types of scarabs and scaraboids have not been found here. This shows that the network of islands that distributed the Egyptian and Egyptian–inspired examples did not necessarily pass through Carthage.

The typological and iconographical origins of scarabs and scaraboids made of green jasper (a variety of quartz) lie in the Orient. Seals made of various hardstone types are first encountered in the Iron Age II (1000-600 BC). They are the harbingers of the production of Phoenician carved stones, which were first produced in the ninth and eighth centuries BC. In addition, they greatly influenced the development of the figurative carvings of scarabs and scaraboids in green jasper and other hardstone types in Oriental workshops. These workshops were extremely productive in the Persian period (sixth to fourth centuries BC). Between the fifth and third centuries BC, craftsmen working in the western Mediterranean region, some of them from Tharros, others from Ibiza or Carthage, made specimens of fine quality from the same raw materials.

From the seventh/sixth centuries BC onwards, carved seals made of green jasper appear sporadically in Carthage in Archaic funerary and votive contexts. They were probably imported from the Orient and display a pronounced mix of Egyptian and Oriental iconography. From the fourth/third centuries BC onwards, the influence of Hellenistic iconography becomes noticeable.

Besides the scarabs and scaraboids carved in green jasper, specimens appeared in Carthage that had been cut in other hardstone types. These have been found in reasonably large quantities in Carthaginian graves dating from the

seventh and sixth centuries BC. Iconographical themes inspired by Egyptian examples are prominent among them. Similar types can be traced to the Phoenician coast in the East. Although specimens with Oriental motifs are found in Carthage from the seventh/sixth centuries BC onwards, they are few in number.

Evidence of ancient Greek stone–carving in Carthage is extremely scarce; the oldest examples date from the sixth century BC. By the usual standards of Greek stone–carving, the specimens assigned to the sixth and fifth centuries BC are remarkable for the care with which the minutest details of the scenes were executed. The only images on the numerous Carthaginian seals with Hellenistic settings dating from the fourth and third centuries BC are warriors and male heads. Though the number of Carthaginian seals from the 4th-3rd c. BC decorated with Hellenistic decor is important, its repertoire is very limited, representing only warriors and male heads.

Thanks to its strong relations with the leading Phoenician merchants, Carthage built up a material culture, in the first millennium BC, that was greatly influenced by the Egyptian civilisation. The iconography of the amulets and the repertoire of carvings are the most important expressions of that influence. With the collapse of the Persian Empire in the last quarter of the fourth century BC, and the advent of Hellenism, several categories of *Aegyptiaca* vanished from the Near East. Even so, Carthage continued to play a leading role in producing imitations. For many years, it would stimulate the distribution and dissemination of the values of Egyptian culture in the western Mediterranean region.

Seal ring with Egyptian scene; Carthage, Byrsa; 7th -6th century BC; Musée National de Carthage.

View to the south
from Byrsa Hill, with
the contours of
the Punic harbours
clearly identifiable
amid the modern villa
landscape.

7 CARTHAGE AS A MARITIME POWER

Fik Meijer

THE SEA WAS IN THE CARTHAGINIANS'
BLOOD. THEY DESCENDED FROM PHOENICIAN
SEAFARERS OF THE PORT OF TYRE. IN 814 BC
THEY HAD BOARDED THEIR SHIPS AND PUT
TO SEA IN SEARCH OF NEW PLACES TO LIVE.
THEY HAD SAILED ALONG THE COAST OF
NORTH AFRICA AND FOUNDED CARTHAGE,
IN WHAT IS NOW TUNISIA. AT LENGTH, THE
CITY'S NEW INHABITANTS FOUNDED OTHER
COLONIES IN THEIR TURN. WITH THE PASSAGE
OF TIME, A NETWORK OF SETTLEMENTS WITHIN
CARTHAGE'S SPHERE OF INFLUENCE GREW
UP ALONG THE COAST OF THE WESTERN
MEDITERRANEAN. FROM THESE BASES, SPAIN,
THE BALEARIC ISLANDS, SARDINIA, CORSICA
AND THE WEST OF SICILY WERE ALL BROUGHT
UNDER CARTHAGINIAN RULE.

Tightly–organised administration was at the heart of this rule. Nothing was left to chance. A largely mercenary army kept firm control of the population in the interior, while the warships' crews did the same for the colonial territories. From the second century BC onwards, the policy on the fleet was coordinated from the war harbour, which was out of bounds for all non–Carthaginians. Foreigners approaching Carthage from the sea sailed into the commercial harbour through a channel and saw only the circular double walls enclosing the war harbour. There were boat sheds on the harbour quaysides and on the little central island, accommodating over two hundred warships in total. On the front of each boat shed stood two Ionian columns, which gave the harbour and the island the appearance of a single continuous arcade. From his house, rising high up on the island, the admiral could see everything that happened at sea.

Other harbours in the territories under Carthaginian rule probably had boat sheds too. From there, the warships patrolled in the immediate surroundings, so that any incipient revolt could be nipped in the bud. When the population became restive, warship crews protected the numerous cargo vessels that sailed in all directions, bringing precious metals to Carthage in exchange for grain, fish and olive oil. The Carthaginians refused to allow their rivals' ships to sail certain routes. The far west of the Mediterranean, in particular, they regarded as their special domain. The passage through the Straits of Gibraltar was closed to non–Carthaginians.

Triremes

The war fleet that served as the primary instrument of Carthaginian imperialism was composed at all times of the most modern types of ships. The Carthaginians kept a close eye on the types of warships being used by other cities, and put their knowledge to good use. They were particularly keen to watch new trends in Greece, Egypt, and Etruria. They themselves also experimented with new types of ships. The transition in the seventh century BC from monoremes (ships with one level of oarsmen) to biremes, with a second level, was prompted in part by such experiments. In the

sixth century BC, the Carthaginians noted the rapid rise of the trireme, a ship with three rows of oarsmen above one another. They immediately expanded their fleet to include the new model.

It is curious how little we know about the trireme, the standard ship of the fleets in the ancient Mediterranean. We are not even sure of its precise length or width. From the dimensions of the boat sheds in Piraeus, the harbour of Athens, it can be inferred that the trireme was 37 to 40 metres long. The full contingent of oarsmen consisted of 170 men seated on three levels: 54 *thalamioi* at the bottom, with 54 *zugioi* above them, and a further 62 *thranitai* on top. The trireme's coat of arms was the ram.

The Carthaginians soon became masters of tactical manoeuvres with the trireme. The object was to disable enemy ships by ramming them, preferably in their vulnerable flanks, and breaking off the oars. The tactics favoured by the attackers – the Carthaginians' most frequent role – were *diekplous* (sailing through the lines and back again) and *periplous* (encirclement). The best results were achieved when triremes forced their way through the lines and then immediately turned in a semicircle. This put them behind the enemy, making it far less hazardous to ram the enemy ships than doing so from their initial positions. Attacking from behind, they smashed their foes' oars, after which they returned to their own lines. The more ships in a fleet performed a *diekplous* of this kind, the greater the chance that the enemy would be forced to engage.

Admirals who found themselves confronting the Carthaginians would tend to keep their ships in a very close, compact formation, primarily as a defensive strategy. They often formed a defensive circle or *kuklos*, the ships radiating like the spokes of a wheel, their sterns close together and battering–rams facing outward. The answer to this formation was encirclement. The Carthaginian helmsmen would row around the defensive circle in the hope of finding weak links. It was always possible that a ship might break away from the circle formation and attack one of the besieging vessels.

Still Larger Warships

At the beginning of the fourth century BC, there was a clear shift in the focus of the experiments with new warships. The primary target was now Sicily. A fierce struggle was taking place between Syracuse, which had gained supremacy over the other Greek cities on the island under the tyrant Dionysius, and the Carthaginians, who controlled the western part of the island. The newly–designed ships were quadriremes/fours, quinqueremes/fives and hexaremes/sixes. Even these new types of ships were never rowed by more than three levels of oarsmen, however. The innovation consisted of placing more oarsmen at each oar. Only the man at the end of the oar needed to possess expertise, in order to set the rowing pace. The other oarsmen simply followed him. A quadrireme could be rowed with three levels of oarsmen by having one man at the lowest and middle oars and two at the top. In some cases, a quadrireme had two layers of oarsmen. In that case there were two oarsmen at the bottom oar and two at the top. Similar arrangements were used for quinqueremes and hexaremes.

Even today we do not know precisely what these ships looked like. It is thought that the quadriremes had approximately 300 oarsmen, while quinqueremes and hexaremes had even more. Almost everything else about these ships is uncertain. The most important reason for this gap in our knowledge is that no substantial remains of war galleys have been found. All our conclusions must be distilled from the few texts we possess by ancient authors and, from the frequently

The battering ram found in 2010, the only one with a Punic inscription; Soprintendenza del Mare, Palermo.

imprecise images on coins, vases and reliefs. The discovery of the hull of a Carthaginian warship off the west coast of Sicily, near Marsala, did not furnish any clarity, since this is a smaller type of vessel without any rowing benches at all.

The Arrival of the Romans

For many centuries, the Carthaginians had ruled over the western Mediterranean. What happened in Carthage and the territories it controlled scarcely registered with people in the outside world. That the Carthaginians were prospering, however, was clear to everyone. The city grew, its population swelling to perhaps 300,000, most of whom were involved in some way in trade and industry. Large squares, the many wide and narrow streets that led to them, and monumental buildings all testified to the city's wealth.

Not a single Carthaginian can have suspected, as the fourth century drew to a close, that their maritime supremacy was almost at an end.

They certainly never entertained the idea that it would be the Romans who would seal their fate. After all, what did the Romans know about the sea? They had conquered the entire Italian peninsula without a single ship. Around 270 BC, looking out from Rhegium (present–day Reggio Calabrio), the Romans could see Sicily lying on the other side of the Strait of Messina. No doubt the thought of sailing to that large island with its plentiful grain occasionally crossed their minds, but not for long. The Carthaginians and the Syracusans struck fear into them. The Romans realised that it was pointless to engage these foes in battle on Sicily if they did not have a real fleet of their own.

In 264 BC the Romans adopted a new strategy. A conflict for the city of Messina in the north of Sicily unleashed a war that would utterly transform the balance of power in the western Mediterranean. There was a rapid escalation of tension between the Romans and Carthaginians. After long hesitation, the Romans finally de-

The battering ram found in 2010 in situ. Photo: Soprintendenza del Mare, Palermo.

cided to dispatch an army to Sicily. It was a risky venture. Defeat on Sicily would give the Carthaginians an opportunity to cross the water in the opposite direction and threaten the coasts of Italy.

The Romans well understood the crucial importance of building up a good fleet. But how could they acquire enough ships? They had neither shipyards nor oarsmen. Yet within the space of six months, they succeeded in stationing 120 new warships in the city harbours of southern Italy. The historian Polybius, who praises the Romans for daring to confront the rulers of the sea, finds it well–nigh impossible to believe that they achieved all this unaided. He suggests that chance played a great role in their victory – the Romans acquired a Carthaginian warship, a quinquereme, that had run aground, and had shipbuilders copy its design. This version is a little too glib to be true; it leaves out of consideration the skill of the Greek shipbuilders in southern Italy. The likeliest explanation is

that the Romans sent orders to ship's architects in several of Italy's Greek cities, commissioning from them dozens of the warships that were most in use – triremes, quadriremes and quinqueremes.

The Battle of Mylae

By 260 BC the Romans had at their disposal a war fleet of 100 quinqueremes and 20 triremes in the waters around Sicily. They had recruited over 30,000 oarsmen from all parts of the peninsula. Still, the chance of success seemed small, since the Roman admirals and their crews were less skilled and experienced than their Carthaginian counterparts. The first skirmishes seemed to confirm the differences in strength. The Roman consul Gnaeus Cornelius Scipio found himself and his seventeen ships hemmed in by twenty ships of the Carthaginian fleet and surrendered. This setback weakened the Romans' morale. Their dejection increased when the Carthaginian admiral Hannibal (not to be confused with the

View from the Byrsa towards the south. The ancient harbours are still visible in the landscape.

PUNIC BRONZE NAVAL BATTERING RAM (Egadi Islands)

Only one of the eleven battering rams that have been found to date in the area of the Battle of the Egadi Islands, to the west of Sicily, is Punic. The others come from Roman ships. This battering ram was found in 2010 at a depth of 81 metres, during a systematic search conducted by the Soprintendenza del Mare (Regione Siciliana) and the RPM Nautical Foundation. Several amphorae, including Greco–Italic and Punic types, were found within a five–mile radius of the battering ram. No large missing parts are discernible; the only damage is a series of V–shaped notches across the horizontal sections. These notches display a furrowed pattern caused by a frontal collision with another ram. This battering ram was made using the 'lost wax' technique, but its lower section, which covered the keel, was evidently added later or repaired, since there are clear signs of parts being welded together.

The carved inscription, in Punic letters, has been studied by the specialist Giovanni Garbini. The inscription consists of one 35–letter line and bears a strong resemblance to biblical Hebrew. It is an adjuration to the god Baal: 'May this [ram] be directed against the ship: with the wrath of Baal, [the god] who makes it possible to reach the mark, may this go and strike the hewn shield in the centre'.
– *Sebastiano Tusa*

Below: The battering ram found in 2010, the only one with a Punic inscription. Left: Drawing of a Carthaginian warship with a battering ram.

Carthaginian general who crossed the Alps with elephants) carried out a reckless manoeuvre with fifty ships against the Roman fleet, which was sailing in a compact formation. The Romans sank several of the rash Carthaginian's ships and were confident that they could overpower him, but Hannibal escaped, since the Roman ships were too slow in pursuit.

At this point the Roman fleet was without a clear commander, since Scipio had been taken captive and the other consul, Gaius Duilius, was commanding the land forces. Duilius was immediately asked to take over the command of the fleet. He naturally complied, although he must have thought it a thankless task. The fleets clashed near Mylae, a little town on a small peninsula of the north coast of Sicily. What could Duilius, an inexperienced admiral who had little affinity with the sea, accomplish against Carthage's veteran admirals, who knew all the tricks in the book and did not doubt for a moment that they were heading for a glorious victory? The Carthaginians also had the numerical advantage, with their 130 ships as against the Romans' 83 galleys. Most importantly, they were masters in executing tactical manoeuvres. To Hannibal, the outcome was a foregone conclusion. What he did not know, however, was that the Romans, knowing that they could not prevail in a traditional sea battle, had made an important modification to their ships, which had the effect of transforming the encounter into something more resembling a land battle. They had constructed a spiked boarding bridge on each ship, which would become known in the history books as the *corvus* ('raven') engine.

The Carthaginian seafarers rowed self–confidently, in closed formation, towards the enemy fleet, full of contempt for the Romans' inexperience. Even when they caught sight of the boarding bridges on the Roman ships, they did not really suspect that anything was amiss, and continued to sail straight

at the foremost Roman ships, full of brash self–belief. Not until the spikes of the first boarding bridges had pierced their decks, and the Roman soldiers had leapt across onto their ships to engage the Carthaginians in hand–to–hand combat, were they gripped by misgivings. The sea battle had become a land battle, and this was a kind of fighting in which the Romans were invincible. By then, however, it was too late to adopt a different strategy; the damage was already done. Hundreds of Carthaginians were killed, while untold others surrendered. Thirty ships were lost. Even then, the Carthaginian admiral still had thoughts of carrying the day. He ordered the crews to carry out a *diekplous*, sailing through the enemy lines. But the Romans defended themselves by turning their boarding bridges in all directions and bringing them down on the enemy ships, sinking another twenty of the Carthaginians' ships.

Aftermath

The defeat at the Battle of Mylae was the greatest humiliation in Carthaginian naval history. The loss of so many ships and men might possibly have been overcome, but the Carthaginians' reputation of invincibility, of power and superiority, a reputation based on many centuries of seamanship, had been dealt a terrible blow. Four years later, their frustrations were increased by a new defeat, this time in the Battle of Ecnomus, off the south coast of Sicily. Over the following few years, the Carthaginians defeated several sections of the Roman fleet, but without gaining a decisive victory. In 241 BC the Romans won the final sea battle in the Egadi islands, to the west of Sicily. The Carthaginians were forced to give up Sicily, Sardinia and Corsica. The Carthaginians' golden age at sea was over, a demise underscored by the Second Punic War (218-201 BC), in which the Carthaginian fleet played a far smaller role than its rich past would have led one to expect. After their surrender in 201 BC, they were left with just ten warships: their naval ambitions were consigned to the past. Once they had dreamed of making the Mediterranean *mare nostrum* ('our sea'). Now the Romans ruled the waves, and they could do nothing about it. More mortifying still was the fact that for every military action they wished to undertake with their fleet, they had to seek the Romans' permission in advance.

The Romans were still not satisfied, however. The spectre of another Carthaginian revival still haunted them. They planned to wipe the city from the face of the earth. In 149 BC the Romans declared war on Carthage once again. There was no Carthaginian fleet to stop the Roman legions from crossing the sea to North Africa. Three years later, Carthage was seized and razed to the ground.

Herm with image of an African; 2nd century AD; Musée National du Bardo, Tunis; Inv. no. 3018.

8 CARTHAGE & THE LOCAL LIBYAN- NUMIDIAN POPULATION

Nabil Kallala

HISTORY IS OFTEN WRITTEN FROM THE ONE-SIDED AND SIMPLISTIC PERSPECTIVE OF DOMINANT NATIONS, WHICH HAVE DETERMINED THE COURSE OF HISTORY AND, TO A CERTAIN EXTENT, "MADE" IT. THIS IS ESPECIALLY TRUE FOR AFRICA DURING THE PRE–ROMAN ERA. IN FACT, THOSE NATIONS LEFT US TWO TYPES OF SOURCES AND STUDY MATERIALS. FIRST, THERE ARE THE ACCOUNTS OF ANCIENT HISTORIANS WHICH PRESENT A FUNDAMENTAL SOURCE OF MATERIAL FOR TODAY'S ANTIQUITY HISTORIANS. SECOND, THERE ARE PHYSICAL TRACES LEFT BEHIND BY ANCIENT PEOPLES.

These tend to be those of conquerors and rulers, who – even where they have not tried to impose their culture outright – have at least sought to create the political, institutional and social framework that would encourage its adoption. Historians and archaeologists necessarily rely on these sources, and have to base their research and reasoning on them. For instance, the history of Carthage is known to us only from the writings of Roman historians (the Punic libraries went up in flames), just as the Libyan–Numidian history is written from the Carthaginian and Roman perspectives.

However, the many and diverse ties that Carthage had with the indigenous Libyan–Numidian peoples may shed light on the history of Carthage. As a matter of fact, history of dominant civilizations – such as Carthage – could only happen at the expense of colonized and dominated peoples that are often acculturated but sometimes are evolving in a cultural interaction mode, generating a hybrid culture that also influences the dominant civilization. This creates a cultural interface that allows us a better knowledge of history.

New approaches within a large number of history disciplines, such as onomastics, toponymy, historical and cultural anthropology, recent developments in the study of pottery and other materials, new prospection methods and the contributions made by history's 'sister disciplines', such as zooarchaeology, archaeobotany, physical anthropology, archaeometry, palynology, carpology etc., have helped improve our knowledge of the history of Ancient peoples. This applies, for instance, to the subjugated Libyan–Numidian peoples who crossed paths – and sometimes swords – with Carthage. Such approaches must also, of course, take the literary sources into account.

Literary sources continue to figure prominently in modern research on Ancient Carthage, in spite of often being mythical, non–Carthaginian, partial, and the fact that they date from a later period. Didn't Justin tell us that when Elissa, the founder of Carthage, anchored in one of the Gulfs of Africa (nowadays known as the Gulf of Tunis), she 'sought to make friends with the locals, who greeted the strangers joyfully and saw their arrival as presenting opportunities to barter and trade'. She bought some land there to found her city in exchange for paying tax on that land, while she refused to marry the Libyan king, Hiarbas, and committed suicide by burning herself alive. In fact, she wanted to remain faithful to her husband, who had been murdered in Tyre, and more importantly, she wanted to pass on her incarnated power to her people. Over the time, people in the region were attracted by the reputation of the new city, and the population rapidly grew. This growth took place in the years following 814/813 BC. After that, we find no traces of the indigenous population for a century and a half; they reappear in the sixth century BC. Justin tells us that the Carthaginians fought the Libyans, gaining a victory that ended the obligation to pay taxes on the land, which they saw as a humiliating imposition.

Such passages offer no more than fleeting glimpses, but their message is clear. Besides bearing witness to the undeniable presence of the local population during the founding of Carthage, they also portray the Carthaginians as interacting with the Libyans and later flourishing at their expense. This interaction took both peaceful and violent forms. The Libyans, who had a certain political, social and possibly civic organisational structure, pursued economic and commercial activities, based largely on agriculture. The newcomers did not intend Carthage to become a simple trading settlement, of course. They planned to build a fully–fledged city, for which Elissa's company had insufficient manpower. She probably brought with her scarcely more than eighty men – which is the number of girls they abducted from Cyprus on the way to Africa and intended to serve as their brides. The oarsmen were left out of consideration in this arithmetic. Thus, we could assume that Libyans were somehow part of the foundation of Carthage as were the Afro–Punic later on part of the founding effort of roman Carthage. Carthage is almost always described as a purely Phoenician venture, an enterprise that developed internally and organically like other Phoenician colonies, but this fails to give credit to the Libyans. It gives the impression that this part of Africa was a kind of empty desert, or that it was populated solely

Detail of a herm with the image of an African; 2nd century AD; Musée National du Bardo.

Herm with image of an African; 2nd century AD; Musée National du Bardo, Tunis; Inv. no. 3018.

by simple nomads. This is clearly contradicted, however, by the ancient texts themselves and more importantly by recent archaeological discoveries.

It is true that no evidence has been found in Carthage of any indigenous habitation earlier than the eighth century BC. But at the same time the kitchen utensils that have been excavated don't disprove the existence of such habitation. For the research into the oldest archaeological layers is impeded by the remains of phases of land use, and by overlaps in the archaeological layers of Carthage's rich history. In addition, Carthage was destroyed and rebuilt several times. The earth–moving and disruptions of the archaeological layers that accompanied such cycles have also hampered research. It is fair to ask whether anyone has ever tried to reach the pre–Phoenician and pre–Carthaginian levels, given that research has always focused on Punic or Roman Carthage. This tendency is also observed for other coastal sites. Of course, starting such a research presupposes the existence of specialists who feel attracted to the material.

In spite of the relative paucity of research on this subject, a hybrid or acculturated population can be shown to have existed. This is clear from diverse burial grounds in the Tunisian Sahel (el–Hakayma among others) which contain evidence of 'Liby–Phoenicians'. It is also demonstrated by imports of Phoenician pottery, which have been found in Carthaginian graves dating from the eighth to sixth centuries BC. In fact, in the interior parts of Tunisia, especially in the "Haut Tell", evidence has also been found of pottery imports: Phoenician items in Althiburos (a sherd of a stylised Phoenician sacrificial bowl in red slip ware dating from the late eighth century BC), pottery from Massalia (Marseille) in Zama (latter half of the sixth century BC), Attic pottery in Mididi (latter half of the fifth century BC), and also a bronze sphinx found in Cirta (sixth century BC, possibly imported by a local leader). Even so, this is far too little to demonstrate the existence of trade relations between the Libyan–Numidian peoples and the Carthaginians in the Archaic period. Mutual exchanges certainly speeded up from the fifth century BC onwards, after the Carthaginians' conquest of the Numidian territory, which probably took place in the aftermath of the Carthaginians' defeat in the Battle of Himera, in Sicily, around 480 BC.

The findings made in the recent excavation project in Althiburos have greatly added to our knowledge of Numidian society, its activities and its organisational structure. This project focuses specifically on studying the social development and formation of Numidian states as well as the relations that existed between the indigenous population and Phoenician–Punic society. It has now been demonstrated that the earliest traces of human habitation there undoubtedly go back to the tenth century BC. Stone structures in Althiburos and exchanges with the Phoenician world on the coast can confidently be dated back to the eighth century BC (based on the pottery found). It has now been established that the region was inhabited almost without interruption up to the Roman period, although the population density varied. There was probably a gap in the seventh century. The region's urban development began as early as the eighth century BC, a period that corresponds to the settlement of the people of Althiburos (modern Abbah Quṣūr), who devoted themselves to a number of crafts and agricultural activities from then on: pottery, ironworking, weaving, livestock breeding, the cultivation of olive trees and grain, as well as winegrowing and various kinds of horticulture (largely fruits).

Althiburos was, in fact, an independent Numidian city, which may have served at some point as a vanguard garrison for Carthage, since it is believed to have been involved in some way in Hannon's expedition to Hecatompylos (Theveste) in the year 247 BC. This means that Carthage, and possibly other Phoenician coastal settlements, had to deal from the beginning not only with nomadic or semi–nomadic peoples, who were naturally there as well, but also with sedentary peoples whose society had a certain degree of organisational structure. These sedentary groups certainly influenced Carthage and the Carthaginians.

We can assume, in fact that a process of acculturation took place in both directions: Carthage, as the dominant entity, most probably imposed Punic as the official language, but Libyan remained in use. This is clear, for instance, from the two bilingual inscriptions of Thugga, including that of the famous mausoleum (late third/ early second century BC) and numerous Libyan inscriptions. Libyan names occurred in the Punic and even the Roman periods, sometimes in their original form and sometimes with Punic influence, or Latinised. A final piece of evidence comes from Libyan toponymy, which was largely adopted by the Romans; the latter probably learned the names from the Carthaginians. In addition, certain institutions, such as the Council of Elders and the tribunal of three suffetes (magistrates) in the Roman period, are reminiscent of Libyan forms of administrative organisation in Punic–Numidian cities such as Mactaris and Althiburos. The Dii Maurii (Moorish gods) continued to be worshipped until the end of the third century AD.

More significant still is the superb synthesis that the Libyan religion underwent in an *interpretatio punica*, expressing a spirit of mutual religious toleration. In this transformation, the Carthaginian god Baal Hammon is actually a Punic–Berber god. His consort Tanit, who is sometimes mis-

takenly identified as Ashtart (Astarte), is said to have been of Libyan origins. Ashtart (Astarte) who is also referred to as Athena, Venus and so forth might also have Libyan origins. Whatever the case may be, the dissemination of the cult of Astarte in the Numidian world was facilitated by the existence of a related Libyan deity. Such examples are numerous.

Some Numidians adopted Punic names or modified their own names in line with Punic examples. They also adopted beliefs and Punic cults, and therefore built tophets dedicated to Baal Hammon in many Numidian cities, such as Mactaris, Zama, Cirta, Henchir Hami, Sicca Veneria, Althiburos, and Mididi. These sacred sites were widespread even after the fall of Carthage, in the second and first centuries BC, and in some places even during the first two centuries AD. Although the iconography of Numidian stelae exhibits Numidian features, the language of the epigraphic inscriptions is Punic – generally neo–Punic. Some cults remained strictly indigenous, however, and continued to be practiced as such during the Punic and Roman periods: these include those of the Dii Maurii, Dii Magifae, Giddabae Deo Augusto (GDA), Ifru, Monna, Bacax, and the worship of the mountains, caves, stone etc. Libyan–Numidian burial customs survived the period of Carthaginian domination: they included the monumental graves in territories controlled by Carthage and adjacent lands, as well as the Hellenistic graves in the Numidian regions of Chemtou, Kbor Klib (near Zama), and more recently Jebel Brouag (near Althiburos).

It may be concluded that – in spite of the aborted plan of marriage between the Phoenician princess Elissa and the Libyan king Hiarbas, and the troubled relation between both people, which sometimes erupted into ferocious violence, such as during the Mercenaries' War after the First Punic War – it appears that there has been, however paradoxical it may seem, a 'cultural marriage' or cultural coexistence, or some form of acculturation, which worked in both directions. Cultures and religions, it is fair to conclude, do not respect administrative or political frontiers. They transcend the world of politics.

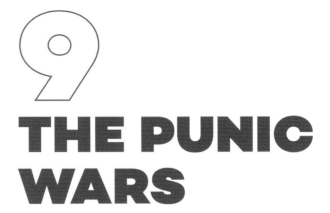

9

THE PUNIC WARS

....

Fik Meijer and Roald Docter

IN THE YEAR 247 OR 246 BC, HANNIBAL WAS BORN IN WHAT WAS THEN THE LARGEST CITY OF THE WESTERN MEDITERRANEAN: CARTHAGE. EXACTLY ONE HUNDRED YEARS LATER, 37 YEARS AFTER HANNIBAL'S DEATH, THIS METROPOLIS CEASED TO EXIST, LAID WASTE IN AN APOCALYPTIC SEA OF FIRE THAT HAD BLAZED FOR SIX DAYS AND NIGHTS. IN THE INTERVENING CENTURY, ROME AND CARTHAGE FOUGHT TWO LONG, BLOODY WARS (218-201 AND 149-146 BC), WHICH ARE KNOWN FROM A ROMAN PERSPECTIVE AS THE PUNIC WARS, BUT WHICH THE CARTHAGINIANS THEMSELVES PROBABLY REGARDED AS THE TWO ROMAN WARS.

A PUNIC COIN MOULD FROM THE SECOND PUNIC WAR

During excavations carried out by the University of Amsterdam in the centre of Carthage, in the year 2000, a limestone mould was found among the rubble of the devastated Punic city. It was almost certainly used to mint coins. Engraved in its surface are at least twelve identical images of horses looking back, the primary symbol of Carthaginian coinage. The Swiss numismatic expert Susanne Frey–Kupper has established that the mould was used to mint bronze coins at the end of the third century BC. The immediate precursors of this specific type of coin were the Carthaginian coins minted between 221 and 210 BC over coins of Hiero II of Syracuse (274-216 BC), seized as spoils of war. At some point the stock of Syracusan coins in use for this purpose evidently ran dry, and coins were therefore minted of the same Punic type, using this mould. The object is also interesting from a technological viewpoint. Research conducted by the Amsterdam metallurgist Hans Koens and Roel Janssen of Amsterdam Medical Centre has demonstrated that it is impossible that bronze was ever cast directly in this limestone mould. This would have caused far too much heat damage to the surface to produce a sharp image. They suspect that the mould was used to make beeswax models. These models were subsequently wrapped in clay, after which the wax was melted out, leaving a mould for bronze coins. This process can easily be repeated ad infinitum, and is known as the 'lost wax' technique.

– *Roald Docter*

Punic mould used to mint coins.

It should be added that the earlier conflict, known as the First Punic War (264-241 BC) – concluding with the Peace of Lutatius in 241 BC – also falls, marginally speaking, within this period of time. For Carthage, this treaty did not mean immediate peace, since immediately afterwards, the discontented mercenaries unleashed a war against Carthage that did not end until 238/237 BC. In the Second Punic War, Hannibal moved the theatre of war to the Italian peninsula, pushing Rome to the edge of ruin. The spectacular campaign in which he crossed the Alps with elephants has continued to fire the imagination for centuries, taking on mythical proportions. The same applies to the destruction of the city at the end of the Third Punic War. Less well known among the public at large, however, are the events that led to the First Punic War and the course it took. Let us start, then, by focusing on these events.

First Punic War

By around 270 BC, the Romans had conquered the entire Italian peninsula. Whether they were already cherishing ambitions to seize Sicily as well is not entirely clear. In any case, they were afraid that the Carthaginians, who controlled part of the island, might cross to Italy. The Carthaginians in their turn feared that the Romans might seek to expand their sphere of influence to include Sicily. The difficulties experienced with former mercenaries from the army of Hiero, the tyrant of Syracuse, kept the mutual fears alive. The mercenaries had entrenched themselves in the northernmost city of the island, Messina. When this city was besieged by Hiero's troops, the Mamertine mercenaries called on the Carthaginians to come to their aid. The Carthaginians came, but then declined to leave, prompting the Mamertines to turn to Rome for assistance. The Romans hesitated for some considerable time, but in 264 BC they crossed to Messina.

At that stage, no one could suspect that the incident would escalate into a major conflict: the First Punic War (264-241 BC). When war erupted, the outcome was almost impossible to predict. The Roman legions were certainly as good as the Carthaginian troops, but the Roman fleet was regarded as far weaker than that of its opponents. It therefore came as a shock when the Romans triumphed in the first confrontation at sea. This was the Battle of Mylae, in 260 BC, which they won thanks to the invention of the boarding bridge.

Fortune continued to favour the Romans. They secured several victories, but their aim of occupying the west of Sicily remained elusive. To bring the Carthaginians to their knees, they adopted an audacious plan in 256 BC, and invaded North Africa. This invasion ended in a debacle for the Romans. The war dragged on over the next few years, without either party securing a decisive advantage. The Romans suffered a blow of a different kind, when violent storms destroyed a large part of their fleet.

The Romans appeared to be staring defeat in the face in 247 BC, when the Carthaginian general Hamilcar Barcas unleashed a new offensive on Sicily, which extended to the very coasts of Italy. Gathering all the forces at their disposal, the Romans mustered a new fleet, which defeated the Carthaginians near the Egadi islands in 241 BC. Cut off from help by sea, the Carthaginian cities on the west coast of Sicily had no choice but to surrender to the Romans.

The battle for hegemony on Sicily had been fought and won. The island became the first province of the Romans. Four years later, the Carthaginians also had to give up Sardinia and Corsica.

Shekel, Heracles/ Melqart on the right, an elephant on the left; 213-210 BC; Sicily; National Numismatic Collection, De Nederlandsche Bank; inv. no. GR-10250.

Tetradrachme, depicting Arethusa on the left and a horse on the right; 320-300 BC; Sicily; National Numismatic Collection, De Nederlandsche Bank; inv. no. GR-01798.

Hannibal: The Second Punic War

Hannibal's political career is fairly well known from the Roman and Greek sources. Born in Carthage as the son of Hamilcar Barcas, he accompanied his father to Iberia, present–day Spain, in 237 BC, when he was almost ten years old. He therefore must have spent his earliest years in Carthage and the immediate surroundings. Although he cannot have consciously experienced the tail–end of the First Punic War against the Romans, the war against the mercenaries – which was fought out in the hinterland of Carthage – will undoubtedly have placed its stamp on his boyhood. Until 224 BC he spent most of his time in Spain, but he may have sometimes stayed in Carthage. After that he became second–in–command to his brother–in–law Hasdrubal. After the latter's death in 221 BC, the troops proclaimed him commander over Libya and Iberia, which decision was later endorsed by Carthage. He was then about twenty–five years of age. Six months after Rome had declared war on Carthage (in the autumn of 219 BC), Hannibal set off with his troops on a long march: they crossed the Ebro, the Pyrenees, and eventually the Alps. Then, in the course of the improbably–long period of fifteen years, he and his army advanced through Italy. In 203 he was called back to Africa when Scipio's armies were threatening Carthage. The decisive battle took place at Zama in the late summer or autumn of 202. Hannibal was defeated, after which a treaty was concluded in 201. At the end of this Second Punic War, Carthage also lost Spain for good; its territory had been reduced to the African hinterland.

Although defeated Carthaginian generals usually came to a bad end – that is, they were murdered or pressured into suicide – Hannibal made a remarkable comeback into Carthaginian politics. In 196 BC he was elected suffete, and immediately set about removing the rot from the system, purging the political institutions and rooting out corruption. The Romans will have watched this vigorous exercise with suspicion, and a year later they were pressuring Carthage to extradite Hannibal to Rome. With this threat hanging over him, he went into exile in Tyre (the 'mother city' of Carthage), in present–day Lebanon, after which he hired himself out as a strategist to Antiochus

III and other Hellenistic rulers in the East. In 183 BC, at almost 64 years old, he committed suicide at the court of King Prusias of Bithynia to avoid the disgrace of falling into the Romans' hands. He thus joined a long line of Carthaginian kings and aristocrats who opted for death, a tradition that started with Elisa/Dido and ended in 146 BC, when the wife of the younger Hasdrubal killed herself and her two small sons.

The Carthaginian elite – and consequently the Barcas family and Hannibal himself – were open to influences from the Greek–Hellenistic culture. Hannibal is known to have received lessons in Greek literature from the Spartan Sosylos, and his retinue also included another Greek, Silenos, from Kale Akte in Sicily. He may have had even more Greeks among his entourage, but this is pure speculation, since the Greek–Roman sources are biased and not very informative. Most of the information about the Spartan Sosylos, for instance, is provided by Polybios (3.20.5), who expresses himself contemptuously about the Spartan's writings: 'the common gossip of the barber's shop.' The fact that Hannibal was able to operate without any problem whatsoever during his period of exile in the Greek–speaking East suggests that he was well versed in Greek. The period he spent in Greek–ruled southern Italy (Magna Graecia) would have been helpful in this respect. He probably spoke Latin as well.

This historical sketch of Hannibal's life is based on the elements that most interested the Romans, which naturally related mainly to military and political events. The accounts convey little about the Punic world in which Hannibal lived and grew up, however. Archaeological finds, most notably in Carthage, have helped to amplify and clarify this picture (see also chapter 3).

Hannibal's Carthage

The Punic archaeology of North Africa is characterised by an 'urban bias', a heavy emphasis on urban culture, especially that of the metropolis of Carthage. This makes perfect sense, since from

Punic cuirass; Ksour Essaf; 3rd -2nd century BC; Musée National du Bardo.

the very moment at which colonists from Tyre founded Carthage (= 'New City') in 814/13 BC, Carthaginian culture was pre–eminently an urban culture with a strong connection to the sea. In this sense it differed fundamentally from virtually all other Mediterranean cultures (Greek, Etruscan, etc.), in which the urban or pre–urban centres were embedded far more clearly in agricultural societies. Hannibal himself is a typical product of this urban culture.

Nowhere in Carthage is the name of Hannibal more clearly linked to archaeological remains than in the so–called 'Hannibal Quarter' on the southeast slope of the Byrsa hill. It was here that French archaeologists excavated a Punic urban district in the 1970s and 1980s, a district that must have been built in the years around 200

BC. This archaeology–based date tallies well with Hannibal's period as suffete of Carthage and the vigorous administration attributed to him. More importantly, it tallies with his reputation as an urban planner during his later exile. Indeed, he is said to have planned the city of Arthashat (Artaxata) in Armenia. In Carthage we can see clearly that the new district is based on a tightly–designed rectangular plan with streets enclosing relatively small blocks of houses: a good example of Hippodamian planning. The urban dwellings are long and narrow, and each has its own small courtyard and a small cistern for water storage. These houses will have been several storeys high, and the analysis of the excavated material reveals that they were inhabited by an affluent middle class, which would have included craftsmen. The French made many discoveries, including the

The Battle of Zama has been the subject of several paintings and prints in European art history. The prints were widely distributed. Cornelis Cort; 1567.

remains of a place for milling grain and a workshop used by a craftsman who fashioned items in red coral. Many of the houses are decorated with Greek–Hellenistic murals in the 'Constructive' style, which is known in the cities around Mount Vesuvius as the First Pompeian Style. It is striking that the streets in the 'Hannibal Quarter' are unpaved. Stone slabs were laid only at the junctions, probably to prevent erosion.

War Debt

In the peace treaty signed in 201 BC, the conditions imposed on the defeated Carthaginians were draconian, particularly in financial terms. Rome demanded that Carthage pay an immediate sum of 1,000 talents, plus an additional sum of 250 Euboic talents annually for fifty years. This Greek monetary unit of weight was used as the international standard and was equivalent to about 26 kilograms of silver. The total debt imposed was therefore 13,500 talents, which amounted to approximately 350,000 kilograms of silver! For purposes of comparison: at the end of the First Punic War in 241 BC, the Carthaginians paid a one–off sum of 1,000 talents to Rome, plus another 2,200 talents spread over a ten–year period. This sum of 3,200 talents (or 83,000 kilos of silver) was already a high price for losing the war, but the quadrupling of that sum in 201 BC produced an astronomical debt. The raising of the annual sum from 220 to 250 talents a year might conceivably be regarded as a kind of correction for inflation; it was above all the duration of the imposed payments that was unprecedented. The Romans' objective was most probably to humiliate Carthage and to incapacitate it for a very long time, both economically and militarily. This latter aspect in particular will certainly have played a role in the setting of the amount and duration of the debt. For Carthage had always relied primarily on mercenaries for its permanent army. An impoverished Carthage would probably be unable to muster a large mercenary army, and would certainly not be able to maintain it for any length of time. Militarily too, Carthage was now bound hand and foot. The war fleet was reduced to the symbolic number of ten triremes, the war elephants had to be handed over, and Carthage was not permitted to wage war outside Africa. Even within its own territory – in other words, in

Africa – it had to seek consent from Rome before engaging in military action.

In spite of all this, and contrary to all Rome's expectations, the heavy war debt did not reduce Carthage to penury. Hannibal's reform of the state's income evidently furnished the Carthaginian state with a larger, constant source of revenue. In addition, the military restrictions imposed by Rome actually gave Carthage a great economic advantage. There was no longer any need to pay for a permanent army of mercenaries or expensive military campaigns. Carthage appears to have redirected its energies to investments in agriculture and trade, as Appian suggests. Another important, albeit speculative, explanation should be mentioned in this context. It can be assumed that far more money was available for such investments since many wealthy citizens from the former Punic territories in Spain and Sicily, now annexed by Rome, had fled to Carthage.

The City that Must be Destroyed: the Third Punic War

In the year 157 or 153 BC, the ageing senator Cato the Elder visited Carthage as a member of a Roman mission. As he walked around the harbour and the city centre he was struck by the prosperity he saw everywhere, and – something that greatly alarmed him – sheds full of timber, which he took to be intended for the construction of new warships. After his return to Rome, he became the spokesman for a group that sought the total destruction of Carthage. Whatever subject was being debated in the Senate, Cato is said to have ended every speech he addressed to the floor with the words: 'Ceterum censeo Carthaginem esse delendam' ('Moreover, I consider that Carthage must be destroyed'). Although this phrase was probably thought up by the German historian Franz Fiedler in the nineteenth century, the message itself certainly chimes with the views held by Cato, who left no stone unturned in his efforts to persuade his fellow senators of the threat posed by Carthage. A few years later, in 149 BC, the Romans decided to wage war against Carthage for the third time within a little over a century. What followed was a series of steps involving provocation, intimidation, deception and a show of strength, geared towards the permanent elimination of the city that had so long been a thorn in the Romans' side.

The Carthaginians resisted doggedly for over two years, which must have astonished the Romans, who had demanded that their opponents hand over all their weapons in exchange for the promise of peace. The Carthaginians had fulfilled these conditions, but the Romans followed it up with a new demand: the Carthaginians were to abandon their city and found a new one, 20 kilometres further inland. For the Carthaginians this was going too far, and they declared war on the Romans. Their city underwent a true metamorphosis. Temples, public buildings and squares were converted into workshops. Men and women worked day and night in shifts, forging new weapons. Every day, they produced 100 shields, 300 swords, 1,000 catapults and 500 javelins and spears. Women cut their long hair and used it to string their bows.

The tide turned in 147 BC, with the arrival of a new Roman consul, Scipio Aemilianus. He ensured that the Carthaginians' supply lines were watched more closely than before. A dam was built, closing off the harbour. After that, food shortages soon became apparent in the city. From the walls, the Carthaginians could see that the Romans were preparing for a massive offensive. But the Romans were not in any hurry. They had watched as people flocked to the city from the countryside over a period of several months, causing serious overcrowding. It was clear to the besieging forces that the Carthaginians – by then the city had a population of several hundred thousand people (estimates vary from 400,000 to 700,000) – were shut up within their walls. They had nowhere to go. In the packed streets, the people became ever more violent in their efforts to get hold of food. Brawls became commonplace. Not just in the street – fighting was even seen in the Carthaginian Senate.

In the spring of 146 BC, Scipio prepared to launch the decisive attack. The Romans knew that victory could not elude them, and with a great sense of theatricality, Scipio persuaded his soldiers that the gods too were on their side. In a solemn ceremony known as *evocatio*, he exhorted the Carthaginian

gods to abandon the city and settle in Rome instead. Now that its gods had forsaken it, Carthage could be seized and plundered without anyone being able to accuse the Romans of sacrilege.

The Carthaginians resisted bravely and even managed to put some of the Romans' battering rams out of action, but eventually the Romans succeeded in cutting them off from the outside world. The Roman troops tore down the walls and ran through the narrow streets, with their high buildings, towards the city centre. Initially they were fired at from the roofs, but once they had taken the first houses, they laid beams and planks over the spaces in between and in this way cleared a path to the market. The rest of the Roman soldiers fought their way through the narrow alleys, spreading death and destruction everywhere. People were shot or stabbed. For a time the Romans were loath to set fire to the city, concerned that their own soldiers on the roofs might be consumed by the flames, but once the operation was progressing steadily, Scipio personally ordered his men to set fire to several alleys.

By then, the city presented a terrifying appearance. Fierce fires blazed everywhere. Any buildings that were still standing were demolished with great ferocity. Women, children and elderly men who had been sheltering inside emerged into the street half–burned or fell from the collapsing roofs. Soon the streets and alleys were littered with bodies. This did not deter the Romans. They had specially trained field engineers who went along efficiently removing obstacles from their path: with pickaxes and spears they cleared the bodies and waste from the streets, tossing them into pits or ditches. The carnage was unspeakable. People lay in pits, some still alive, while Roman horsemen rode over them. The fighting and slaughter carried on for over a week, until the Carthaginians finally capitulated. By then, most of the population were dead. Fifty thousand men, women and children surrendered, and would be taken as slaves. The city continued to burn for days. All that remained was an expanse of blackened ruins. Meanwhile, the Roman war machine thundered relentlessly on. In due course, Scipio ordered his troops to demolish any building that was still standing. The soldiers were given permission to ransack the city until there was nothing left. Many precious items that came into the hands of the generals were sent to Rome to be displayed in public as a permanent memorial to one of the greatest triumphs of Roman history.

According to the Greek historian Polybius, Scipio could not suppress his emotion when he saw the old city lying in ruins. Scipio, when he looked upon the city as it was utterly perishing and in the last throes of its complete destruction, is said to have shed tears and wept openly for his enemies. After being wrapped in thought for long, and realizing that all cities, nations, and authorities must, like men, meet their doom; that this happened to Ilium, once a prosperous city, to the empires of Assyria, Media, and Persia, the greatest of their time, and to Macedonia itself, the brilliance of which was so recent, either deliberately or the verses escaping him, he said:

"A day will come when sacred Troy shall perish,
And Priam and his people shall be slain."

And when Polybius speaking with freedom to him, for he was his teacher, asked him what he meant by the words, they say that without any attempt at concealment he named his own country, for which he feared when he reflected on the fate of all things human. - Translation: Loeb Classical Library

When news of the victory reached Rome, people rushed out of their houses to celebrate in the street. For over a century they had lived in constant fear of the Carthaginians. Now it was finally over. They now felt assured that no state would ever be capable of stopping the Romans' ambitions.

Map of Hannibal's march (white line). The dotted line shows the route followed by Hannibal's brother, Hasdrubal, who brought reinforcements but was defeated by the Romans. The red dots indicate the places where major battles between Hannibal's army and the Roman legions took place.

Basemap by NASA/Goddard Space Flight Center – Wikimedia Commons

Bronze Eros with lamp; shipwreck of Mahdia; 100 BC; Musée National du Bardo (photo: E. van den Bandt).

10
THE MAHDIA SHIPWRECK

Ruurd Halbertsma

THE DESTRUCTION OF CARTHAGE IN 146 BC BY THE ROMAN LEGIONS WAS NOT AN ISOLATED EVENT IN THE HISTORY OF THE MEDITERRANEAN REGION. ONCE THE PUNIC THREAT HAD BEEN EXTINGUISHED, THE ROMANS TURNED THEIR ATTENTION TO SUBDUING POCKETS OF RESISTANCE IN THE EAST. A NUMBER OF GREEK CITY-STATES OF THE ACHAEAN LEAGUE WERE IN REVOLT AGAINST ROMAN RULE. THE SENATE SENT TWO LEGIONS COMMANDED BY LUCIUS MUMMIUS TO GREECE. OUTSIDE THE WALLS OF CORINTH, THE ROMAN AND GREEK TROOPS ENGAGED IN BATTLE.

› Bronze figure of a dwarf; shipwreck of Mahdia, 100 BC; Musée National du Bardo.

The Greek general Diaeus fled, leaving Corinth undefended. To set an example, Mummius razed the city of Corinth to the ground. The news that both Carthage and Corinth had been destroyed in the same year struck fear into many rulers, who were concerned for their own territories. King Attalus III drew up a will stating that upon his death the kingdom of Pergamon was to come under Roman rule. This took place in 133 BC.

Sixty years after the Battle of Corinth, another battle raged in Greece. King Mithridates VI of Pontus had unleashed a revolt against Rome and had conquered several parts of Greece. He had placed Athens under the rule of one Aristion, a Greek ally. General Lucius Cornelius Sulla advanced from Rome to halt the advance of Mithridates and to punish the Greek insurgents. After a long siege, Sulla took Athens in 86 BC and ordered his troops to plunder the cultural capital of antiquity for several days. The finest works of art were taken to Rome as spoils of war, to be sold there. But not all the ships carrying their precious cargoes safely reached the Italian harbours for which they were bound.

In 1907, Greek sponge divers off the coast of Tunisia discovered the wreck of a ship from antiquity. The ship was not carrying the usual cargo of transport amphorae: the divers saw bronze and marble limbs poking out between pieces of seaweed and coral. They retrieved some statues of exceptional beauty and brought them on land at the little port of Mahdia. The Tunisian archaeological service subsequently launched a number of diving expeditions, which continued until 1913. The finds were outstanding: Greek sculptures in bronze and marble from the Hellenistic period, luxury items of furniture, intact columns and capitals, inscriptions, decorative vases, candelabras and lead ingots. Items of 'ordinary', everyday pottery dated the shipwreck to the first half of the first century BC. This soon led the scholars to link the finds to the plundering of Athens and the artworks shipped to Rome. They put forward the theory that the ship may have been

⌄ Bronze Eros with lamp; shipwreck of Mahdia; 100 BC; Musée National du Bardo.

blown off course in a gale, and when the cargo started to slide (it included 60 stone columns!) it capsized off the coast of Tunisia. It is thought unlikely that the ship was actually heading for North Africa. Carthage was in ruins and there were no other cities in the vicinity with wealthy local elites. The 'treasure of Mahdia' was displayed in the Bardo Museum in Tunis. In 1994 all the finds were exhibited at the Rheinisches Landesmuseum in Bonn, after first undergoing restoration there.

The exhibition *Carthage* includes three remarkable bronze pieces from the shipwreck: a satyr, a dancing female dwarf, and an Eros bearing a torch. According to the German scholar Werner Fuchs, who published an inventory of the ship's contents in 1963, these three bronze statues originate from a studio in Athens that was run by the famous sculptor Boethus of Calchedon. His signature is found on another piece from the shipwreck.

The satyr, half man, half animal, is a fine example of Hellenistic sculpture. This was a period in which sculptors experimented with depicting human bodies in the most complicated of poses. The satyr in the exhibition exemplifies a surprising blend of movement and stillness. He appears to have come to a sudden halt after rushing at top speed, stopped in his tracks by something he sees in the distance. His eyes have an alert expression, his mouth is open, gasping for air, and his arms are thrown forward by the sudden stop. His hair is unruly and bristly. He is one of the followers of the god of wine, Dionysus. Has he glimpsed his lord and master in the distance? Or has he seen a beautiful girl, a maenad, for which satyrs are constantly searching? Possibly the satyr once belonged to a larger group of sculptures.

The dancing girl has all the features associated with dwarfism: short legs, a long torso, short arms and a disproportionately large head. Dressed in a long robe she executes dance steps. Her head is thrown back towards her neck, almost in ecstasy. She dances to the rhythmic accompaniment of the *krotala* or castanets in her hand. Renderings of human beings with unusual proportions were also popular in Hellenistic sculpture. After the

classical period with its perfect representation of the perfect body, Greek artists turned their attention to different, distinctive kinds of bodies: they depicted children, for instance, but also people with disabilities or deformities. People afflicted by dwarfism provided musical and acrobatic performances at festivities in antiquity. Egypt had a long tradition in this regard. This figure belonged to a group of three small dancers found in the shipwreck of Mahdia. They were dancing to the music of a fourth figure, a winged Eros with a splendid lyre. There is a ring on his back, to which a chain must originally have been attached. One of the dwarf figures also has a ring of this kind. Perhaps the entire group was once suspended as a kind of mobile, depicting Eros playing music, surrounded by 'comical' dancing dwarfs.

The third figure from the shipwreck of Mahdia is an Eros with a torch. This is an androgynous figure, carrying the torch in the left hand. This Eros has a companion–piece: a hermaphrodite depicted running, also carrying a torch. The two runners allude to the typical Athenian sports event *Lampadedromia*, a relay race between the boys' teams of the different districts or *phylai* of Attica. The boys would start their race outside the city towards dusk, at the altar of Prometheus and Hephaestus. The 'baton' was a burning torch. At set times during the two–kilometre race they had to hand the torch to the next member of the team until they reached the finish in the city. They were not permitted to allow the fire to go out. Upon reaching the finishing line, the winner would use his torch to light a fire on the altar. The spectacle appealed to the Greeks' aesthetic tastes, their love of the sight of young athletes, and was frequently depicted in the art of ancient Attica, in various periods. The running Eros discussed here combines male and female beauty, which – like the fire in the torch – is only transient. The torch of this statue could really burn. The back of Eros's head (which has been lost) was actually a lid into which oil could be poured. This oil passed through the left arm into the torch, where it could be ignited with a taper. These torch–bearers, standing in banquet halls with an abundance of food and drink, recalled the ephemeral nature of earthly delights.

In his collection of poems *Catacomben* ('Catacombs'; 1980) the Dutch poet, archaeologist and former curator of the National Museum of Antiquities, Frédéric Bastet, wrote a poem inspired by the shipwreck of Mahdia. He was fascinated by the tragic fate of these ancient masterpieces, while at the same time he was well aware that the shipwreck ultimately led to their preservation. He compares the descent into the sea and the eventual retrieval of the art treasures by divers to the descent and retrieval of his most personal feelings – which he prefers to keep to himself:

The Shipwreck of Mahdia

Two thousand years ago
the ship of Mahdia sank.
the bronze god of love,
lying in seaweed and coral,
sang as a water gong –
with ever open lips.

Two thousand years ago
the ship of Mahdia sank.
The great marble urn
with its satyrs and its maenads,
whispering, whelk–like, sank –
and all their feet danced on.

Two thousand years later
the ship of my thoughts sinks
to an unfathomable depth,
and let no diver ever dive there
to retrieve the timber wreck –
their imaginings live on.

Bronze satyr; shipwreck of Mahdia; 125-100 BC; Musée National du Bardo.

Particularly in Roman times the art of mosaic making reached exceptional quality. Often the richness and wealth of northern Tunisia is depicted. Collection: Musée National du Bardo, Tunis.

11
ROMAN CARTHAGE: HISTORY AND MONUMENTS

Samir Aounallah

AFTER SCIPIO AEMILIANUS HAD WON A GREAT VICTORY OVER CARTHAGE IN 146 BC, HE ADDRESSED THE SENATE, ASKING: 'I HAVE CONQUERED CARTHAGE. WHAT WOULD YOU HAVE ME DO WITH IT?' THE REST OF THE STORY IS WELL KNOWN. CATO'S WARNING WAS HEEDED (POSTHUMOUSLY) AND VELLEIUS PATERCULUS RELATES (IN HIS HISTORIAE BOOK 1, 12:L. 27): 'EVEN AFTER ROME HAD CONQUERED THE WORLD, SHE COULD NOT HOPE FOR SECURITY SO LONG AS THE NAME OF CARTHAGE REMAINED AS OF A CITY STILL STANDING'. A TEN–MAN COMMITTEE OR DECEMVIRATE WAS ORDERED TO RAZE THE CITY TO THE GROUND.

The tale of the ensuing expedition is told by Appian (in *Punica* 135.639-642): 'They decreed that if anything was still left of Carthage, Scipio should obliterate it and that nobody should be allowed to live there. Direful threats were levelled against any who should disobey and chiefly against the rebuilding of Byrsa or Megara'.

Carthage remained out of bounds for almost twenty–five years. In the meantime, a major epidemic swept through Africa in 125-124 BC, killing animals and crops. In this region it claimed 200,000 human lives, opening up large swathes of empty land (Orosius Book 5, 11.4). Meanwhile, in Rome it was reported that the suspension of grain supplies had led to famine and insurgency. In 123-122 BC conflicts erupted between *optimates* and *populares* (roughly: aristocrats and populists) over the vacant tracts of land. The tribune Gracchus, who belonged to the latter group, put several draft laws to the vote in the Senate. Two of them provided for the redistribution of part of the Italian public land to the Roman citizenry (plebs) and for the founding of new colonies. The idea of founding a colony in Carthage was born.

Gracchus sailed to Africa with 6,000 colonists to found a new colony there. If we are to believed Plutarch (*Caius Gracchus*, 32), the new colony was set up in just seventy days, with each colonist being assigned 50 hectares of land. It enjoyed the protection of the goddess Juno, and was named 'colonia Junonia Carthago'. The land thus allocated in this ambitious project covered a total of 300,000 hectares, a surface area comparable to the peninsula of Cap Bon, opposite Carthage. It foundered, however, because of political conflicts in Rome and the assassination of Gracchus, and just twelve months later the colony was abandoned.

Ten years later, in 111 BC, an agricultural law, lex Thoria, privatised the public land, to the clear benefit of the Roman aristocracy. A large number of colonists sold the lands thus obtained and either returned to Rome or opted to go and live in Utica, then the capital city of Africa.

What happened to this first colony? Was it abandoned, or was it simply its status as a colony that was abolished? There is some archaeological evidence, but none of it conclusive: the existence of a large rural land allocation (*centuratio*) that is attributed to Gracchus; the discovery, some five kilometres to the west of the Byrsa Hill, of walls that can be connected to Gracchus's colony; and a series of anepigraphic gravestones that may have belonged to these early colonists. The systematic archaeological excavations that took place as part of the 'Save Carthage Campaign' did not yield anything from the pre–Augustan Roman era.

The literary evidence is scarcely more illuminating. The testimony of Eutropius and of Solinus points to the continued existence of the 'city' after the abortive venture led by Gracchus: a Roman presence in the form of a village, possibly mixed with Africans and Romans, survived the colonia Iunonia Carthago, but the significance of their presence cannot be evaluated on the basis of today's knowledge.

Golden Age: From Caesar to Commodus: 46 BC - AD 192

The situation remained unchanged until Caesar's victory over King Juba I of Numidia in 46 BC. Rome, with rather more verve this time, finally decided to found a colony in Carthage: colonia Concordia Iulia Carthago. Appian (136) and Solinus (27.9) relate that having destroyed Carthage, the Romans rebuilt it 102 years later – that is, in 44 BC. At Caesar's instigation, the project was carried out by his adopted son, Octavius, the future Emperor Augustus (27 BC - AD 14). Octavius consolidated this colony in 29 BC by sending more settlers and lifting the curse that had lain on the land since 146 BC. From the moment of its

‹ Stela of Saturn; AD 323; Musée National du Bardo. In the Roman period, the Phoenician god Baal–Hammon was transformed into Saturn.

⌄ The Roman amphitheatre of Carthage.

Byrsa Hill. On the remains of Punic houses and workshops stand the foundations of Roman buildings. The concrete pillars used to 'reinforce' the enormous platform are visible here.

foundation, Carthage was allocated a vast territory (the *pertica Carthaginiensium*) with a circumference of over a hundred kilometres, and granted immunity from taxation. Several settlements in Africa, including Dougga and Thibar, were partly annexed to Carthage.

This meant that Carthage had everything it needed to become one of the largest cities in the Roman Empire and the capital city of Africa. The first public works began on the Byrsa Hill and were undoubtedly devoted to building the residence of the proconsul of Africa and the administrative buildings in which he could perform his duties. A Latin inscription excavated here refers to 'proconsular baths' (ILTun. 1093). An amphora wall found on the southeastern flanks attests to this initial construction work. It was erected between 43 and 19 BC at the earliest: seven to eight layers of horizontal nesting amphorae that were filled with soil and separated by a thick layer of soil (some 50 to 60 cm). The wall was about 4.4 metres wide.

The construction work evidently went on for decades, since the governor of Africa was still living in Utica in 12 BC. This proconsul's house may well be the residence mentioned by Victor de Vita (*Bellum Vandalorum*, 1.20): 'the building dominates the city and serves as a residence for the kings of the Vandals; there is a prison in the cellars'. The hill's development began with two symbolic acts. The remains of Punic Carthage and everything that bore witness to the past, to the city's former power and the curse on the land, had to be erased. The Punic buildings were not removed but buried beneath enormous artificial embankments and foundations that levelled out the terrain: thousands of tons of material, reinforced with concrete pillars, were needed to elevate the ground level. This is one of the largest artificial platforms in the Roman world: at 336x223 metres, an area slightly over three hectares, it is three times the size of Augustus's Roman Forum.

The growing city also needed a framework in which to construct new buildings: essentially an urban development plan, with the central point corresponding to the choir screen of the present–day St Louis Cathedral. This map defines the spaces designated for public buildings and private houses. It is almost a perfect square, measuring 1,776 metres from north to south and 1,656 metres from east to west, approximately 250 hectares of four large rectangles, each of which is divided into 120 smaller ones. The small and large rectangles are separated by roads, some of which are wide (11.8 metres) and others narrow (7 metres), depending on the adjacent rectangles. The road network of Roman Carthage covered an estimated length of 60 kilometres. Although few excavations have been conducted there, the most important development phases of the settlement can be deduced from the results.

The first phase started with the founding of the colony and lasted about a hundred years, the second witnessed the building of the library in the west and the basilica in the east. Eventually the settlement would be divided into three parts. In the north was a large forum, with a surface area of over 13,000 m², the long sides of which were flanked by porticos while its east side was dominated by the basilica, of which only the foundations and a few elements of the floor can still be seen today. This monumental structure measured 3,600 m², making it the third largest basilica in the Roman Empire, after the Basilica Ulpia and the Basilica Julia in Rome. In the south was a large terrace. This was probably a promenade, to which a temple was added in the second century AD. In the middle of the settlement was a second square, almost as large as the forum, with a temple dedicated to Aesculapius. In the second century AD a large library was added to this structure.

This, in a nutshell, is all that can be said about this settlement, which retains its symbolic significance to this day: from the earliest excavation and foundations to the almost complete restoration after the fire that destroyed the city under the principate of Antoninus Pius (138-161). The central square, like the rest of the urban space, was undoubtedly an enormous construction site for many years, given that many buildings had to be constructed. It seems likely that this situation continued for half of century, or more.

1.

2.

3.

'it is said that Caesar . . . when he had pursued Pompey . . . was troubled by a dream in which he saw a whole army weeping, and that he immediately made a memorandum in writing that Carthage should be colonised. Returning to Rome not long after, and while making a distribution of lands to the poor, he arranged to send some of them to Carthage and some to Corinth. But he was assassinated shortly afterward . . . and his son Augustus, finding this memorandum, built the present Carthage, not on the site of the old one, but very near it, in order to avoid the ancient curse. I have ascertained that he sent some 3000 colonists from Rome and that the rest came from the neighbouring country. – Appian, Punica, 136

The prosperity and opulence that returned to Carthage in the Roman period often found expression in superb mosaics; Roman period; Musée National du Bardo.

• •

One of the episodes [in Virgil's *Aeneid*] that the Romans will certainly have found moving is that in which Virgil describes the love between Dido and Aeneas. The African land on which the queen and the hero first met, and this luxurious city that was being built there, fired the imagination. By a fortunate coincidence, Augustus happened to be extremely interested in Carthage at that time; he invited his subjects to rescue the city from its wretched state and to restore it to its former glory. The Emperor and the poet agreed; the Muses conspired with political ambition. This was all that was needed to make the reconstruction of Carthage a fashionable venture, rather than the partisan undertaking it had been in the past.'– *Audollent 1901.* [transl. BJ]

• •

In Hadrian's biography, we read: 'Though he cared nothing for inscriptions on his public works, he gave the name of Hadrianopolis to many cities, as, for example, even to Carthage and a section of Athens; and he also gave his name to aqueducts without number'. – *Historia Augusta, The Life of Hadrian,* 20.4-5.

When we study the city plans in detail, we see that nothing was left to chance. From the latter half of the second century AD onwards, most of the public buildings, such as the theatre, the amphitheatre and the circus were in use, They were located on the outskirts of the city, probably to spare the city centre the nuisance that necessarily accompanied large crowds, chariots and wild animals.

The role played by the Antonine emperors in enhancing the splendour of Carthage is confirmed by several texts. One of the city's inhabitants, Apuleius (AD 125-175), wrote: 'Behold these charming buildings, so superb in construction, so beautiful in decoration, in which they have invested their capital; behold these villas built on a scale that vies with cities, these houses that are embellished in the manner of temples, these hordes of countless adorned slaves, these sumptuous furnishings. Everything accrues to them, everything breathes opulence' (*On the God of Socrates*, 22.171; transl. BJ)'.

One of the monuments that were built in this dynasty was the aqueduct of Zaghouan, which appears to have been an initiative of Hadrian and which was completed under Antoninus Pius in AD 157. The large Antonine Baths were dedicated in the same year and completed in AD 162. The aqueduct assured Carthage of a daily water supply of 32,000 cubic metres. The other monument that should be mentioned is the harbour complex that was completed under Commodus (AD 180-192). The old Punic harbours were completely redesigned and given a different function. Between AD 98 and 138, the rectangular harbour was enlarged and modified, acquiring a hexagonal shape resembling that of Trajan's inland harbour in Ostia. The circular harbour was completed in the second century AD, when the quayside around the harbour was constructed and the old 'admiralty island' was converted into an open square surrounded by columns, with a small temple and an octagonal building in the middle. This ensemble, built in grand imperial style, was further embellished by a triumphal arch with four openings. This work undoubtedly took place under Commodus, who created, in AD 186, the 'grain fleet' (that is, the fleet that imported grain from Africa), which was probably stationed in Carthage.

Emperor Commodus named the city 'Carthage Alexandria Commodiana Togata' (*togata* signifying 'clad in a Roman toga'. While the large complexes were being constructed on the Byrsa Hill and in the harbour area, it appears that from an early stage the Carthaginian authorities also indulged their love of spectacle by building monumental recreational structures. None of them is precisely dated, but Tertullian (AD 155/170-222) refers to four monumental structures used to stage games or plays: the circus, the theatre, het amphitheatre, and the stadium (*De spectaculis*). Later, Augustinus refers to hunting in the amphitheatre, pantomime in the theatre, chariot races in the circus, and a *naumachia* (sea battle in the theatre, or in the amphitheatre at an earlier stage). If we are to believe the literary sources, this love of games and plays endured, even when King Gaiseric of the Vandals appeared at the gates of the city in AD 439.

The End of Prosperity

All the conditions were in place for the birth of a real Rome – a Rome in Africa, wrote Salvian, in his treatise *On the Government of God* (7.13-17). Carthage was never a rival for the glory of Rome, but from the early third century AD onwards, according to the ancient scribes, it was one of the candidates for the second place, alongside illustrious cities such as Constantinople and Alexandria. From Septimius Severus (193-211) onwards, however, we see the progressive dismantlement of the *pertica* of Carthage: the old cities that had been placed under its authority, such as Dougga, became independent. The regional dignitaries who had previously been required to pay tribute to Carthage for the performance of certain tasks and positions in the Magistracy left the city almost immediately.

To compensate Carthage for these losses, Emperor Caracalla conferred the *ius italicum* on the colony, which was renamed Colonia Concordia Iulia Aurelia Antoniniana Carthago. This placed it on the same footing, with the same fiscal benefits, as a city in Italy. This measure did not suffice, however, since with the exception of the Odeon, which Tertullian tells us was built under Septimius Severus, no more really large public buildings were registered that are comparable to what was achieved in the Antonine period. This grand Carthage would continue to exist for some time. Aurelius Victor (*De Caesaribus* 39.45) writes that Diocletian (284-305) built monumental structures in several cities including Carthage. Under Constantine the Great (307-337), inscriptions refer to multiple instances of restoration work on buildings that were probably destroyed in AD 310 when the soldiers of Maxentius (306-312) plundered the city. The last great structure is the city wall, which the *chronica Gallica* (AD 452) attribute to Theodosius II and Galla Placidia. The wall was evidently not very effective, since Gaiseric had little trouble taking the city in AD 439.

Mosaics from the collection of the Musée National du Bardo, Tunis.

Ruins of Roman Carthage. Baths of Antoninus Pius. Built in the Second century AD (© Canonman29 | dreamstime.com).

In the Christian period, many buildings were decorated with tiles depicting Biblical scenes. Musée National de Carthage.

12
CHRISTIAN CARTHAGE

Fathi Bejaoui

THE EARLIEST RELIABLE EVIDENCE OF THE DEVELOPMENT OF CHRISTIANITY IN AFRICA, AS FAR AS WE KNOW TODAY, DATES FROM THE SECOND CENTURY. UNDERSTANDABLY, IT ORIGINATES FROM CARTHAGE, WHICH WAS THE REGIONAL CAPITAL AT THAT TIME. THE DOCUMENTATION ALL RELATES TO THE PERSECUTION OF CHRISTIANS. IN AD 180, TWELVE CHRISTIANS (SEVEN MEN AND FIVE WOMEN) WERE BEHEADED IN CARTHAGE, BECOMING THE FIRST KNOWN AFRICAN MARTYRS IN CHRISTENDOM. TWO OTHERS – THE FAMOUS PERPETUA AND FELICITAS – MET THE SAME FATE IN AD 203, POSSIBLY, AS LEGEND HAS IT, IN THE CITY'S AMPHITHEATRE.

These dramatic events have come down to us primarily through the copious writings of Tertullian (before 160-122), the first Christian to have written in Latin. An orator, legal scholar, priest and early Christian apologist, Tertullian was known for his rigour and steadfastness. From his work and from that of Cyprian, another African Church scholar, we can be certain that Carthage already had a fairly large Christian community in the third century. Cyprian was an ecclesiastical writer who rose to become bishop of Carthage, and organised a major Episcopal Synod in 256, which was attended by the representatives of over eighty African dioceses. We can therefore conclude that Christianity had become firmly embedded in this part of the Empire by this point in time. Cyprian himself died a martyr's death under Emperor Valerian in the year 258.

At some point in the fourth century, we find that an official ban on paganism had been in force for several decades, and Carthage had converted almost entirely to the new religion. This is clear from the writings of St Augustine (354-430), one of the most important Church Fathers, who left not only a voluminous body of correspondence but several works that are central to Christian orthodoxy, of which he was a passionate champion. Throughout his life, Augustine fought against schisms within the African Church that were caused by the Manichaean, Pelagian and most notably the Donatist heresies.

Donatism, a separatist movement named after bishop Donatus Magnus, which originated in Carthage in response to the persecutions of Christians under Diocletian, precipitated a serious religious crisis. It made itself felt in urban and rural settlements alike, and at some point almost every city had buildings dedicated to both sides in the controversy, in which the rival parties celebrated their cults. This information can be distilled from the report of the Conference of Carthage, held on the initiative of St Augustine in 411 and attended by just under 600 bishops, almost half of whom were Catholic and the other half Donatist. This was the beginning of the movement, which did not vanish entirely until the advent of the Vandals, who reached Carthage in 439 and settled there for a hundred years. The writings of Victor de Vita, bishop of Byzacena (in present–day central Tunisia) describe the years 480-484, and tell of the razing of buildings, abuses of power and persecutions in the city of Carthage that ensued from this invasion. The Odeon district and the theatre, for instance, were partly laid waste at the beginning of this occupation, as the archaeological record confirms.

With the Byzantine reconquest of Africa, at the behest of Justinian in 533, the Bishop of Carthage was once again Primate and guardian of the unity of the African Church. This position was gradually lost, however, after the city fell to Arab–Islamic armies in the years 697-698. From certain sources, however – papal correspondence in particular – we know that the old metropolis still had bishops well into the tenth century. Thanks to the writings of such learned clerics and the rapid and effective organisation of the local Church, the name of Carthage has been inscribed forever in the annals of history alongside those of Rome and Constantinople, as the place where the Latin Bible was first created and developed.

Daniel in the den of lions; ivory; Musée National de Carthage.

The archaeological records of Christian Carthage

A large quantity of diverse archaeological evidence has been preserved of the Christian era of Carthage: architecture, epigraphs, diverse art forms, such as sculptures, mosaics, pottery, glass, jewellery in precious metals etc. Excavations and research that started in the nineteenth century (with Alfred Louis Delattre and Paul Gauckler) and continued to the end of the twentieth century (mainly conducted by Noël Duval, Susan Stevens and especially Liliane Ennabli, who produced several treatises on Christian Carthage that examine Christian inscriptions and religious architecture, teach us that no fewer than 23 or 24 churches were established here. Some are named, for instance in sermons and in the letters of St Augustine.

Today, more than ten religious buildings are visible in the known area of the ancient city, which was divided into seven or eight ecclesiastical regions. They include the basilica of Damous El Karita, which was probably one of the largest in Africa (65 metres long and 45 metres wide, not counting the numerous annexes),the basilica of St Cyprian, which was built on the site of the saint's grave, and the Dermech complex near Anthony's thermal baths. There were also chapels and monasteries. Most of the floors of these buildings were decorated with mosaics in various geometrical, floral, animal or symbolic motifs (cross, peacock, kantharos etc.) or with illustrations of Biblical stories, after the example of the theme of the rivers of

Late Antique tile, with an image of Adam and Eve. Collection: Musée National de Carthage.

Paradise, three examples of which were found in a single church, namely Bir Ftouha. The roofs, and undoubtedly the walls too, were covered with terracotta tiles (an African specialty) on which believers could admire images of the most popular subjects from Early Christian art: Adam and Eve, the sacrifice of Abraham, Daniel in the lion's den, Jonas in the whale, the Miracles of Christ, and the Virgin Mary. These same subjects were fashionable towards the end of the fourth century for the decorations on African pottery lamps. Thousands of these objects, which were made virtually in an assembly line, were discovered during excavations on this site. Epigraphs (thousands of inscriptions in stone or mosaic documented in inventories) have provided us with important information about the role played in Carthage by the cults of saints and martyrs, the apostles Peter and Paul, the martyrs Perpetua and Felicitas, Stephen and Menas. These epigraphs and dedications have also acquainted us with the names of bishops and other clerics who are mentioned in the reports of the numerous councils and synods that were organised in this city. The precise date of the first of these meetings is not known, but it was probably in the early third century.

This distinguished past of the greatest Christian metropolis in Africa is reflected today in the historic buildings that are open to the public. The memory of this past is also preserved in two museums, one on the Byrsa Hill, close to the cathedral that was built in the nineteenth century to commemorate St Louis, and another that is dedicated to Christian Carthage.

Byzantine basilica of Dermech I, to the west of the Antonine Thermal Baths.

Scipio weeping for Carthage; Ludwig Gottlieb Portman; 1797; Rijksmuseum Amsterdam; inv. no. RP-P-1905-2181.

13
DIDO AND HANNIBAL THROUGH WESTERN EYES

....

Eric M. Moormann

THE HISTORY OF CARTHAGE HAS FIRED THE IMAGINATIONS OF WRITERS AND ARTISTS SINCE THE MIDDLE AGES, BECAUSE OF THE CITY'S HEROIC RESISTANCE TO THE ROMANS. MANY TRIED TO DEPICT OR DESCRIBE EPISODES FROM CARTHAGE'S PAST WITHOUT ANY KNOWLEDGE OF NORTH AFRICA. THE SOURCES THEY CONSULTED WERE FIRST AND FOREMOST ROMAN TEXTS SUCH AS VIRGIL'S *AENEID* AND LIVY'S HISTORY OF ROME, *AB URBE CONDITA*. THEY ALSO DREW ON BIOGRAPHIES OF THE PROTAGONISTS BY THE GREEK WRITER PLUTARCH, WHICH WERE WIDELY DISSEMINATED (LARGELY IN FRENCH TRANSLATION) THROUGHOUT WESTERN EUROPE. FOR MANY CENTURIES, SOURCES ILLUMINATING THE PUNIC SIDE OF EVENTS WERE ENTIRELY ABSENT.

Part of the appeal of Dido, Hannibal, Sophonisba, Massinissa and others who were involved in the wars between Rome and Carthage was the exoticism of these men and women, who were sometimes portrayed as dark–skinned Africans and who were 'nonetheless' capable of wreaking havoc among the forces of the noble Romans. Dido was the mysterious queen who succeeded in detaining Aeneas at her court until the gods sent their messenger, Mercury, ordering him to return to Italy. She was clever, beautiful and alluring, as courageous as a man, and she consequently possessed almost superhuman gifts. She could serve as an example to kings and queens alike, but she was also described in the sources as an immoral and perverse temptress and a suicide. Dido's Carthage would later

become the powerful opponent of Aeneas's descendants. The Queen cursed the future Rome as she burned at the stake.

Dido was seen as the equal of rulers and soldiers of military fame. She built a city, fought against the surrounding tribes, and went hunting, all supposedly 'male' activities. Aeneas broke into this happy pioneering world, and his passion seems initially to have enriched it. One of the high points in their stormy relationship, as related by Virgil, is a hunting trip during which a torrential downpour and thunderstorm force them to take shelter in a cave. The two are in every respect a match for each other, and in the sketch produced by Romeijn de Hooghe, Dido wears a suit of armour over her royal robe. This

Female personification of Africa; Crispijn van de Passe; 1589-1611; Rijksmuseum Amsterdam; inv. no. RP–P–1938-1492.

is a highly atmospheric sketch, with its sarcophagi bearing imaginary inscriptions in Greek. Dido's assistant Anna withdraws discreetly, and the heroes have laid their weapons aside.

Her counterpart, Aeneas, was generally described in glowing terms, despite his weakness in succumbing to Dido's charms. His first meeting with Dido was sometimes depicted in cycles of paintings or tapestries, such as the series made for the negotiations of the Peace of Nijmegen in 1678 (now in Museum Het Valkhof, Nijmegen). The pictures were reproduced in cheap copies – prints, sold separately or included as illustrations in books. Crispijn de Passe's series, one print of which is included in the exhibition, consisted of at least thirteen prints. It is clear from the caption to the anonymous classicist print dating from around 1700 that Aeneas is also depicted here as devious. He plays the gallant when the queen meets him in the harbour or in her throne room, but meanwhile he pursues his own goals. For Dido, the future has only death in store.

Aeneas's entrance into Carthage is in itself a miraculous event. Tiepolo depicts Venus showing Aeneas and Achates the way to the city, in his sketch for a ceiling painting. She is sitting on a cloud that obscures Aeneas's fleet. In the print by Thomassin, dating from the middle or late seventeenth century, two lines from the *Aeneid* (1.588-589) clarify the action: Achates asks Dido to come to the aid of the castaways, and after he has spoken, Aeneas appears to descend from the clouds. Dido's throne is in front of some buildings that are under construction; on the left, a labourer is busying himself with a marble column. The eighteenth–century fan depicts the same scene; for its erudite owner, the allusion to the storm in which Aeneas appears may have been a delightful association with the fan that cooled her brow, and that was furthermore an important instrument in lovemaking. All these scenes emphasise the contrast between Aeneas's fiery temperament and Dido's restraint.

Dus deerlyk fneuvelde Kartagoos koningin.
Men fchrikke, en wachte zich voor d'ongebonde min.

∧ *Dido in the throes of death, with a moralistic caption beneath the print. Rijksmuseum Amsterdam.*

> *Dido and Aeneas; Paper; Romeyn de Hooghe; 17th century; Leiden University Libraries; inv. no. PK-T-306.*

Crispy van pas scul

112

Prima luce feras dire, Carthaginis arces
martius armata vicit prope littora turma
Scipio, et oblatum metit Insatiabilis agmen.

A la puissante Cite Cartago
par scipio de grand force, voya
fist tant q̃ ladite Cite, au prem

donna
son auātage.
na.

Scipio beſtormpt Cartago die ſtercke Stadt
Inde zee plat ondiep, hy ſyn voerdeel aenſach
Sulcx ſonder verdrach, dat hyſe want den i.ᵉⁿ dach.

Raph. Vrbin inu.
Cornelio Cort fe.

The Dutch tragedy *Didoos doot* ('The Death of Dido'), written in 1668 by Andries Pels, served in turn as a source of inspiration well into the eighteenth century, when the play was still being performed. In a print by Simon Fokke, dating from 1758, Dido is burning at the stake in front of a canal house, while Aeneas is depicted as a modern burgher, complete with the long wig that was fashionable at the time. The aim was probably to ridicule Pels's play, which was regarded as pompous. The scene included several minor characters: a urinating figure of Amor, Dido's wet nurse Anna in the doorway, and Juno riding a chariot across the clouds. None of the artists who produced any of these paintings or prints made the slightest effort to portray Carthage or Dido as foreign. The architecture is classicist, and the characters' dress is quasi–Roman, probably based on stage costumes.

Another popular theme, second only to the dramatic love between Dido and Aeneas, was the history of the Carthaginian Princess Sophonisba, who was forbidden to marry her beloved Massinissa. Sophonisba was Hannibal's niece, while Prince Massinissa was one of Scipio's allies. The Roman general would not countenance this relationship between Massinissa and his arch–enemy's kinswoman, and the couple sealed their suicide pact by drinking poison mixed with wine. This exemplum of lovers driven to seek death by the constancy of their love is frequently depicted in frescoes and paintings. The setting for the tale is a sumptuous palace hall, with a hint at Oriental decadence. Even so, all attention focuses on the couple and their admirable loyalty to one another.

The military qualities of the Carthaginians, starting with valiant Dido herself, greatly appealed to the Baroque artists who worked for kings and other rulers. Hannibal was seen in antiquity as one of the two greatest generals of all time (the other being Alexander the Great), endowed with a mix of tactical insight and great courage. The deployment of elephants gave his battles an added air of spectacle: Cornelis Cort's print of 1567 depicts the Romans utterly unmanned, scarcely capable of defeating any of their opponents. However, the attentive viewer

The Battle of Zama; 1567; Cornelis Cort; Leiden University Library; inv. no. PK–P– 102.455.

CVM CIRCVMFVSA
REPENTE
SCINDIT SE
NVBES

Vn des Tableaux de la grande Gallerie du Palais Royal.

knew that Publius Cornelius Scipio would eventually secure a decisive victory here, at Zama, following peace negotiations with Hannibal that also found their way into prints. In honour of his victory, Scipio was surnamed Africanus.

Scipio himself was also a popular subject in Baroque art. His life history was always closely linked to the slow decline in the power of Carthage. Besides being an effective military commander, he is also depicted in the sources – and therefore by the artists who portrayed him – as a wise man, someone who did not pursue gain for himself. The *continentia Scipionis* (Scipio's self–restraint) is one of the episodes of his life that is depicted most frequently: when a girl was given to him as part of the spoils of war after the conquest of the Spanish city of Numantia, he returned her to the young man to whom she was betrothed. Some versions refer to the couple as Lucretia and Allucius.

Other Roman soldiers, Marcus Atilius Regulus and Fabius Maximus Cunctator, served in art as exemplars of patience and caution, their actions furnishing monarchs and others in positions of leadership with food for thought. Fabius refused to rush into battle against Hannibal; his long delay and wary approach averted much greater losses, eventually weakening Hannibal's forces. He was also a paragon of fearlessness, as is clear from a print by Portman dating from 1795, one of a series depicting figures of extraordinarily noble character, the others being Hannibal and Regulus.

When we look at the images of these figures, it is striking that they always served as examples: the scenes demonstrated the true meaning of courage and virtue. Rulers possessed precious artworks such as tapestries, fresco cycles and series of paintings depicting leaders that could serve as examples. Sequences of episodes from the lives of Hannibal and other heroic commanders, if displayed in great palace halls used for audiences and meetings, might encourage those attending to emulate their great deeds. On a smaller scale, some paintings and prints, or other products derived from them, served to inspire conversations in the home, or in clubs and societies, about themes such as courage and virtue, faithfulness and sincerity, or vices such as falseness and hypocrisy. In images such as these, Carthage was an 'ordinary' classical city. Its Oriental features would not become attractive until the nineteenth century. Until the Enlightenment, two nations – the Carthaginians and the Romans – were constantly held up as shining examples of virtue. Aeneas was generally forgiven for his youthful lapses, but as a military commander he would never achieve the glory of the later heroes.

The arrival of Aeneas in Carthage; Simon Henri Thomassin; 18th century; Leiden University Libraries; inv. no. PK–P–126.471.

Roman statues from Utica, purchased by J.E. Humbert in 1823; Collection of the National Museum of Antiquities.

14

FOREIGNERS ON AN UNFAMILIAR COAST: THE REDISCOVERY OF CARTHAGE

Ruurd Halbertsma

ON 18 AUGUST 1815, THE FRENCH FRIGATE FLEUR DE LYS ARRIVED IN TUNISIA. ONE OF THOSE TO DISEMBARK WAS A POLITICAL REFUGEE NAMED CAMILLO BORGIA, A DESCENDANT OF AN OLD NOBLE FAMILY FROM VELLETRI. DURING THE POLITICAL CONVULSIONS TRIGGERED BY NAPOLEON'S CONQUESTS IN EUROPE, COUNT BORGIA HAD SIDED WITH THE FRENCH. IN ROME HE HAD SERVED AS COMMISSIONER OF POLICE, AND LATER HE BECAME THE CONFIDANT OF THE 'REVOLUTIONARY' KING JOACHIM MURAT.

After the fall of Napoleon in 1815, Murat was taken prisoner and executed by firing squad. Borgia managed to escape, but was sentenced to death in absentia. He had no choice but to leave his wife Adelaide and their two children behind in Naples.

Because of the old ties between his family and the Danish royal house, Borgia had been issued with a Danish passport in Naples, and upon arrival in Tunisia he was received and given accommodation by the Danish consul, A.C. Gierlew. In the first weeks of his stay in Tunis, Borgia concentrated on introducing himself to the local *corps diplomatique* and an array of dignitaries. He enjoyed watching wrestling matches and was astonished by the voluptuousness of the belly dancers. In the letters he wrote to his wife, he praised the tolerant attitudes towards the Jewish and Christian communities that prevailed in Tunis, and the people's moderate approach to 'the laws of the prophet'. It was his first visit to a North African country, and he included vivid descriptions of the rich flora and fauna of these exotic parts. He accompanied the Danish consul Gierlew on a visit to the ruins of Carthage and Utica, and the visit rekindled his old passion for archaeology. In Velletri the Borgia family had built up a large collection, including objects of ethnological and archaeological interest[1]. Camillo Borgia, who had grown up amid these art treasures, had never lost his love for objects that resonated with history, and he decided to spend his time in Tunisia usefully by researching the country's ancient history.

The Count and the Engineer

During a reception at the Dutch Consulate, the consul Antoine Nijssen introduced Borgia to a Dutch engineer who had been working in Tunisia for almost twenty years: Jean–Émile Humbert. Humbert, born in The Hague in 1771, had trained as a military engineer, but as a supporter of the House of Orange he had been compelled to leave the Netherlands after the Batavian Revolution of 1795. The following year, he and two other Dutch soldiers arrived in Tunis, where the Bey had commissioned them to build a new harbour. Within the space of ten years, the three

engineers built a modern harbour that was called La Goulette ('gullet'), after the bottleneck channel between Lake Tunis and the Mediterranean. Life in Tunisia agreed with Humbert: he married one of the younger sisters of the Dutch consul Nijssen, and once the harbour was complete, he was offered the position of chief engineer by Hamouda Pascha, Bey of Tunis. In his leisure time, Humbert studied geography and ethnology and explored the Carthaginian peninsula.

The difficult relations that existed between the North African or 'Barbary' states and the Europeans made studying Carthaginian topography awkward and sometimes dangerous terrain, and few travellers had ventured into it. The first serious researcher had been the Englishman Thomas Shaw, who had sailed to Tunisia in 1727. Shaw had studied theology in Oxford before being appointed chaplain at the British trade mission in Algiers. From there he travelled to Egypt, the Levant, Cyprus and the coast of North Africa. In 1738 he published his *Travels, or, Observations Relating to Several Parts of Barbary and the Levant*, an encyclopaedic work with accurate descriptions of the natural history, customs and traditions, and antiquities of the countries he visited. The second edition of his book was translated into Dutch, French and German. Shaw was the first to formulate the question of where the famous Byrsa Hill, the centre of Punic Carthage, was located: was it the low, southern hill that still bore this name, or could it be the high, northern Cape Carthage, on which perched the little village of Sidi Bou Said? According to the writings of ancient authors, whom Shaw quoted at length, the famous double harbour lay close to the Byrsa. This meant that determining which of the hills had been the Byrsa would also have implications for the location of the double harbour.

Humbert's long stay in Tunisia and his position as engineer at the court gave him ample opportunity to study the topography of Carthage. When foreigners arrived in Tunisia, he took them on tours of ancient Carthage: excursions that might take up an entire day, made especially enjoyable by the generous lunches that were served at the Roman cisterns, where Humbert regaled his guests with

Portrait of Jean Émile Humbert; artist unknown; 1800-1824; Netherlands Institute of Art History (RKD); inv. no. IB71282.

1. The collection was later purchased by Museo Borbonico in Napels, now the Museo Nazionale.

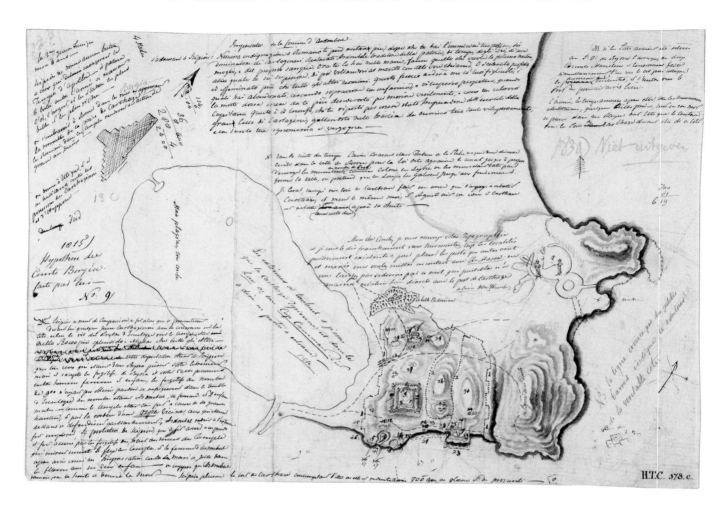

Sketch of the Carthaginian peninsula by J.E. Humbert, with topographical notes; Archives of the National Museum of Antiquities.

songs about the famous queens of Carthage. One of these guests was the French writer François René de Chateaubriand, whose ship docked in the harbour of La Goulette on 12 January 1807 on the way back from his pilgrimage to Jerusalem, which he later turned into a literary travel journal, *Itinéraire de Paris à Jérusalem* (1812).

Humbert's theory, that it was the southern hill that was the famous Byrsa, was adopted by Chateaubriand. Borgia too was impressed by Humbert's topographical knowledge, and suggested that they produce a joint publication on Tunisian antiquity: a collection of all the material remains, with separate chapters on the topography of Carthage and Utica, the two cities that had played such an important role in antiquity.

As an engineer, Humbert undertook frequent working trips into the interior of Tunisia. He built a series of fortresses there to protect the frontier

with Algeria. For security, he always travelled under military escort. Camillo Borgia was granted permission to join these excursions into the interior. Humbert and Borgia went on three major expeditions around Tunisia. The records of these journeys can be found in Borgia's diaries and travel papers, which were to serve as the basis for their joint publication: sketches of ruins, drawings of inscriptions, detailed floor plans of temples, triumphal arches and Christian basilicas. The notes made by Borgia and Humbert provide a rich overview of the antiquities that could still be seen in the interior of Tunisia around 1815. In 1817, Camillo Borgia received news from Naples. The king had revoked his sentence, and he was free to return to his family in Italy. He composed a poem about 'Carthage and Humbert', which he inscribed at the back of his Dutch friend's album, took all his notes and set sail for Naples, where he planned to have the drawings engraved and the notes elaborated into a book. Sadly, the project was never completed: Borgia died shortly after arriving in Naples, probably from the effects of malaria, which he had contracted in the swampy regions around Utica.

That same year, 1817, Humbert made the discovery of his life. In excavations between the Roman amphitheatre and the village of La Malga, he discovered six objects from the Punic period of Carthage: four virtually intact stelae with inscriptions and sculptural work, and two fragments of similar stones. These were the first Punic objects to have been discovered on the site of the Punic city, and provided important clues to the location of the oldest settlement on the peninsula. Now that his hopes for a joint publication with Borgia had been dashed, Humbert decided to present the stelae and his portfolio with notes to the Dutch government, to have them published by a Dutch scholar. In 1819 the Bey granted him an honourable discharge from his service, and Humbert sailed to The Hague to find a buyer for his important collection.

Caspar Reuvens and Archaeology

In 1818 the young scholar C.J.C. Reuvens was appointed by royal decree to an endowed chair at the University of Leiden (fig. 9). His field of study was 'Archaeology, or the knowledge of antiquity, as illuminated by surviving monuments, a subject that has thus far never been the explicit subject of instruction'. He became the first professor of archaeology in the world. He was also given responsibility for the Archaeological Cabinet, consisting of Greek and Roman sculptures, some Egyptian antiquities, and prehistoric finds, all of which were the property of the university. Reuvens created order in the collection and made an inventory of its contents. He was given a modest–sized museum building to put it in.

Inspired by the great examples of the Louvre and the British Museum, Reuvens dreamt of a large, national collection of antiquities to rival the institutions that existed in other countries. At the end of 1820, the education minister, Anton Falck, wrote to say that one Major Humbert had come to see him in The Hague, claiming to possess a remarkable collection of antiquities. Reuvens was asked to determine the collection's value to scholarship. On a freezing winter's day, the professor and the major met in Leiden. Looking at the Punic stelae and the files full of drawings, and listening Humbert's stories, Reuvens felt his head begin to spin. He described the experience as 'catching sight of a new horizon'. He suddenly glimpsed the possibility that he might become the first scholar to unveil the topography of Carthage, and the first museum director to possess those Punic objects from Carthage in his collection. The education minister agreed to purchase the entire collection from the public purse. Reuvens proposed to Humbert that the latter return to Tunisia in the service of the Dutch government, to conduct archaeological research and to purchase antiquities. The Dutch winter almost threw a spanner in the wheels of these new plans: Humbert fell gravely ill, and through his feverish dreams he could speak only two words: 'Carthage' and 'Reuvens'!

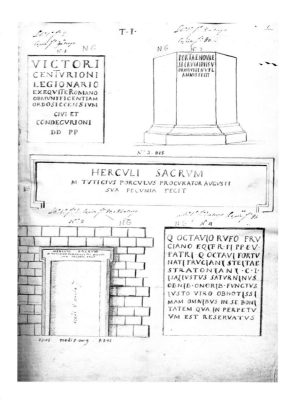

Drawing by Camillo Borgia: Latin inscriptions from the interior of Tunisia; Archives of the National Museum of Antiquities.

Expeditions to Tunisia and Italy

Humbert received a royal distinction for his scholarly achievements, was promoted in rank to lieutenant–colonel, and set sail for Tunisia in 1822. The Bey granted him permission to conduct excavations in Carthage and Utica, in exchange for some work on the harbour of La Goulette. With the authorities' consent, he purchased a large number of objects for the Leiden museum. Besides a superb collection of eight imperial statues from Utica (fig.10), these also included Punic–Roman art from the interior and objects used in everyday life: plates, drink-ing bowls, tableware, cutlery and oil lamps. The provenance was noted down in each case, as far as it was known. Excavations brought to light more Punic material. Humbert also solved the topographical questions that Reuvens had for-mulated. In the hope that sufficient material had been collected for a publication, Humbert re-turned to the Netherlands in 1824. But Reuvens had the ambition to achieve a complete picture. Rather than confining himself to Carthage, he wanted to incorporate the other antiquities of Tunisia into his publication. Furthermore, he

Drawing by Camillo Borgia: Nymphaeum near Zaghouan; c. 1815; Archives of the National Museum of Antiquities.

wanted to present Tunisia in the context of the surrounding regions. In short, a second expedition was called for, the aim being to chart the entire north coast of Africa in archaeological terms. Reuvens also wanted to purchase Camillo Borgia's notes, as a supplement to Humbert's notes and floor plans. Humbert himself, who was by then 55 years of age and in poor health, sighed that 'an armchair scholar could have no idea' how hard it was to achieve all these objectives in reality. He set off nonetheless, in 1826, on a mission that would last for four years. Arriving in Livorno, he was informed that some important Etruscan collections were being offered for sale in Volterra and Cortona. There was also an Egyptian collection from Livorno. He obtained permission to remain in Italy for a year to secure these purchases. In 1827 he had an opportunity to acquire an extremely large Egyptian collection – the third largest in Europe, after those in Paris and Turin. Reuvens set his sights on gaining possession of it. The negotiations

lasted a year, and were finally concluded successfully. Humbert spent the final year of the mission travelling around Italy, picking up smaller purchases. By then, Leiden had already acquired several magnificent Etruscan and Egyptian collections through his exertions.

Reuvens's publication never materialised. In 1834 the Danish researcher Christian Falbe published his study 'Recherches sur l'emplacement de Carthage', after which Reuvens lost interest in the subject. His time was now taken up with the publication of the Egyptian collections and excavations in the Netherlands. His sudden death in 1835 brought the Tunisian adventure to an end. Humbert spent the last few years of his life in Livorno, where he died in 1839. In his will he had expressed his desire to have the name of Carthage included in the inscription on his gravestone. He bequeathed his private collection of antiquities to the National Museum of Antiquities in Leiden.

15
REFLECTIONS OF CARTHAGE IN NINETEENTH-CENTURY ART

Eric Gubel

THE 1858 PUBLICATION OF THE BOOK VERSION OF THÉOPHILE GAUTIER'S *LE ROMAN DE LA MOMIE*, WHICH HAD ORIGINALLY BEEN SERIALISED IN NEWSPAPERS, WAS A LANDMARK IN THE EGYPTOMANIA THAT HAD SPREAD THROUGH VIRTUALLY ALL BRANCHES OF WESTERN ART SINCE THE CAMPAIGNS OF NAPOLEON BONAPARTE. ARMED WITH A THOROUGH KNOWLEDGE OF THE WRITINGS OF CLASSICAL AUTHORS ON ANCIENT CARTHAGE, ONE OF GAUTIER'S MOST ARDENT ADMIRERS, GUSTAVE FLAUBERT – WHO HAD GARNERED SUCH SUCCESS (AND SCANDAL) WITH HIS NOVEL *MADAME BOVARY* (1857) – SET OFF TO TUNIS THE FOLLOWING SPRING TO ACQUIRE A CERTAIN *COULEUR LOCALE* WITH WHICH TO SPICE UP HIS NOVEL *SALAMMBÔ*.

Et là–bas, sous le pont, adossé contre une arche,
Hannibal écoutait, pensif et triomphant,
Le piétinement sourd des légions en marche.

J–M. de Heredia (1842-1905), 'La Trebbia' (from Les Trophées, 1893).

The 1858 publication of the book version of Théophile Gautier's *Le roman de la momie*, which had originally been serialised in newspapers, was a landmark in the Egyptomania that had spread through virtually all branches of Western art since the campaigns of Napoleon Bonaparte. Armed with a thorough knowledge of the writings of classical authors on ancient Carthage, one of Gautier's most ardent admirers, Gustave Flaubert – who had garnered such success (and scandal) with his novel *Madame Bovary* (1857) – set off to Tunis the following spring to acquire a certain *couleur locale* with which to spice up his novel *Salammbô*. While it is true that Flaubert succeeded in finding details that would bring to life the city's topography (including information derived from Charles–Ernest Beulé), his correspondence repeatedly boils over with frustration: he was distressed to find so few traces of the material culture of Hamilcar and Hannibal's contemporaries. 'We know nothing about Carthage', he wrote in one letter, dated October 1858, to the disconcerted writer and archaeologist Ernest Feydau, and writing to the critic Charles–Augustin Sainte–Beuve in December 1862, he declared: 'Archaeology makes me laugh'.

Flaubert's *Salammbô* immediately joined the steamy ranks of *femmes fatales* in world literature, inspiring numerous artists to depict her: Mucha (lithograph in Paris, compositional sculpture in Karlsruhe), Rodin (watercolour in Paris, Musée Rodin), Rochegrosse (Paris, Bibliothèque nationale de France) and Prouvé (Nancy), the latter two as illustrators of editions of his novel in the age of Art Nouveau. Among the most striking sculptures of Salammbô were those by Ferrary (Liverpool), Rivière (Paris, Musée d'Orsay; Cologne, Wallraff–Richartz) and Idrac (Toulouse, Musée des Augustins), while Constant and Strathmann (Weimar) depicted her in paintings. In 1863, Paris indulged

in unbridled mockery with the operetta parody *Folammbô ou les Cocasseries carthaginoises* (Mad–ammbô, or Carthaginian High Jinks) by De Clairville and Laurencin long before Ernest Reyer's opera *Salammbô* (1890) was performed in the theatres of London, Paris and Brussels. In Anatole France's *Le crime de Sylvestre Bonnard*, the protagonist's two cats, Hamilcar and Hannibal, doze contentedly, utterly unmoved by the action going on around them. Salammbô also became a popular mannequin at French *bals masqués*, and possibly supplied welcome fodder for the Frisian self–styled 'baron' Tinco Martinus Lycklama à Nijeholt, who had a weakness for such entertainments. Through all these representations, the fictional tragic heroine Salammbô acquired a permanent place alongside the heroic Punic generals Hamilcar and Hannibal (and their antagonist Scipio).

Ever since the Middle Ages and throughout the Renaissance, these generals' glorious deeds (Zama, Cannae, the crossing of the Alps) had been etched into the collective memory with numerous incunabula, frescoes, tapestries and other artworks, by artists who were all too eager to depict the siege and fall of mighty Carthage from the Judeo–Christian viewpoint that blamed its downfall on hubris. Partly from this perspective, Salammbô was a version of the mythical founder of Carthage, Elissa (also known as Dido, 'the refugee'), whose doomed love for Aeneas had been a popular motif in the arts since classical antiquity (Macrobius, *Saturnalia*, v,17, 5), a popularity that endured well into the nineteenth century. Her supposed blood ties with the Phoenician royal family of Tyre, as the daughter of King Mattan I (840-832) and the sister of his successor, Pygmalion (known to the Phoenicians as Pumayyaton, 831-738 BC), often inspired paintings by European artists. Another popular subject for painters was the cunning trick she used to secure a large piece of land after her flight to North Africa. After first agreeing to accept a piece of land that could be encompassed by an ox's hide, she had the hide cut into tiny strips with which she encircled the entire hill of Byrsa, creating the centre of what would become Carthage. The English artist William Turner (1775-1851) regarded his 1815 oil painting *Dido building Carthage* (London, National Gallery) as his greatest masterpiece. Other artists added a dramatic dimension to their images of Dido by focusing on her romance with Aeneas as described by Virgil. These images frequently feature the bitter end of her life: Dido is shown burning herself on the pyre just as Carthage is poised to acquire a key role in embedding Phoenician power in the Western Mediterranean. As far as artists from the Netherlands are concerned, the painting *The Death of Dido* by Jozef Stallaert (c. 1872) cannot be omitted from this brief survey. For Stallaert depicts the palace of the first queen of Carthage decorated with Egyptian columns (an allusion to the work *The Death of Cleopatra* by Alexandre Cabanel, now hangs the Museum of Fine Arts, Antwerp). The attentive viewer will also discern an Assyrian *lamassu* (a winged sphinx with the body of a bull) as well as an embroidered hunting scene copied after an example of an Assyrian relief in the British Museum. This painting may therefore rightly be classified as a visionary work, since it would not be for another decade that the excavations at Carthage would prove that the Phoenician founders of Carthage (the name derived from Qrt–hdšt or Kart–Hadasht, meaning 'new city') had introduced traditions from the East that were grafted onto centuries–old ties with the civilisations of the Nile, just as in the region between the Tigris and Euphrates. Stallaert's painting thus heralded the assumptions encapsulated in *Ex Oriente Lux*!

It remains difficult to give a concise impression of Carthage as seen through nineteenth–century eyes. Indeed, such an enterprise is as doomed as the frustrating love life of Salammbô and her distant ancestor Elissa. Fortunately, nowadays we have the benefit of powerful internet search engines that I hope the reader will use to delve into the life and 'afterlife' of Carthage and to enjoy, each in his or her own way, the myriad facets of this fascinating subject.

130

Cover of the comic book Les voyages d'Alix: Carthage (V. Henin & J. Martin 2000; © Jacques Martin / Casterman 2014).

16

IMAGES OF CARTHAGE IN THE 20TH AND 21ST CENTURIES: FILMS, COMICS AND GAMES

Vanessa Boschloos

DIDO AND AENEAS, SALAMMBÔ AND MATHÔ, HANNIBAL ... IN THE TWENTIETH AND TWENTY–FIRST CENTURIES, TRAGIC LOVE STORIES AND WARS HAVE REMAINED THE PRIMARY THEMES THAT INSPIRE ARTISTS SEEKING TO REVIVE ANCIENT CARTHAGE. SINCE THE LATE NINETEENTH CENTURY, ANY REFERENCE TO CARTHAGE HAS AUTOMATICALLY EVOKED THE NAMES OF LARGER–THAN–LIFE CHARACTERS SUCH AS SALAMMBÔ, HANNIBAL AND BAAL–MOLOCH, AS A RESULT OF FLAUBERT'S TREATMENT OF THE SUBJECT AND THE TRAGIC HISTORY OF THE CITY THAT VIED FOR SUPREMACY WITH ROME.

Add a dash of Orientalism, and it is immediately apparent why Carthage makes such frequent appearances in paintings and operas, and later in films, comic strips and graphic novels. Furthermore, our knowledge of the ancient city and its history is still growing today, thanks to archaeological and epigraphical research, producing more accurate and detailed representations – or at least preparing the ground for them in the future.

In the early twentieth century, Flaubert's novel *Salammbô* (1862) was still inspiring Orientalist painters such as Adrien Henri Tanoux (1921) and the French symbolist painter Gaston Bussière (1907), who also illustrated several of Flaubert's novels. To this day, the novel continues to inspire the composers of operas, from Josef Matthias Hauer (1929) to Philippe Fénelon (1998), but it is in comic books and films that Carthage appears most frequently.

The silent movie *Cabiria* by Giovanni Pastrone (Italy, 1914), as well as the films *Salammbo*

by Arturo Ambrosio (Italy, 1911), Domenica Gaido (Italy, 1914), Pierre Marodon (France–Austria, 1925) and Sergio Grieco (Italy–France, 1959/1960) are based on Flaubert. Inspired by the imposing scenography, exotic costumes and dramatic personifications from opera (and possibly even the references to them in Orson Welles's *Citizen Kane*, 1941) and the cinema, the first adaptations of the story started to appear in comics in the 1940s: comic strip magazines published short stories or weekly episodes depicting events from the novel, by comic book artists such as René Gahou (in *Cendrillon* no. 26 of 1943), Raymond Poïvet (in *Vaillant* nos. 248-265 of 1950), Christo (in *Héroïc Albums* no. 29 of 1952), Novi (in *Mondial Aventures* no. 2 of 1953) and Chevanel & Deverchin (*La revolte des mercenaires* in *Tintin* no. 40, 1965). The temptress Salammbô and the horrific scenes of human sacrifice were central features of these versions, set in a Roman or Arabising scenery. Christo wrote in a note that he had drawn on an opera libretto, whereas Poïvet used cinematic camera angles and gave every episode a title, by

Album cover of Les voyages d'Alix: Carthage (V. Henin & J. Martin 2000; © Jacques Martin / Casterman 2014).

analogy to a scene or act. Thierry Robin plainly stated that in making his comic strip *Koblenz 2: Marcher dans Carthage une nuit sans lune* (2000), he had drawn inspiration from the films of Pierre Marodon and Sergio Grieco about Salammbô as well as Flaubert and the Orientalist paintings of the nineteenth century. Robin was one of the few authors of comic strips who actually travelled to Tunis to make sketches and to get a feel of the ancient city, as Flaubert had done. Of course, in 1999 he was able to see far more archaeological remains than Flaubert and he could study objects in the local museums.

We also encounter museum objects in the comic strip *Les voleurs de Carthage* by Apollo and Hervé Tanquerelle (2013). This two–part series revolved around several characters presented as caricatures (the anti–heroes, a Gallic and a Numidian mercenary, recall Matho and Spendius, whereas the thief who accompanies them could hold her own with Salammbô). In the background we recognise architectural remains, stelae and reliefs from Tunisian museums, including the sculpted lion–headed Tanit that – though of gigantic proportions – serves as a cult statue in the temple they are trying to rob. To the three main characters from Flaubert's novel is also referred to in the flashbacks that Freddy Lombard, the hero in the comic strip series by Yves Chaland and Yann Lepennetier has in a delirious dream (*Freddy Lombard: La comète de Carthage, 1986*).

The Carthage series by Fabrice David, Grégory Lassablière and Mauro De Luca is very well illustrated and documented. Two albums have appeared to date: *Le souffle de Baal* (2010) tells the story of the aftermath of the First Punic War and the revolt of the mercenaries in Carthage. We are shown the harbour and the temple of Tanit, where child sacrifices take place. In *La flamme de Vénus* (2011), we read about Hannibal and the Second Punic War. This is also the backdrop for the story in which Sirius's hero Timour sees Hannibal's city and imposing army (*Les Timour: Le captif de Carthage*, 1956).

133

Sacrifices to Moloch in Les voyages d'Alix: Carthage (V. Henin & J. Martin 2000; © Jacques Martin / Casterman 2014)

HUMAN SACRIFICES TO MOLOCH IN COMIC STRIPS

In comic books, neither children nor beautiful maidens are safe from the gaping, fire-breathing jaws of the statue of Moloch. The story owes a debt to Flaubert, who in turn drew on classical sources, coloured by Roman propaganda. The statue turns up in various places: Carthage (*Salammbo* in Héroïc-Albums no. 29-1952; Alix : *l'Ile maudite*, 1957; Alix : *Le spectre de Carthage*, 1977; Freddy Lombard: *La comète de Carthage*, 1986; Carthage: *Le souffle de Baal*, 2010); but also in Rome (Alix: *Le tombeau etrusque*, 1968; Alix: *La conjuration de Baal*, 2011); Egypt (Aviorix le Gaulois: *Dans l'antre des sacrifices* in Héroïc-Albums no. 43-1956); and Phoenicia (Alix: *Le tombeau étrusque*, 1969; *Le triérarque sans nom*, 1985; Corian: *Les fous de Baal*, 1989; Silvain de Rochefort: *Prisonniers de Baalbek*, 1993). For the overview of the Moloch cult given in Alix: *Le tombeau étrusque*, Jacques Martin went so far as to consult the *Dictionnaire des antiquités grecques et romaines* (Daremberg & Saglio 1870-1911).

Scenes set in Atlantis (Jean d'Armor in Wrill nos. 103-133-1947/1948), parallel dimensions (Koblenz: *Marcher dans Carthage une nuit sans lune*, 2000) and futuristic cities (Res Punica: *Baal*, 2001; *Le dernier troyen: Carthago*, 2006) have an even stronger appeal to the imagination. Finally, because of the association with fire, the name 'Moloch' is often chosen to denote active volcanoes: (Alix: *les proies du volcan*, 1978; Bernard Prince: *Le souffle de Moloch*, 1976) and man-eating monsters (De Rode Ridder: *De Moloch*, 1977).
– *Vanessa Boschloos*

Alix and his friend Enak in Carthage (© Jacques Martin / Casterman).

Alix and Enak overlooking the tophet (© Jacques Martin / Casterman).

The best–documented comics that pay tribute to Punic and Roman Carthage are without a doubt those created by Jacques Martin. When the grand master of historical comic strips was asked what had first aroused his passion for history and antiquity, he replied without hesitation: Flaubert's novel! The impact of this work on Martin's oeuvre is already visible in the third album in the Alix series, *L'Ile maudite* (1957), in which Caesar sends Alix to Carthage to investigate some mysterious events, which are eventually found to be the work of his nemesis, Arbaces. in this work the cityscapes still allude to Roman models or spring from the artist's own imagination, Martin will adjust this in *Alix: Le spectre de Carthage* (1977). In this album we recognise diverse monuments, while Alix and Enak wander around the city, which is ruled by a Roman governor, with flashbacks to its Punic past (the harbour, the Byrsa hill, the Tophet). Alix's adventures in Carthage reached an apogee in 2000 with the publication of *Les voyages d'Alix: Carthage*, prepared by Martin and written and drawn by his assistant Vincent Hénin. The latter based the detailed reconstructions on books about Phoenician and Punic art and history, on studies and accurate reconstructions of Roman architecture (by scholars such as Jean–Claude Golvin and Pierre Gros) and the ruins and scale models he saw in Tunis during a study trip in the late 1990s. Only in the pictures of the sacrifices to Moloch and the siege of the mercenaries in the valley 'of the Axe' do any lingering echoes of Flaubert's novel remain.

We catch a glimpse of Carthage and Utica in the age of the late Roman Republic and the Numidian kings in the first Jugurtha album (*Le lionceau des sables,* 1967), drawn by Hermann with a script by Jean–Luc Vernal. It seems that only ruins remain of ancient Carthage. The same applies to medieval Carthage, which we barely get to see when Karel Biddeloo's Red Knight goes off on a treasure hunt, accompanied by a beautiful Berber princess (*De Rode Ridder: De schat van Carthage,* 2002). Finally, we should mention that Robin's *Koblenz: Marcher dans Carthage une nuit sans lune* (2000) is the only comic strip with views of the nineteenth–century city (including the ruins of the military harbour, the souq and Bab el–Bahar, casually embellished with antiquities such as double bull capitals, ivory furniture elements, Phoenician–Punic masks, and funerary stelae. Each chapter of the story is prefaced by a bookplate designed in art nouveau style, depicting Elissa and Salammbô.

It is apt to conclude with futuristic visions of Carthage, in particular the comic picturing the city in the 2814th year after its foundation, created by the Cosset brothers in *Res Punica: Baal* (2001). Here, a class society is oppressed by a Council of Elders that seeks to reintroduce the tradition of sacrificing young children to the god Baal. Also worth mentioning is the double planet 'Carthago–Ogahtrac' in *Le dernier troyen: Carthago* (2006) by the artist Thierry Démarez and the historian Valérie Mangin. This is loosely based on Virgil's *Aeneid* and is one of the few examples of comic–book art in which Elissa/Dido plays the leading role: Aeneas's spaceship is stranded on the planet and the queen seals the fate of her city by falling in love with the last Trojan, whose descendants will found Carthage's nemesis, the city of Rome.

The comic book artist Philippe Druillet, a pupil of Poïvet's who published a three–part science fiction version of Flaubert's story in the early 1980s, was neither aiming for historical accuracy. Rather, he set out to produce a space opera that confronted human beings with their ambitions and their weaknesses. Druillet was closely involved in the development of a video game based on his series, *Salammbo: Battle for Carthage* (Cryo Interactive Entertainment, 2003). Finally, the extent to which Carthage – including its rivalry with Rome – lives on in the popular imagination is clear from the theme's popularity in board games: *Hannibal: Rome vs. Carthage* (Valley Games, 1996), *Carthage: The First Punic War* (GMT Games, 2005), *Traders of Carthage* (Japon Brand Z–man Games, 2006) and *Porto Carthago* (Irongames, 2010).

The personification of Africa. Note the wealth and at the same time the dangerous, evil elements of the image. Crispin van de Passe; 1589-1611; Rijksmuseum Amsterdam; inv. no. RP-P-1938-1492.

17

ANCIENT CARTHAGE IN THE 21ST CENTURY: A TIMELESS MESSAGE

Mustapha Khanoussi

THE WORLD OF THE EARLY TWENTY–FIRST CENTURY WORLD IS INCREASINGLY DOMINATED BY GLOBALISATION. SOMETIMES OUR PLANET SEEMS TO HAVE SHRUNK TO THE DIMENSIONS OF ONE LARGE VILLAGE. DOES THE ANCIENT CITY OF CARTHAGE, OF WHICH ONLY ARCHAEOLOGICAL RUINS REMAIN, MANY OF THEM SUBMERGED BENEATH A MODERN CITY, NONETHELESS HAVE A MESSAGE FOR US? WE MAY INITIALLY BE INCLINED TO THINK IT DOES NOT. UPON REFLECTION, HOWEVER, WE ARE MOVED TO RECONSIDER.

Carthage, which Aristotle praised as a democracy, was the home of Hannibal Barca and 'a melting pot of illicit passions' to the young Augustine, the future bishop of Hippo and a fervent opponent of the Donatists. Today, UNESCO recognises Carthage as a World Heritage Site of outstanding universal value. This means that it is inscribed on the World Heritage List under criteria II, III and VI of the Operational Guidelines for the Implementation of the World Heritage Convention.

Under criterion III, UNESCO explains that 'The site of Carthage bears exceptional testimony to the Phoenico–Punic civilisation, being at the time the central hub in the western basin of the Mediterranean. It was also one of the most brilliant centres of Afro–Roman civilisation'. Under criterion VI, it states: 'The historic and literary renown of Carthage has always nourished the universal imagination. The site of Carthage is notably associated with the legendary princess of Tyre, Elyssa–Dido, founder of the town, [whose praises were sung] by Virgil in the *Aeneid*; with the great navigator–explorer, Hannon, with Hannibal, one of the greatest military strategists of history; with writers such as Apuleius, founder of Latin–African literature; with the martyr St Cyprian; and with St Augustine, who was trained there and visited [the city] several times.'

This recognition of the importance of Carthage serves to illustrate the vitality and topicality of the message that the ancient city of Elissa–Dido continues to propagate, many centuries after the city's repeated destruction. It is a memorable site, on which the archaeological remains of Carthage and its present–day historic buildings and monuments constitute the tangible evidence of almost three thousand years of history. A history that was frequently racked by conflict, but that had an abundance of glorious moments. Still, many of these are scarcely known to the world beyond Tunisia, and even within it.

Most people are familiar with the legend that Carthage was founded by a princess who had fled from Phoenicia, the country of her birth. This female initiative in the city's origins can be said to be reflected in the prominent position of

women within society. Today's Tunisian women lay claim to be the lawful heirs to the legacy of Elissa and all the great female figures who have played key roles in the country's changing fortunes. The general public is also well aware that Hannibal Barka was born in Carthage. Hannibal has been universally recognised since antiquity as one of the greatest military geniuses of all time. His crossing of the Pyrenees and the Alps with elephants has become embedded in the collective imagination.

Other facts are less well known, however. One is the role of Punic Carthage as a beacon of light in the benighted Western Mediterranean region, which forged its place in history by introducing and consolidating alphabetical script throughout the region, and disseminating written documents. The role of Carthage in agriculture is also little known. One name stands out here: that of Mago the agriculturalist. Mago's major work on agriculture was a seminal textbook that remained the primary reference work in this field for many centuries. Such was its value that it was the only book in the Punic library to be taken back to Rome by order of the Roman Senate after the destruction of Carthage in 146 BC. The Romans translated it into Latin, in which version it became the most important source of inspiration for many other works of this kind.

Another topical message from Carthage is personified by Apuleius. He came from Madaure (today M'daourouch in Algeria) and was proud to be 'half Numidian and half Gaetulian'. However, he was raised in the Roman–Carthaginian mould, with a Graeco–Roman cultural background. In this respect he was the precursor of what would become, many centuries later, a fixed identity for a growing multitude.

One of the most famous Carthaginians is Augustine. He rose to a position of great esteem in the Mediterranean region and his message was universal in its scope. He was born in Thagaste (Souk Ahras in eastern Algeria), to a pagan father and a Christian mother. He spent his boyhood years in Carthage and later studied there. In his *Confessions*, he described Carthage as a 'melting pot of illicit passions', in open acknowledgement that he had strayed from the path of virtue more than once in his youth. 'At times the desire rose in me to saturate the universe of my youth with infernal pleasures, and I did not turn aside from voluptuous passions, which are as fickle as they are bleak'. After some time in Roman Italy, where he converted to Christianity, he returned to Africa, eventually becoming Bishop of Hippo. But the face he chiefly showed to the world was that of the indefatigable traveller who went from one city to the next proclaiming the Gospel and defending the Catholic Church.

For the Tunisians living in today's post–revolutionary times, the Carthage of the age of the Philaeni brothers is important. They were known for their heroic patriotism, something that today's Tunisians may well wish to emulate. Their self–sacrifice, which was frequently related by the writers of antiquity, took place against the backdrop of a border conflict between the Punic metropolis and the Greek city of Cyrene (in the vicinity of Benghazi, on the east coast of Libya). Sallustius tells the story in his work *The Jugurthine War*. The Cyrenian and Carthaginian envoys had agreed to set out at the same time from their respective regions and to fix the frontier between their territories at the place where they met. When the Cyrenians realised that they had been too slow, they dreaded the vengeance of their countrymen, who might blame them for the failure of their mission. They began to wrangle with the Carthaginians, whom they accused of setting out before the appointed time, and declared they would submit to any terms, rather than depart defeated. The Philaeni brothers, on behalf of the Carthaginians, asked them to set fresh conditions, provided these were fair and reasonable, but the Cyrenians gave them only one choice: either to be buried alive on the spot which they required as the boundary of their dominions, or to allow them to advance as far as they thought proper, on the same terms as before. The brothers accepted these terms and, sacrificing their lives to the good of their country, were buried alive there. The Carthaginians erected an altar on this site in memory of the Philaeni brothers and bestowed other honours upon them in Carthage.

Carthage has been a UNESCO World Heritage Site since 1979.

USED LITERATURE AND SUGGESTIONS FOR FURTHER READING PER CHAPTER

Chapter 1

Goldsworthy A., 2000, *The Fall of Carthage. The Punic Wars 265-146 BC.*, London. (Translated as: *Carthago*, Amsterdam, 2008).

Hoyos D., 2010, *The Carthaginians*, Oxford.

Miles R., 2010, *Carthage Must Be Destroyed. The Rise and Fall of an Ancient Civilization*, London. (Translated as: *Carthago. Opkomst en ondergang van een stad*, Amsterdam, 2010).

Chapter 2

Aubet M.E., 1993, *The Phoenicians and the West. Politics, colonies and trade*, Cambridge.

Markoe G.E., 2000, *Phoenicians* (Peoples of the Past), London (2nd edition 2002).

Tubb J.N., 1998, *Canaanites* (Peoples of the Past), London.

Chapter 3

Aubet M.E., 1993, *The Phoenicians and the West. Politics, colonies and trade*, Cambridge.

Bechtold B., Docter R.F., 2011, Transport Amphorae from Carthage: an Overview, in: Nigro L. (ed.), *The Phoenician Keramic Repertoire between the Levant and the West 9th - 6th century BC. Proceedings of the International Conference held in Rome, 26th February 2010* (Quaderni di Fenici-Punica), Roma, 85-116.

Benichou-Safar H., 1982, *Les tombes puniques de Carthage. Topographie, structures, inscriptions et rites funéraires*, Paris.

Bénichou-Safar H., 2004, *Le tophet de Salammbô à Carthage. Essai de reconstition* (Collection de l'École Française de Rome 342), Rome.

Bonnet C., 2006, Identité et altérité religieuses. À propos de l'hellénisation de Carthage, *Pallas* 70, 365-379.

Carandini A., Cappelli R., 2000, *Roma. Romolo, Remo e la fondazione della città*, Roma.

Chelbi F., Maraoui Telmini B., Docter R.F., 2006, Découverte d'une nécropole du huitième siècle av. J.-C. à Carthage (Bir Massouda). Rapport préliminaire sur les fouilles de l'Institut National du Patrimoine (Tunis) et l'Université de Gand, *CEDAC Carthage* 22, 13-25.

Docter R.F., 2000, Pottery, Graves and Ritual I: Phoenicians of the First Generation in Pithekoussai, in: Bartoloni P., Campanella L. (eds), *La Keramica Fenicia di Sardegna: Dati, Problematiche, Confronti. Atti del Primo Congresso Internazionale Sulcitano, Sant'Antioco, 19-21 Settembre 1997*, Roma, 135-149.

Docter R.F., 2002/2003, The topography of archaic Carthage. Preliminary results of recent excavations and some prospects, *TALANTA. Proceedings of the Dutch Archaeological and Historical Society* 34-35 [2004], 113-133.

Docter R.F., 2005a, The *koprologoi* of Carthage. On the scarcity of settlement finds in Carthage between c. 550 and 480 BC, in: Spanò Giammellaro A. (ed.), *Atti del V Congresso Internazionale di Studi Fenici e Punici. Marsala – Palermo, 2-8 ottobre 2000*, Palermo, 269-276.

Docter R.F., 2005b, Een spectaculair einde: Carthago en Rome 246-146 voor Chr., *Lampas* 38,3, 313-329.

Docter R.F., 2007, Published Settlement Contexts of Punic Carthage, *Carthage Studies* 1, 37-76.

Docter R.F., 2007, Carthage and its hinterland, in: Helas S., Marzoli D. (eds), *Phönizisches und punisches Städtewesen* (Iberia Archaeologica 13), Mainz a.R., 179-189.

Docter R.F., 2013, Archäologische Stadtforschung. II. Die griechische und punische Welt, in: Mieg H.A., Heil C. (eds), *Stadt. Ein Interdisziplinärisches Handbuch*, Stuttgart, Weimar, 164-173.

Docter R.F., Chelbi F., Maraoui Telmini B., Nijboer A.J., Van der Plicht J., Van Neer W., Mansel K., Garsallah S., 2008, New radiocarbon dates from Carthage: Bridging the gap between history and archaeology?, in: Sagona C. (ed.), *Beyond the Homeland. Markers in*

Phoenician Chronology (Ancient Near Eastern Studies 28), Leuven, Paris, Dudley, 379-422.

Fumadó Ortega I., 2009, *Cartago. Historia de la investigación*, Madrid.

Fumadó Ortega I., 2013, *Cartago Fenicio-Púnica. Arqueología de la forma urbana*, Madrid.

Greene J.A., 1986, *The Carthaginian Countryside. Archaeological Reconnaissance in the Hinterland of Ancient Carthage*, Chicago.

Horden P., Purcell N., 2000, *The Corrupting Sea: A Study of Mediterranean History*, Oxford.

Hurst H., Stager L.E., 1978, A Metropolitan Landscape: The Late Punic Port of Carthage, *World Archaeology* 9, 334-346.

Lancel S., 1995, *Carthage. A History*, Oxford, Cambridge MA.

Maaß M., 2004, Ceterum censeo … oder so, in: *Hannibal ad portas. Macht und Reichtum Karthagos*, Stuttgart, 380-382.

Maraoui Telmini B., 2011, Découverte de latrines puniques du 5ème siècle av. J.-C. à Carthage (Bir Massouda), *BABESCH. Annual Papers on Mediterranean Archaeology* 86, 53-70.

Maraoui Telmini B., Docter R.F., Bechtold B., Chelbi F., Van de Put W., 2014, Defining Punic Carthage, in: Quinn J.C., Vella N.C. (eds), *The Punic Mediterranean: identities and identification from Phoenician settlement to Roman rule*, Cambridge [in press].

Niemeyer H.G., Docter R.F., Schmidt K., Bechtold B. *et alii*, 2007, *Karthago. Die Ergebnisse der Hamburger Grabung unter dem Decumanus Maximus* (Hamburger Forschungen zur Archäologie 2), Mainz a.R.

Scheid J., Svenbo J., 1985, Byrsa. La ruse d'Élissa et la fondation de Carthage, *Annales. Économies, Sociétés, Civilisations* 40, 2, 328-342.

Slopsma J., Van Wijngaarden-Bakker L., Maliepaard R., 2009, Animal Remains from the Bir Messaouda Excavations 2000/2001 and other Carthaginian Settlement Contexts, *Carthage Studies* 3, 21-63.

Smith P., Stager L.E., Greene J.A., Avishai G., 2013, Cemetery or Sacrifice? Infant burials at the Carthage *Tophet, Antiquity* 87, 1191-1207.

Stuijts I., 1990, Kinderoffers in de *tophet* (Carthago). Houtskoolonderzoek, *Paleo-Aktueel* 2, 58-61.

Tang B., 2005, *Delos, Carthage, Ampurias. The Housing of Three Mediterranean Trading Centres*, Rome.

Van Zeist W., Bottema S., Van der Veen M., 2001, *Diet and Vegetation at Ancient Carthage. The Archaeobotanical Evidence*, Groningen.

Xella P. (ed.), 2014, *The Tophet in the Phoenician Mediterranean* (Studi Epigrafici e Linguistici sul Vicino Oriente antico, Nuova Serie - Ricerche storiche e filologiche sulle culture del Vicino Oriente e del Mediterraneo antico 29-30 [2012-2013]), Verona.

The Blacksmith's Secret

Docter R.F., Carthago: opgravingen van de Universiteit van Amsterdam in 2000 en 2001, *TMA Tijdschrift voor Mediterrane Archeologie* 26, 2002, 43-49.

Docter, R.F., The topography of archaic Carthage Preliminary results of recent excavations and prospects, TALANTA. *Proceedings of the Dutch Archaeological and Historical Society* 34-35 (2002-2003) [2004], 113-133.

Chapter 4

Donner H., Röllig W., 1973-1979, *Kanaanäische und aramäische Inschriften* (mit einem Beitrag von O. Rössler), 3rd/4th ed., Wiesbaden.

Ferjaoui A., 1993, *Recherches sur les relations entre l'Orient phénicien et Carthage* (Orbis biblicus et orientalis), Göttingen.

Guzzo Amadasi M.G., 1967, *Le iscrizioni fenicie e puniche delle colonie in occidente*, Roma.

Harris W.V., 1989, *Ancient Literacy*, Cambridge, Mass.

Hoftijzer J., Jongeling K., 1995, *Dictionary of the North-West Semitic Inscriptions* (Handbuch der Orientalistik 1. Nahe und der Mittler Osten 21.1-2), Leiden, New York, Cologne.

Peckham J.B., 1968, *The Development of the Late Phoenician Scripts*, Cambridge, Mass.

Chapter 5

Bartoloni P., 1976, *Le stele arcaiche del tofet di Cartagine*, Roma.

Bénichou-Safar H., 2004, *Le tophet de Salammbô* à *Carthage. Essai de reconstition* (Collection de l'École Française de Rome 342), Rome.

Moscati S., 1987, *Il sacrificio punici dei fanciulli: realtà o invenzione?*, Roma.

Ribicchini S., 1987, *Il tofet e il sacrificio dei fanciuli*, Sassari.

Smith P., Stager L.E., Greene J.A., Avishai G., 2013, Cemetery or Sacrifice? Infant burials at the Carthage *Tophet, Antiquity* 87, 1191-1207.

Xella P. (ed.), 2014, *The Tophet in the Phoenician Mediterranean* (Studi Epigrafici e Linguistici sul Vicino Oriente antico, Nuova Serie - Ricerche storiche e filologiche sulle culture del Vicino Oriente e del Mediterraneo antico 29-30 [2012-2013]), Verona.

An Urn in Leiden and the Excavations of Kelsey and Khun De Prorok

Docter R.F., Smits E., Hakbijl T., Stuijts I.L.M., van der Plicht J., 2001/2002, Interdisciplinary Research on Urns from the Carthaginian *Tophet* and their Contents, *Palaeohistoria* 43/44 [2003], 417-433.

Chapter 6

Berges D., 1997, Die Tonsiegel aus dem karthagischen Tempelarchiv, in: Rakob F. (ed.), *Karthago II. Die Deutschen Ausgrabungen in Karthago*, Mainz a.R., 10-214.

Gorton A.F., 1996, *Egyptian and Egyptianizing Scarabs. A Typology of steatite, faience and paste scarabs from Punic and other Mediterranean Sites* (Oxford University Committee for Archaeology Monograph 44), Oxford.

Hölbl G., 1986, Ägyptisches *Kulturgut im phönikischen und punischen Sardinien* II (Études préliminaires aux religions orientales dans l'empire romain 102), Leiden.

Hölbl G., 1989, *Ägyptisches Kulturgut auf den Inseln Malta und Gozo in phönikischer und punischer Zeit. Die Objekte im Archäologischen Museum von Valetta*, Wien.

Quillard B., 1979, *Bijoux carthaginois. I. Les colliers d'après les collections du Musée national du Bardo et du Musée national de Carthage*, Louvain-La-Neuve.

Quillard B., 1987, *Bijoux carthaginois. II. Porte-amulettes, sceaux pendentifs, pendents, boucles, anneaux et bagues d'après les collections du Musée national du Bardo et du Musée national de Carthage*, Louvain-la-Neuve.

Redissi T., 1990, Les amulettes de Carthage représentant les divinités leontocephales et les lions, *REPPAL* 5, 163-216.

Redissi, T., 1999, Étude des empreintes de sceaux de Carthage, in: Rakob F. (ed.), *Karthago III. Die deutschen Ausgrabungen in Karthago*, Mainz a.R, 4-92.

Chapter 7

Cintas P., 1973, *Le port de Carthage*, Paris.

Frost H., *et alii*, 1981, Lilybaeum (Marsala). The punic ship: final excavation report, *Notizie degli Scavi di Antichita* XXX, supplemento, Roma [1976].

Goldsworthy A., 2007, *The Fall of Carthage: The Punic Wars 265-146 BC*, London.

Hurst H., 1992, L'îlot de l'Amirauté, le port circulaire et l'avenue Bourguiba, in: Ennabli A. (ed.), *Pour sauver Carthage. Exploration et conservation de la cité punique, romaine et byzantine*, Tunis, 79-94.

Meijer F., 1995, *De trireme, klassiek-Grieks oorlogsschip weer te water*, Amsterdam.

Punic Bronze Naval Battering Ram (Egadi Islands)

Tusa S., Royal J., 2012, The landscape of the naval battle at the Egadi Islands (241 B.C.), *Journal of Roman Archaeology* 25, 7-48.

Chapter 8

Brett M., Fentress E., 1996, *The Berbers. The Peoples of Africa*, Oxford.

Camps G., 1980, *Berbères. Aux marges de l'Histoire*, Toulouse.

Ferjaoui A. (ed.), 2010, *Carthage et les autochtones de son* empire du temps de Zama. Colloque international organisé à Siliana et Tunis du 10 au 13 mars 2004 par l'Institut National du Patrimoine et l'Association de Sauvegarde du site de Zama. Hommage à Mhamed Hassine Fantar, Tunis.

Horn H.G., Rüger C.B., 1979, *Die Numider. Reiter und Könige nördlich der Sahara*, Köln, Bonn.

Kallala N., Sanmartí J., Ramon Torres J., 2008, Présentation du projet tuniso-catalan sur le site d'*Althiburos* et sa région, in: González J., Ruggeri P., Vismara C., Zucca R. (eds), *L'Africa romana. Le richezze dell'Africa. Risorse, produzioni, scambi. Atti del XVII Convegno di studio. Sevilla, 14-17 dicembre 2006*, Roma, 2253-2263.

Kallala N., Sanmartí J., 2011, *Althiburos I : la fouille dans l'aire du capitole et dans la nécropole méridionale*, Tarragona.

Khanoussi M., Maurin L. (eds), 2002, *Mourir à Dougga. Recueil des Inscriptions funéraires*, Bordeaux.

Krandel-Ben Younès A., 2002, *La présence punique en pays Numide*, Tunis.

Chapter 9 (see also chapter 7)
Docter R.F., 2005, Een spectaculair einde: Carthago en Rome 246-146 voor Chr., *Lampas* 38,3, 313-329.

Goldsworthy A., 2006, *The Fall of Carthage*, London.

Hoyos D., 2007, *Truceless War. Carthage's Fight for Survival, 241 to 237 B.C.*, Leiden.

Lancel S. (ed.), 1979, *Byrsa I. Rapports préliminaires des fouilles (1974-1976). Mission Archéologique française à Carthage*, Rome.

Lancel S. (ed.), 1982, *Byrsa II. Rapports préliminaires sur les fouilles 1977-1978: niveaux et vestiges puniques. Mission Archéologique française à Carthage*, Rome.

Lancel. S. 1995, *Carthage. A History* (vertaling A. Nevill), Oxford/Cambridge.

Lancel, S., 1998, *Hannibal* (vertaling A. Nevill), Oxford.

Miles R., 2010, *Carthage Must Be Destroyed. The Rise and Fall of an Ancient Civilization*, London. (vertaald als: *Carthago. Opkomst en ondergang van een stad*, Amsterdam, 2010).

A Punic Coin Mould from the Second Punic War
Frey-Kupper S., 2009, A stone mould from Bir Messaouda (Carthage) for bronze coins of the Second Punic War. Preliminary notes, *Schweizerische Numismatische Rundschau* 88, 185-192.

Chapter 10
Fuchs W., 1963, *Der Schiffsfund von Mahdia*, Tübingen.

Klages C., 1994, Die Satyrstatuetten, in: Hellenkemper Salies G. (ed.), *Das Wrack – Der antike Schiffsfund von Mahdia*, Köln, 531-538.

Pfisterer-Haas S., 1994, Die bronzenen Zwergtänzer, in: Hellenkemper Salies G. (ed.), *Das Wrack – Der antike Schiffsfund von Mahdia*, Köln, 483-504.

Hiller H., 1994, Zwei bronze Figurenlampen, in: Hellenkemper Salies, G. (ed.), *Das Wrack – Der antike Schiffsfund von Mahdia*, Köln, 515-530.

Chapter 11
Audollent A., 1901. *Carthage romaine*. Paris.

Balmelle C., Bourgeois A., Broise H., Darmon J.-P., Ennaïfer M., 2012, *Carthage, colline de l'Odéon: maison de la rotonde et du cryptoportique: (recherches 1987-2000)* (Collection de l École française de Rome 457), Rome.

Ben Abed Khader A. *et al.*, 1999, *Les mosaïques du Parc archéologique des Thermes d'Antonin* (Corpus des Mosaïques de Tunisie IV, Carthage 1; Atlas Archéologique de la Tunisie 81), Tunis, Washington.

Bullo S., 2002, *Provincia Africa. Le città e il territorio dalla caduta di Cartagine a Nerone*, Roma.

Ferchiou N., 1989, *L'evolution du décor architectonique en Afrique Proconsulaire des derniers temps de Carthage aux Antonins. L'Hellenisme africain, son déclin, ses mutations et le triomphe de l'art romano-africain*, Gap.

Ferchiou N., 2008, *Le chant des nymphes: Les aqueducs et les temples des eaux de Zaghouan à Carthage*, Tunis.

Gros P., 1985, *Byrsa III. Rapport sur les campagnes de

fouilles de 1977 à 1980: la basilique orientale et ses abords. Mission Archéologique française à Carthage*, Rome.

Hurst H.R. *et al.*, 1994, *Excavations at Carthage. The British Mission II,1. The Circular Harbour, North Side. The Site and Finds other than Pottery* (British Academy Monographs in Archaeology 4), Oxford.

Hurst H. *et al.*, 1999, *The Sanctuary of Tanit at Carthage in the Roman Period. A Re-Interpretation* (Journal of Roman Archaeology Supplementary Series 30), Portsmouth, RI.

Iciek A., Jagodziński A., Kolendo J., Przenioslo J., 1974, *Carthage. Cirque. Colline dite de Junon. Doar Chott. Recherches archéologiques et géophysiques polonaises effectuées en 1972*, Wrocław, Varsovie, Cracovie, Gdańsk.

Jaïdi H., 1990, *L'Afrique et le blé de Rome aux IVe et Ve siècles*, Tunis.

Ladjmi Sebaï L., 2005, *La colline de Byrsa à l'époque romaine. Étude épigraphique et état de la question* (Karthago. Revue d'Archéologie Méditerranéenne 26), Paris.

Lézine A., 1968. *Carthage. Utique. Études d'architecture et d'urbanisme*. Paris.

Mills P., 2013, *The Ancient Mediterranean Trade in Keramic Building Materials. A Case Study in Carthage and Beirut* (Roman and Late Antique Mediterranean Pottery 2), Oxford.

Rakob F., 2000, The making of Augustan Carthage, in: *Romanization and the City. Creation, Transformations, and Failures. Proceedings of a Conference held at the American Academy in Rome 14-16 May 1998*, Portsmouth, 72-82.

Wells C.M., 1992, Le Mur de Théodose et le secteur nord-est de la ville romaine, in: Ennabli A. (ed.), *Pour sauver Carthage. Exploration et conservation de la cité punique, romaine et byzantine*, Tunis, 115-123.

Chapter 12 (see also chapter 11)
Bejaoui F., 1997, *Céramique et religion chrétienne. Les thèmes bibliques sur la sigillée africaine*, Tunis.

Brown P., 1967, *Augustine of Hippo. A Biography*, London.

Dolenz H., 2001, *Damous el-Karita. Die österreichisch-tunesischen Ausgrabungen der Jahre 1996 und 1997 im Saalbau und der Memoria des Pilgerheiligtumes Damous el-Karita in Karthago* (Österreichisches Archäologisches Institut Sonderschriften 35), Wien.

Ennabli L., 1997, *Carthage. Une métropole chrétienne du IVè à la fin du VIIè siècle* (Études d'Antiquités africaines), Paris.

Ennabli L., 2000, *La basilique de Carthagenna et le locus des sept moines de Gafsa. Nouveaux edifices chrétiens de Carthage* (Études d'Antiquités africaines), Paris.

Hattler C. (ed.), 2009, *Das Königreich der Vandalen. Erben des Imperiums in Nordafrika*, Mainz a.R. (Franse versie van teksten: *Le royaume des Vandales. Les héritiers de l'Empire en Afrique du Nord*).

Miles R., 2006, British Excavations at Bir Messaouda, Carthage 2000-2004: the Byzantine Basilica, *BABESCH Annual Papers on Mediterranean Archaeology* 81, 199-226.

Seney P. (ed.), 2000, *Carthage XI. À la basilique dite «triconque» de l'Ædes Memoriæ. Fouilles 1994-2000* (Cahiers des Études Anciennes 36), Trois-Rivières.

Stevens S.T. (ed.), 1993, *Bir El Knissia at Carthage: a rediscovered cemetery church Report no. 1* (Journal of Roman Archaeology Supplementary Series 7), Ann Arbor MI.

Stevens S.T., Garrison M.B., Freed J., 2009, *A Cemetery of Vandalic Date at Carthage* (Journal of Roman Archaeology Supplementary Series 75), Portsmouth Rhode Island.

Stevens S.T., Kalinowski A.V., VanderLeest H., 2005, *Bir Ftouha: A Pilgrimage Church Complex at Carthage* (Journal of Roman Archaeology Supplementary Series 59), Portsmouth Rhode Island.

Chapter 13
Kruijsen B., Moormann E.M., 2011, *Vergilius en Ovidius in Nijmegen. Wandtapijten voor de Vrede van Nijmegen (1678-1679)*, Nijmegen.

Moormann E.M., Uitterhoeve W.J., 2007, *Van Alexander tot Zeus. Figuren uit de klassieke mythologie en geschiedenis, met hun voorleven na de oudheid*, Amsterdam.

Hermeneus 54 (1982) aflevering 4, 252-333, bevat verschillende artikelen over Aeneas uitbeeldingen, o.a. van Ilja Veldman over de prenten van Crispijn de Passe.

Chapter 14
Ciccotti V., 1999, *Camillo Borgia (1773-1817), soldato ed archeologo*, Velletri.

Ciccotti V. (ed.), 2000, *Atti del convegno internazionale di studi Camillo Borgia (1773-1817)*, Velletri.

Debergh J., 2000, L'aurore de l'archéologie à Carthage au temps d'Hamouda bey et de Mahmoud bey (1782-1824): Frank, Humbert, Caronni, Gierlew, Borgia, in: *Geografi, viaggiatori, militari nel Maghreb: alle origini dell'archeologia del Nord Africa. L'Africa romana. XIII convegno internazionale di studi, Djerba, 10-13 dicembre 1998*, Roma, 457-474.

Debergh J., 2000, L'esilio in Tunisia. Il fascino dell'antichità, in: *Atti del convegno internazionale di studi Camillo Borgia*, Velletri, 45-71.

Debergh J., 2001, Camillo Borgia. Ricerche archeologiche in un esule in Tunisia (1818-1816), in: *Tunisia: archeologi, mercanti e medici italiani (Levante XLVIII,3)*, 7-26.

Falbe C.T., 1833, *Recherches sur l'emplacement de Carthage*, Paris.

Halbertsma R.B., 1991, Benefit and honour: the archaeological travels of Jean Emile Humbert (1771-1839) in North-Africa and Italy in service of the Kingdom of the Netherlands, *MededRom* 50, 301-316.

Halbertsma R.B., 1995, *Le solitaire des ruines: de archeologische reizen van Jean Emile Humbert (1771-1839) in dienst van het Koninkrijk der Nederlanden*, Leiden.

Halbertsma R.B., 2000, Il fondo Borgiano di Leida, in: *Atti del convegno internazionale di studi Camillo Borgia*, Velletri, 37-44.

Halbertsma R.B., 2003, *Scholars, Travellers and Trade – The Pioneer Years of the National Museum of Antiquities in Leiden, 1818-1840*, London.

Lund J., 1986, The archaeological activities of Christian Tuxen Falbe in Carthage in 1838, *Cahiers des études anciennes* 18, 8-24.

Lund J., 2000, Il console Gierlew e il conte Borgia in terra d'Africa, in: *Atti del convegno internazionale di studi Camillo Borgia*, Velletri, 75-84.

Chapter 15
Daguerre de Hureaux, Pelletier-Hornby P., Moatti Cl., Lefébure A., De Los Llanos J., 1995, *Salammbô: entre l'Orient des romantiques et l'orientalisme fin-de-siècle?* in: *Carthage, l'histoire sa trace et son écho*, Paris (Musée du Petit Palais), 128-181.

Siebenmorgen A.H., Hattler Cl., Krause B., 2004, Karthago - eine Erinnerung, in: *Hannibal ad portas. Macht und Reichtum Karthagos*, Stuttgart, 362-379.

Chapter 16
Siebenmorgen H., Hattler C., Krause B., 2004, Karthago – eine Erinnerung, in: *Hannibal ad portas. Macht und Reichtum Karthagos*, Stuttgart, 362-379.

Chapter 17
30 ans au service du patrimoine 1986: Exposition catalogue *30 ans au service du patrimoine. De la Carthage des Phéniciens à la Carthage de Bourguiba (18 Octobre 1986 – 18 Octobre 1987. Année du Patrimoine)*, Tunis.

Ennabli A. (ed.), 1992, *Pour sauver Carthage. Exploration et conservation de la cité punique, romaine et byzantine*, Tunis.

Gutron C., 2010, *L'Archéologie en Tunisie (XIXe-XXe siècles). Jeux généalogiques sur l'Antiquité*, Paris.

Vitelli G., 1981, *Islamic Carthage. The Archaeological, Historical and Keramic Evidence*, Carthage.

INDEX

Michael Tomkinson's

GAMBIA

First published 1987 by
Michael Tomkinson Publishing
Hammamet Tunisia &
POB 215 Oxford OX2 0NR
Reprinted 1991
Second edition 2000

Designed by
Roger Davies Gregory Taylor

Photograph page 108 by Tony
Baker/Picturepoint; pages 28 left, 29 upper
left, 33, 34, 35 right, 36, 71 lower, 76 left, 104 by
Eddie Brewer OBE; pages 81, 92 inset by Ann
Hills; pages 71 upper, 118 by Michael Kirtley;
pages 1, 3 upper left & lower right, 7 upper left
& lower right, 18 centre & upper, 20, 21 right,
22, 22-23, 31 right, 46 upper, 48 upper right
and lower, 50, 51, 52 upper & left, 53 upper, 55,
62 left, 69 lower, 73 upper, 75 upper, 76 right,
80 upper, 81 inset, 90-91, 90 left & centre, 91,
96, 119 lower, 126-27 lower, facing page 128 by
Michel Renaudeau/Hoa-Qui; pages 1, 3 upper
right & lower left, 4-5, 4 upper left, 5 right, 6
upper right, 7 centre left, 14-15, 18 lower right,
19, 21 left, 25 inset, 26 inset, 28 centre, 28-29,
32, 44-45, 46 left, 52 lower, 54 left, 58-59, 62-
63, 84 lower right, 98-99, 100-101, 103 upper,
106 upper, 110 lower, 115, 116-17 by The
Gambia Experience; pages 7 upper right &
centre, 45 centre, 59 right, 72 lower, 82 lower,
84 lower left, 85 lower by Thomson Holidays;
pages 38, 39 by James Walford; all others by
the author

Printed in Singapore by
Star Standard Industries
ISBN 0 905500 59 8 (hardback)
ISBN 0 905500 64 4 (paperback)

Contents

Introduction

In a world where racial discrimination, ethnic violence, sectarian strife and civil war are all too frequent, finding a country free of all these is refreshing. It is perhaps a sign of the times that such havens of peace go unnoticed. That in The Gambia more ethnic groups than Bosnia's cohabit uneventfully does not interest the media. The press is not impressed by the fact that Gambian Muslims, Christians and animists – a divergence of faiths far wider than Ulster's – live and work together unconcerned by each other's beliefs. That religious, racial and sexual abuses are unknown here is not news.

More and more visitors are discovering individually what the mass media ignore. Despite continuing economic decline and a recent peacable change of regime, this smallest nation in Africa is attracting an ever greater number of holidaymakers from Europe.

Their destination is the closest of the English-speaking Commonwealth countries, Britain's first and last West African colony and the tropical resort within easiest reach of Europe in which winter sun and warmth are guaranteed. The Gambia's island-capital borders the estuary of the magnificent watercourse from which the modern state takes its name, shape and *raison d'être*. Early adventurers sailed up this 'Golden River' in search of legendary mines. Later traders came, lured by gold and ivory, but soon turning their attention more to lading slaves. For Mungo Park and his lesser-known contemporaries the river was the long-sought route to the riches of Timbuktu, to the source of the Niger and even the Nile. While 19th-century officials on the spot palavered and pacified, their governments, scrambling for Africa, haggled and aggrandized, encompassing the Gambia in artificial frontiers. The legacy today is Senegambian families in which, beside their local languages, some speak English, some French. And a relaxed and peaceful river that, by pleasure boat, dug-out or converted pirogue, you can travel in relative comfort

two arterial roads criss-cross the country. There are roughly a dozen accessible ancient sites, a half-dozen interesting churches and mosques, three national parks (one out of bounds), three nature reserves and only three townships with fridges and cold drinks in The Gambia's whole northern half.

But neither should the attractions be under-estimated. The broad sandy beaches,

sufferance, a post-colonial anachronism. It has a character and identity of its own. Here people have moved and married so freely, so blithely ignoring what authorities call porous borders, that the country's smallness is compensated by its 'quintessential' richness, by the insight it offers into the region around. You can holiday in Kenya and learn nothing of its neighbours, visit Tunisia without suffering the side-effects

viewing villages and wildlife little changed by the 20th century.

In sunshine rarely interrupted between October and May, in a welcome winter average of 24°C, modern beach hotels stand for the most part in gardens ablaze with flowers: hibiscus, frangipani, bougainvillea and Morning glory, Golden shower, lantana, jacaranda and canna lilies come as a dazzling contrast to British winter-grey. The Gambians' everyday dress is equally colourful and, usually just as brightly flamboyant, birds abound everywhere, in a profusion that has made the country famous.

Outside the hotels, standards should not be overstated: the capital, Banjul, is the largest town – with 45,000 inhabitants. Just

strewn with shells, are everywhere uncrowded. Cottonsilk and baobab trees tower over villages where fishermen and farmers gather at the *bantaba*; women pound coos or pump water, their babies on their backs, while dewlapped cattle graze by mountains of groundnuts and high-piled kapok or cotton. Baboons patrol and palm-trees dominate the half-farmed savanna around, which gives way to lush 'jungle' beside the streams and hollows. And through all this runs one of Africa's great waterways, tapering eastward for some 300 miles.

Even more than the bird life and flora, I find the population fascinating. Though small and endowed with few natural resources, The Gambia is by no means a state on

of Libya or Algeria, but The Gambia means an encounter with all the colourfulness, friendliness and penury of West Africa.

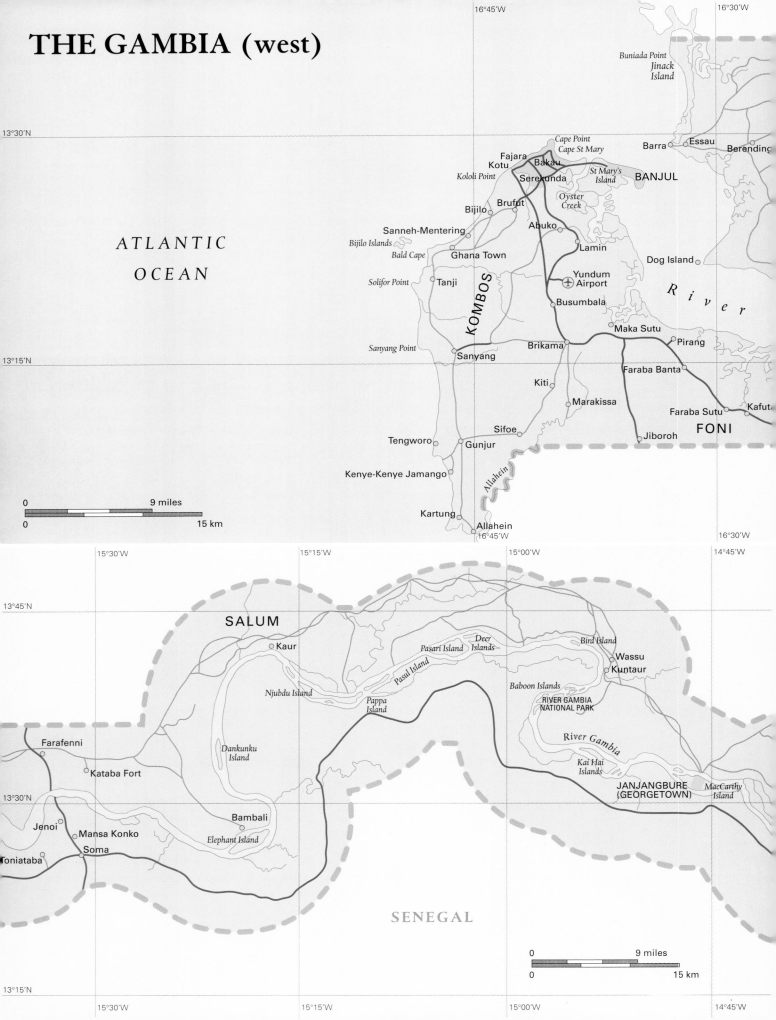

THE GAMBIA (west)

16°45'W
16°30'W

Buniada Point
Jinack Island

ATLANTIC
OCEAN

13°30'N

Cape Point
Cape St Mary
Fajara
Kotu Bakau
Kololi Point
Serekunda
St Mary's Island
Barra
Essau
Berending
BANJUL
Bijilo
Brufut
Oyster Creek
Sanneh-Mentering
Abuko
Bijilo Islands
Bald Cape
Ghana Town
Lamin
Dog Island
KOMBOS
Solifor Point
Tanji
Yundum Airport
River
Busumbala
13°15'N
Maka Sutu
Pirang
Sanyang Point
Brikama
Sanyang
Faraba Banta
Kiti
Marakissa
Faraba Sutu
Kafut
Sifoe
Jiboroh
FONI
Tengworo
Gunjur
Allahein
Kenye-Kenye Jamango

0   9 miles
0   15 km

Kartung
Allahein
16°45'W
16°30'W

15°30'W
15°15'W
15°00'W
14°45'W

13°45'N

SALUM
Kaur
Pasari Island
Deer Islands
Bird Island
Wassu
Kuntaur
Njubdu Island
Pasul Island
Baboon Islands
RIVER GAMBIA NATIONAL PARK
Pappa Island
River Gambia
Farafenni
Dankunku Island
Kai Hai Islands
JANJANGBURE (GEORGETOWN)
MacCarthy Island
Kataba Fort
13°30'N
Jenoi
Bambali
Mansa Konko
Elephant Island
Toniataba
Soma

SENEGAL

0   9 miles
0   15 km

13°15'N
15°30'W
15°15'W
15°00'W
14°45'W

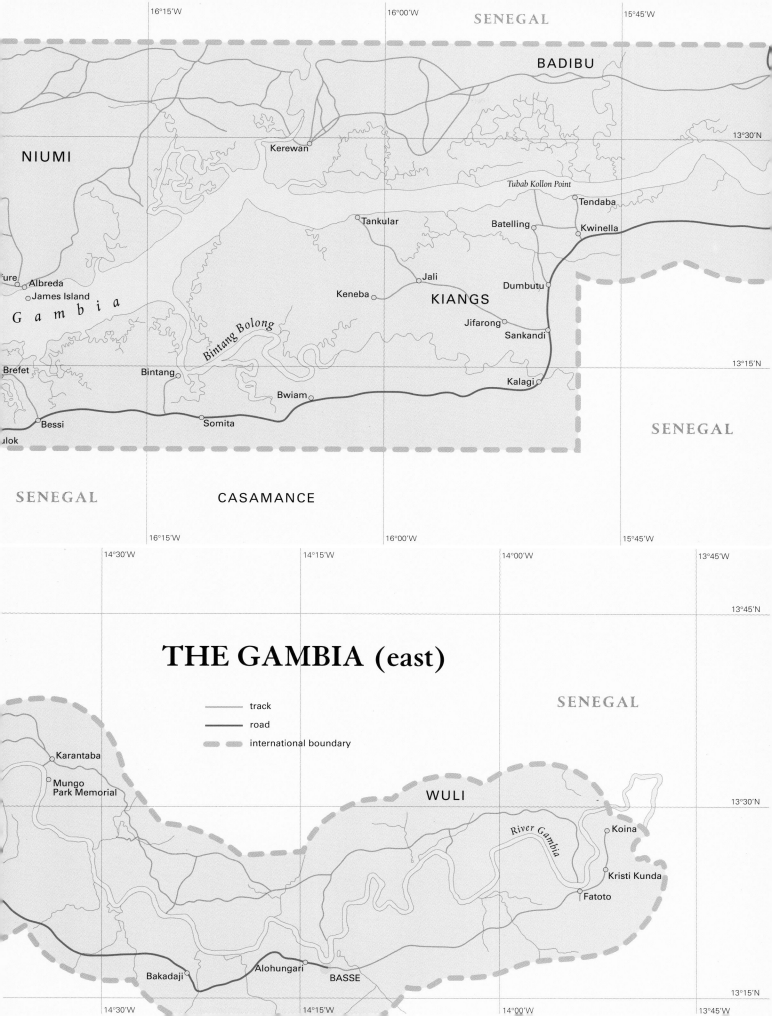

SENEGAL

BADIBU

NIUMI

Kerewan

Tubab Kollon Point

Tankular

Tendaba

Batelling

Kwinella

'ure

Albreda

James Island

Jali

G a m b i a

Keneba

KIANGS

Dumbutu

Bintang Bolong

Jifarong

Sankandi

Brefet

Bintang

Kalagi

Bwiam

SENEGAL

Somita

Bessi

ulok

SENEGAL

CASAMANCE

13°30'N

13°15'N

16°15'W

16°00'W

15°45'W

14°30'W

14°15'W

14°00'W

13°45'W

13°45'N

THE GAMBIA (east)

———— track

———— road

– – – – international boundary

SENEGAL

Karantaba

Mungo
Park Memorial

WULI

River Gambia

13°30'N

Koina

Kristi Kunda

Fatoto

Bakadaji

Alohungari

BASSE

13°15'N

14°30'W

14°15'W

14°00'W

13°45'W

Geography

The Gambia is the westernmost country of Africa (which is why Lufthansa chose it in 1934 as base for the first-ever transatlantic flights) and lies astride longitude 15°W (which is why today's six-hour flight from Britain causes very little jet-lag). It is equidistant from the Equator and the Tropic of Cancer, 13°15'-13°30'N being the approximate latitudinal extent. In common with many of its African neighbours, the country is the victim of some geodetic incertitude: elastic dimensions and an area that varies with each official source. It fares best on the Internet and in guide-books, with '11,300 square kilometres' in the *Rough Guide*, '11,295 sq km (4,361 sq mi)' on Microsoft's *Encarta* and 'around

Lagoon behind the beach at Tanji

11,000 sq km' chez *Lonely Planet*. More authoritative, the *Commonwealth Fact Sheet* gives a total of 4049 square miles (10,367 square kilometres) and the government's *The Gambia in Brief* 4045 square miles (10,356 km²). With its 4003 square miles (10,247 km²), the *Encyclopædia Britannica* further reduces the country's size. Which is the last thing it needs. Whatever its actual extent, The Gambia is easily half as large again as Lincolnshire.

The northern and southern boundaries, both with Senegal, are at their widest 30 miles (48 kms) apart. From this distance on the coast they narrow inland to fifteen miles (24 kms) – the maximum range, according to

Whitehall wags, of British gunboats on the river. State and river stretch eastward for 304 miles/487 kms (or 201 miles/322 kms or 288 miles/460 kms viz. the above authorities) as far as the Barrakunda Falls, whereas landfall in the other direction is in the West Indies, 3000 miles away. The last remark is not fatuous: it helps explain The Gambia's involvement with the slave-trade. Wind and water aided and abetted: the Canary current carried ships from Europe south to the mouth of the river. While the doldrums then impeded their further passage around Africa, the north equatorial current and the prevailing north-east trade winds (not named that for nothing) combined to assist them across the Atlantic.

Venturing southward beyond Cape Non ('No further'), European navigators faced the flat inhospitable coast of the Western Sahara and Mauritania, 1100 miles with little water and few natural harbours, until the Senegal, Gambia and Casamance rivers were reached. All three rise in the Guinea plateau of Futa Jallon, the Gambia twelve miles from the 'town' of Labe. From here the distance to the sea is as the crow flies 150 miles, to the actual estuary about 300, but the river's meanderings protract its total length to over 1000 miles.

In The Gambia, the river's initial width of 600 feet is constricted to a twenty-foot channel by the Barrakunda Falls. For most writers these ledges of laterite rock are an 'obstacle to navigation': the presentday scarcity of boats above Fatoto makes the comment academic. For The Gambia the falls' significance is as the country's easternmost limit, below which the river is tidal. Koina is the first 'port' (viz. rickety jetty), Kristi Kunda ('Christ's Place') the first, now-defunct Anglican mission. At Fatoto is the first (small-dinghy) ferry.

Here the picturesque riverbanks impress with an average height of 40 feet, which varies with the rainfall and the tide. They illustrate how for the last one million years the river has gouged its course through the tertiary sandstone of the Senegambian plateau. Islands of harder ironstone

Flooded banto faros, near Farafenni

Air-roots of the mangroves, along any bolong

and gneiss have resisted erosion and now stand as isolated, flat-topped hills; pockets of kaolin supply the cottage-potteries near Basse. From here to the Atlantic, on terra firma everywhere, the topsoil is in general red laterite, an infertile 'ferruginous crust' that frustrates farmers but, like East Africa's murram, makes good 'roads'. It covers all too much of the country and, on any dry-season drive, the wayside vegetation, your vehicle and you.

A Barrakunda-like formation, the Buruko Rocks, again constricts the river. Squeezed into a channel only 100 feet wide, the faster current sweeps with it a mass of silt and sand; this alluvium removed in the upper reaches reforms as islands in the rambling middle river. Below Janjangbure (the late MacCarthy Island) they are named either from their part-extinct fauna – Baboon, Bird, Deer and Elephant – or, with many an alias, in the vernacular: Kai Hai, Pasari, Pasul and Pappa, Njubdu and Dankunku. Human habitation consists of Janjangbure (Georgetown) on the same-named island and, on the Baboon Islands, the national park wardens in remote confinement and the occasional privileged visitor to a study-group of chimpanzees.

The river's meanderings round these sometimes water-logged obstacles meant 80 miles of difficult tacking in the days of sail: only with the advent of steam could Georgetown be easily reached and developed. Kuntaur is the all-time limit for ocean-going vessels and marks the

Timeless in The Gambia, a dig-out on the river

approximate point at which salinity yields to fresh water. (Salt water, to be precise, reaches in the dry season 140 miles up stream, and half that far during the rains.)

In riverside clearings decrepit piers step from the water to narrow mud causeways that run straight to villages built high and dry behind. These stand on slight rises, amidst the *banto faros*. Meaning in Mandinka 'beyond the swamp', these grasslands, often flooded by river and rain, are for the rest cultivable if salinity permits. In its final 93 miles below Elephant Island the broader, straighter river sidles off into larger creeks, here called bolons/bolongs. Many, like the

A groundnut cutter tacks up stream

13

largest Bintang Bolong, straggle north or south into Senegal; tortuous tributaries, they contribute fresh water when replenished by rain. Their banks, like those of the mainstream, are a tangle of mangrove swamps: not the Indian Ocean's lowly growth but off-shore forests in which air-roots arc symmetrically high and timber-straight trunks stand 60 feet tall.

As fertility deteriorates towards the river mouth – clay alluvium and sand predominating – the Gambia grows busier and more magnificent. Fishermen cast hand-nets from mahogany dug-outs and painted-plank pirogues. Tugs chug down in season with lighters of groundnuts in tow. Birds, as everywhere, astonish at every turn and dolphins frolic or bask like shark as you sail by.

En route you pass, as did the earliest settlers, two islands of not alluvium but rock. If the river is the axis round which the country's life turns, James Island was for centuries the hub. Dog Island, down stream, was first manned by Britain in 1661. St Andrew's/James Island – in mid-river, more extensive and defensible – had been frequented by the Portuguese since 1456. And sailing in untroubled by sandbanks or reefs (the estuary's bar is navigable and in the river's silt no coral grows), Hollanders, Frenchmen and the Duke of Courland's Germans had fought with them and died for these petty arid outcrops.

On the last and largest island stands the capital, Banjul. Despite a swampy, once-waterlogged site which, in Sir Richard Burton's words, was 'selected for proximity to mud, mangoes, malaria and miasma', Britain in 1816 established colonial Bathurst. From twelve miles at its widest, between Cape St Mary and Buniada Point, the Gambia estuary narrows here to under three. Thus initially of strategic importance, the new capital acquired both commercial and administrative significance as the British colony/protectorate took shape. Finally demarcated in 1889, that shape prompted the Victorian comment that 'its very appearance on the map is an invitation to the zealous reformer'. American journalists prefer the analogy of 'a long crooked finger poked into Senegal'.

Crossing the Gambia by ferry at Farafenni, the Trans-Gambia Highway is Senegal's strategic link between its capital, Dakar, and the Casamance

Sunset at Tendaba (inset)

14

Climate

Weather-wise,
The Gambia is
Europe's antipodes,
Britain's better half

In September or October here the rains ease off and there starts a sunny season that lasts until April or May. Sea-breezes (the north-east trade winds) keep temperatures on the coast at an equable and pleasant average of 24°Centigrade/76° Fahrenheit. During the eight-month tourist season the thermometer drops to December, with the last 30 years' median *minimum* of 16°C/61°F. From January to May it climbs back to the October-November peak, measured over the same period as a *maximum* 32°C/91°F. At this time of year humidity is at an ideal 50-60%. Days are warm and nights cool.

which induces the south-west monsoons. Blowing from the ocean, these arrive laden with rain. In their first encounter with the weakening north-east trades (what scientists call the Inter-tropical Front) they deposit it on The Gambia in spectacular storms and tornados. (Wind and water have similar confrontations: when the cool Canary

The Gambia teeters climatically on the edge of the arid Sahel zone. The coast generally benefits from the ocean's tempering effect, but inland the Atlantic's sphere of influence is soon replaced by the Sahel's. The heat increases as humidity and even visibility drop. Especially when the north wind blows – the hazy *harmattan*, between February and May, for a week or two at a time – throats parch, lips crack and static is crisp in the atmosphere. Sensitive skins inland need dowsing with moisturizer. At such times the baobab tree prevents loss of water by shedding its leaves: man's only recourse is drink.

A word about the wet season may be of deterrent interest. As every A-level pupil knows, the air in the Sahara rises with the heat of summer, causing an area of low pressure

After August rains, on Jinack Island (left) and the Wassu 'road'
Tendaba sundowner (centre)
Offloading a cutter at Oyster Creek (opposite)

current meets the warmer Guinea stream, fogs occur off the Senegambian coast.) As the monsoons set in, ousting the trade winds between May and August, the rainfall is welcome but variable in force. While regular short showers leave clear skies, cloudbursts bring inches in minutes (or, as in August 1999, last hours and cause catastrophic damage). Though the sand and permeable soils drain too fast for streams and pools to survive for long, the vegetation then is at its most luxuriant. Nature-lovers not averse to sustained rain enjoy this season best.

The Gambia is lacking in mineral resources. The gold-mines for which it enjoyed chimeric fame have proved as elusive as the Philosopher's stone; ilmenite workings have been abandoned; the 'immense deposits of iron ore on the cliffs overhanging the river' are exploited only by armchair geographers, and salt – dried from the shallows and bolongs and packed in roadside baskets for transportation to market – is the only claim to geological wealth.

Agriculture

The rainfall during the monsoon season is a *sine qua non* for The Gambia's farmers, whose bane is its unpredictable start and finish, its occasional failure to appear at all or, as in 1999, its calamitous excess. Farming is none the less the nation's mainstay, accounting for 60% of per capita income and, with fishing, 74% of the work-force.

The varied topography described above – rich banto faros subject to floods, light sandy soils vitiated by salinity, fertile river silt often clogged with laterite – has as much

effect as the climate on crops. The principal of these are groundnuts, rice and cotton, maize, millet and sorghum, market-garden produce and sesame, recently introduced.

Groundnuts are the corner-stone of agriculture, the economy and, in a sense, The Gambia itself. Known as *tio* in Mandinka, the 'peanut' or 'monkey nut' is the country's only significant export and principal cash crop. So vital are the unsightly swellings on the roots of this legume that books like Lady Southern's *The Gambia* are subtitled *The Story of the Groundnut Colony*. And when that colony became independent the plant was chosen to top its coat of arms, which featured *dibongo*s and *dabandingo*s, the coop coops/hoes used to till it.

The Portuguese in the 16th century introduced the species from Brazil; the Gambians until the 1830s cultivated it for their own consumption only. Several odd

quirks of colonial history were to be the cause and effect of its rapid development. Soap came into fashion in France (more so, it seems, than in Britain) and demand for groundnuts as its raw material grew: from 100 baskets in 1830 to a record 8636 tons in 1848. Soon overtaking hides, ivory and beeswax, the crop constituted by the 1850s over two thirds of the colony's export total. Production increased with Britain's colonial commitment. Agricultural advisers brought in new strains like the Rio Fresco/Rufisque, spread the use of fertilizers and implemented 'oxenization', prevailing upon villagers to use animals in lieu of the coop coop. By resisting the enticement to mechanize – tractors break down – The Gambia was able to progress simply while other African projects like Tanganyika's Groundnut Scheme turned into costly fiascos.

For three pence (50 buluts) the women on sidewalks and in market-places everywhere will measure you out,

from their cheap Chinese bowls, a tomato puree tinful of crisp fresh-roasted nuts. Such 'Hand Picked Selected' and 'Philippine Pinks' may still be grown 'exclusively for the confectionery trade' but peanuts, neat, have long been of less importance than the oil pressed from them. The basis for French soap and the crop's initial success, this side-product soon so dominated the market that already in the 1860s Gambian nuts were hit by competition from American petroleum and 'belmontine'. After the Second World War, the Tanganyikan scheme had been designed to relieve a worldwide shortage of margarine; edible oil from Senegambian groundnut kernels, refined without odour or taste,

fights a losing battle with olive-oil on the European market. Partly to reduce our dependence on petroleum, partly to avert a produce 'mountain' (caused by the USA, West Africa and India), American scientists are looking to the groundnut as a source of new foodstuffs and ersatz petrol, paper, cosmetics and even industrial diamonds.

The farmers up river would be flattered if they knew. Each season they clear the bush where necessary in the time-honoured African way, by the ubiquitous 'slash and burn' technique. Joined seasonally by 'strange farmers' – share-cropping *nawettanes* from Mali, the Guineas and Senegal – they brush the fields ready for the first soil-softening

rain. They sometimes fertilize, then they (or more often now their oxen) plough. Planting takes place at the start of the monsoon; weeding is easy (which may be why this is all-male work) and picking begins as the wet season ends (given the requisite 750mm of rain and a minimum temperature of 24°C). After two or three seasons of this, and a one-year sortie into cereals, natural nutrients in the sandy soil are exhausted and the land, if not fertilized, should be left to lie fallow and revert to bush.

The plants are laid to dry on platforms, raised and covered to safeguard them respectively from vermin and belated rain. The villagers next beat the nuts free with forked sticks; they

'winnow' them either in loose-meshed panniers or in the rotating *passoires*, the long perforated cylinders seen in many villages. Collected and piled in open-air *seccos* or the larger centres' hangar-like 'bins', then graded, weighed and transported by lorry or lighter, 'quality' nuts – from December to March – should go for decortication at Kaur or Banjul; to these towns' wharves for direct shipment overseas or, for crushing into oil and 'cake', to Banjul's Denton Bridge.

For generations groundnut growers here had been an unwitting object-lesson for Rabelais' *Discourses in the Praise of Borrowers and Lenders*. The need to feed families through each

The Gambia and Senegal were still the world's largest commercial producers of groundnuts.

All this is history. Bankrupted by mismanagement and a slump in world market-prices, the board was privatised as the Gambia Groundnut Corporation, which was itself shut down by presidential decree in 1999. With this, the principal vehicle of the country's main crop, removed; with the IMF reducing aid pending a solution, and with fields flooded by exceptional rains in 1999, the immediate future for The Gambia's groundnuts looks bleak.

year's rainy season, to buy seed for sowing and to wait months for any return had made them dependent on advances of food and/or funds. Crop failure put them irretrievably in debt: to pioneer French firms like the CFAO, Maurel Frères and (until 1978) Maurel & Prom, to Lebanese traders and less scrupulous 'julamen' – Mungo Park's *Juli* – lending at 100% plus.

To keep hungry growers from eating the seed-nuts, and reducing the crop by picking prematurely for the sake of an early return, the colonial government in 1903 stepped in to subsidize, store and distribute. Which resulted simply in a transfer of the farmers' debt from the dealers to HMG. Owed £50,000 by 1921, Britain altered course. In 1924 an Agriculture Department was started, later a programme of expatriate advisers and local extension workers to organise seed-storage on a village basis, to encourage mixed farming and – the most far-reaching move – to form co-operatives.

The Gambia Co-operative Union lived longest of the many well-meant initiatives taken for the sake of the groundnut in recent years. After drought

in the early 1960s, better harvests and higher world prices helped The Gambia survive, against expectations, following independence in 1965. In 1973 the Gambia Produce Marketing Board took over the crop (like that of palm-kernels, rice and cotton), building depots, setting up annual buying stations, subsidizing fertilizers and holding 'price stabilization reserves'. A Gambia Commercial & Development Bank made the much-needed advances to farmers. The Gambia River Transport Company's seven barges provided lighterage at fixed 'zonal freight rates'. In the 1980s

Besides giving front-page prominence to the groundnut 'results', Banjul's letterpress dailies used to exhort readers to 'Light up with Briquettes'. This solid fuel, from compacted groundnut-shells, was sold cheaply in lieu of the charcoal with which too many village housewives cook and heat. (Hoardings around Banjul announcing the 'EEC/Sahel Butane Gas Programme' are all that survives of a similarly short-lived alternative.) For charcoal-makers cut and burn whole forests, destroying the habitat of many wildlife species and also the vegetation cover. This causes steady desertification and The Gambia, like many African states, has banned random charcoal-burning. The sackloads seen for sale by roadsides now should have been brought in from the Casamance.

The need to conserve the oil-palm explains the attempted prohibition of another once-popular product: palm-toddy. Bainunka men, especially in the Kombos, you can still see scaling the footholed trunk with their fixed elliptical sling, the *kajandak* resembling a windsurfing boom. They tap the tree just below the flower-stalk, fill a gourd or two and, lax Muslims, sell off what little they leave unconsumed of the fast-fermenting liquor. (A dance done by Jola women depicts *Cassa*-tappers in their *daaka*, palm-wine

Palms, and palm-wine tapper

'brewery'.) Strictly, only small-time tapping is allowed now, just enough to jollify friends and family. For removal of the sap not only impairs the oil, it has also made of the palm itself an endangered species. Some fruit is boiled and crushed, the palm-oil you taste in local dishes exuding from the flesh, the mesocarp. But the oil from the kernels being worth more, these were in better times bagged for export to Europe.

Longer heads have always thought that The Gambia's reliance on the 'cash monoculture' of groundnuts was unwise. The alternative, or rather adjunct, of cotton has often been mooted – especially in the 19th century when Americans were prospering on southern plantations and Victorian Britain, rich from India, was turning Egypt from self-sufficiency in wheat to dependence on international cotton-price fluctuations. Here the crop has a long and chequered history. Reaching the Gambia in 1455, the

Portuguese explorer Luiz de Cadamosto was 'astonished to find the inhabitants clothed'. For centuries the Serahulis, Fulas and Mandinkas had grown 'tree cotton' from which to make the *pagnes* they dyed with indigo (the secret of weaving, so they say, having come from a fisherman who learned it from a jinn). In 1760, impressed by Senegambian samples, the London Society of Arts had offered a gold medal for the importer of the greatest quantity, 'not less than two tons', but only in 1833 was that amount attained. Settling the Liberated Africans up river, the 'Home Government' in London supplied them with Sea Island cotton-seed. An official report of 1860 gave 206 tons as grown and traded annually: 'If cultivation . . . is now taken up seriously,' it said, 'the export return should shortly become substantial'. 'Shortly' was not until 1904, when 70 tons left Bathurst for London. There the British Cotton Growing Association had been set up in 1902; in 1903 £500,000 were found for advances to planters and experimental farms, for seed, ginneries and baling machines; King Edward in 1904 gave his blessing by way of a Royal

Ample manpower and scant funds means more manual labour than mechanization (right) Picking cotton near Basse (below)

Charter . . . and in 1906 all Bathurst could report was that 'cotton might be taken up . . . if it is seen to pay'.

Replacing the endemic 'tree' with hardier 'hairy' cotton, planters moved to Nigerian varieties then settled on 'American Upland'. Ploughing and harrowing for sowing must be deep. Sowing must be done by hand, in precisely the right week or two, with the soil just sufficiently moist. No moisture must touch the bolls during picking . . . Growing only on the well-drained sandy soils of the middle and upper river, where groundnuts also fare best (and require much less effort of the selfsame workforce), cotton looked likely to remain for some time a perenially 'promising' crop.

That The Gambia's cotton has not gone the way of its groundnuts is due to the *Compagnie française pour le Développement des Fibres textiles*. Established in Paris in 1948 and now operating in most of Africa's cotton-growing countries, the CFDT in 1992 established with the Gambian government the Gambian Cotton Company, GAMCOT. In a project financed by the French and Gambian govern-

ments, growers are supplied with insecticides, implements, fertilizer and seeds on credit. The hub of this joint enterprise is the Basse ginnery: the lorryloads of seed cotton delivered from local growers, and north-west Guinea's, are here reduced to lint (the seeds left going for cattlefeed or oil), then roadfreighted to Banjul for export. After disappointing crops in 1998 and '99, an optimistic GAMCOT manager in Basse hopes for an annual export average of 1500 tonnes of cotton lint.

Rubber and gum are bygones. Exports of the former stopped in 1901, 'no doubt because . . . the trees, not being judiciously tapped, withered and died'. The rubber-trees seen nowadays – *Funtumia elastica* or imported *Ficus elastica* – are ornamental relics. Humble gum (*gomme arabique*) became a Franco-British *casus belli* in the 18th and 19th centuries, when each country's African Company took up arms over this bacterial pus of the *Acacia senegalensis*. In moments of truce they traded the commodity for slaves: 360,000 pounds of the one for 100 of the other 'in their prime'. So important was the gum of Portendic that, although in 1783 all Senegal was surrendered, British rights to the trade were conceded by the French (who demanded

and obtained in return the enclave of Albreda). Contending nevertheless with French seizure of their ships and sabotage of supplies, Bathurst's merchants maintained the commerce until in 1857 Albreda and the rights at Portendic were re-exchanged.

Rice, short grained, is a staple of long standing. As its cultivation needs care, men entrust it to the women. Traditionally they have utilized the upland areas where the banto faros are no longer too salt and the riverbanks not yet too high for flooding. Though covering only one tenth of the area under such 'rainfed' cultivation, irrigated paddies are the hope for the future. The men accept to help build the bunds, the banks of mud bound with grass around each paddy. The women plough; sometimes plant stake-fences to deter hungry hippos; transplant from the nurseries the six-inch seedlings, and weed – at the same time of year as their men tend the groundnuts. In December, with the waters subsided, the ripe stalks are cut one by one. Each day's harvest is then threshed: on the

ground, thrashed with sticks in the villages, churned in some centres' hand-operated drums or milled, in privileged places like Basse, by machine.

These techniques are basically Indian, but presentday Chinese were an obvious choice for advice. One of The Gambia's few memorials, by the south-bank ferry on Janjangbure Island, honours the Mr Lee who in 1966-69 led the first team of Taiwanese. These made way in 1974-75 for mainland Chinese (all of them but one, that is, who stayed on to run Fajara's Bamboo Restaurant). Sailing past Sapu, you still see perched on the river's edge the Chinese pumps which, with the first seeds, came free.

In 1973 the government's Development Project was started, and in 1984 the first harvest reaped at Jahali Pachaar. A showpiece of successful irrigation, the 3700 acres around these two centres promptly repaid a £23-million investment with a twice-yearly crop averaging seventeen tonnes per acre. This, to the amazement not only of its Euroconsult supervisers, was a rice output unparalleled anywhere in the world. And not since paralleled in The Gambia either.

There was momentary glory when Jahali Pachaar featured in *Time*, then a return to the customary gulf between planning and reality. An ambitious scheme to dam the River Gambia (to keep salinity down stream and maintain the supply of fresh water to the paddies) was dropped. RIDEP, another rice-development project, suffered 'changes in administration which created unforeseen negative impact'. And despite a further six-year plan – the Small-scale Water Control Project launched in 1991 – 'the most urgent concerns of farmers have not been met' (not least of which is day-care centres for working mothers). The perennial problems of rice-growing here are at present being tackled again by communist Chinese, their Agricultural Technical Mission providing advisers, machinery and high-yield seed.

Growing thickly on tall trees around Banjul, The Gambia's grapefruit and Java oranges are in spring a surprising sight. They are also for the most part pip (which is why the latter are usually peeled, sold off-white in the thick pith and just sucked). Limes are more amenable: a 100-acre estate at Yundum supplied for a while a factory producing 'single strength juice' and, from the peel, lime-oil.

Sheep and goats straggle everywhere, especially over your road by night. Their skins and hides, no longer wild animals', are a minor item on the country's list of exports. Odd domestic pigs are an unexpected sight around Barra, salvaging on sufferance amongst Muslim compounds.

Chickens were the victim of a Gambian fiasco to match Tanganyika's Groundnut Scheme. In 1948 Britain's Colonial Development Corporation allotted funds for a Mass Production Poultry Scheme at Yundum. An American director was appointed but his knowledge of local conditions was nil. Fowl typhoid in 1950 killed 80,000 chickens; the project depended on local feedstuffs which it proved impossible to find; Gambians objected that their short supplies of food were made even scarcer by the scheme, and in 1951 it was abandoned. Losses were £628,000: the 38,520 eggs produced had cost the British taxpayer £20.77 apiece. The late Yundum College was installed in the premises. The government has ever since left poultry to the private sector.

Raising livestock alongside crops was an obvious corollary to the government's encouragement of home meat-production (and of the use of fertilizers, since cattle in particular guarantee an instant, on-the-spot supply). Almost all of The Gambia's cattle are either zebus or smaller, tsetse-resistant *ndamas* cross-bred from the zebu and the West African Dwarf. The country's cowboys are for the most part Fulas, sometimes owning a few head themselves, more often tending the collective herds of others. They traditionally see their scrawny kine as a token of wealth, not a source of food. Though it could often improve the stock, they (like Kenya's Masai) would no more cull their herds than you would take three clean pounds for a dirty fiver

Vegetation

The agricultural décor to your travels up country is enhanced, naturally, by the vegetation. To the north of The Gambia, Sudan savanna deteriorates into desert; to the south, gallery and tropical rain forest engulfs equatorial Africa. The *cordon sanitaire* of these botanical extremes is formed by their lesser-scale counterparts: South Guinea savanna and South Guinea woodland. Ecologically the country extends into both, and its flora in particular is correspondingly rich.

Flowers are so delightful a part of the Gambian scene that only a botanical boor would dismiss them as mostly imported hybrids. Though slightly (and literally) gone to seed, the Botanic Garden at Cape St Mary is a rustic introduction to The Gambia's commercially cultivated species.

The hibiscus, dying daily, adorns most hotel gardens: yellow, orange, red, pink and white, 'Sleeping', Korean and the Japanese *Grandiflora*.

Bougainvillea, in the tropics and the Mediterranean area, is an unpredictable boon. In East Africa it spreads, entwined on wire frames, as a multicoloured carpet – mauve, magenta, mustard, salmon or white – but often declines to climb up or cascade down walls. Which is the only way it will grow around the Mediterranean, stockily covering vertical surfaces but refusing to grow low along the ground. In The Gambia it not only creeps and leans but also, as bushes, forms lengthy hedges: like English privet at Bungalow Beach or in solid circles of colour. The tamarisk, too, is clipped and trimmed into hedges.

Walls and corrugated-iron roofs are camouflaged convolvulus-mauve, with not convolvulus but *Thunbergia grandiflora*. The orchid-like Dutchman's Pipe climbs; Golden shower descends like orange honeysuckle. Convolvulus and honeysuckle, poinsettias, jasmin and sturdy oleander, night-fragrant *Datura* ('Angel's trumpet') and *Lagastroemia* ('Queen of the Flowers'), all flourish beside the jacaranda and banana-plant, its flowers weird-obscene, the long-podded flame-tree, and oddities like the Century palm which lives for 100 years, flowers once and dies.

Ground orchid & African crocus (upper left)

Thunbergia grandiflora (upper centre)

Golden shower on a restaurant pergola

Canna lily (left)

Natural forests have suffered, as everywhere, from the 20th century. One third of The Gambia's has vanished since independence, burned, cut or cleared for charcoal, timber or farms. But impressive patches survive: in forest parks which cover three per cent of the country and, easily accessible, at Bijilo and Abuko. In the latter reserve, lowlier savanna growth yields to closer riverine 'jungle'. The Grey plum's buttress-roots block the way like fallen trunks. Aerial and stilt-roots from the parasitic figs rise, entwined with dangling lianas. Tallos and Elephant trees ('African breadfruit') stand massive. With incredible foliage, the Cabbage or Candelabra trees add to the natural chiaroscuro.

Gallery forest in the Abuko Nature Reserve

The savanna, more widespread than woodland, is also less dramatic: low, loose-knit bush over which lone trees tower, grass-green in our autumn, parched brown by Christmas and often burned black in the spring. Scattered amidst the tracts scarred by shifting cultivation stand trees such as the Custard apple and the West African Gum copal; the African locust bean, the emetic Guinea peach and the much sought-after kola; the Black and the Gingerbread plum; ironwood, rosewood and Velvet tamarind; acacias like the fire-resistant winterthorn which, a perverse exception, sheds its leaves in the rainy season, and cassias like the West African laburnum, its seed-pods poisonous and its roots an aphrodisiac. (This last is local lore which I have not verified.)

Baobabs, on James Island (left) and *passim* on the savanna

The baobab, that tropical oddity, stands as the sentinel (or marks the long-gone spot) of every settlement. With boughs like roots, it is obviously growing upside down . . . doomed to do so, Africans say, because it would not stay where God placed it. They nevertheless make cold drinks and lollipops from the crisp white contents of its pods; grind flour from its 'monkey-bread' fruit; boil and eat its young leaves and strip it symmetrically, like cork-oaks in the Atlas, of the bark which is shredded for fibre.

The raffia-palm provides fibre for fencing, matting and furniture, sap for palm-toddy and polished seeds as beads for bracelets and ornamental knick-knacks. The rhun or fan-palm is easily recognized by the leaf-form from which it takes its name and from the standard borassus-bulge in its 100-foot trunk. Insect repelling and not rotting in salt water, this last goes into bridges, wharves and roofing, while lower leaves serve as fencing or poles. The Swamp date-palm prefers freshwater swamps, where it forms impenetrable clumps. Like the straggling rattan from which furniture is made, it is technically a vine.

The bamboo's 1000 species are the fastest growing of all living things, and 1000 known applications make it the world's most versatile. Here it helps bind the soil against erosion, and was widely burned until the recent ban – for charcoal, no longer as a cure for prickly heat. From the bamboo's stalk comes The Gambia's *krinting* which for walls and fencing vies with corrugated iron. The plant bursts into blossom only once, before dying, each decade or two.

The cottonsilk/kapok-tree dominates the savanna, in both abundance and size. The Gambia's White-flowered silk cotton is larger and more striking than its namesake in East Africa. Like the mango there, it often guards the 'village square': by the *bentengo* (platform) in the shade of this *bantango* is the *bantaba*, meeting-place. Buttressed by astonishing 'natural planks', its six-foot-wide trunk rises over 100 feet, providing a mass of albeit inferior timber for dug-outs, drums and not very durable coffins. From the seed-pods bursts the white floss (kapok) which fills mattresses, pillows and unreliable lifebelts.

Wildlife

With the Banjul Declaration a new concern for wildlife became Gambian government policy

Though the Gambian savanna boasts the tallest African trees, its surviving animals are, apart from hippos, smaller scale. The elephant, as collectors of colonial postage stamps know, was once the national emblem, and ivory was traded here in bulk. Since 1913 the only memento is the place-name Elephant Island. The last of the once-common Western giraffes was drowned near MacCarthy Island in 1899; in 1911 the last Giant or 'Derbian' eland was killed. The West African and the 'bastard' Korrigum hartebeest, the buffalo, Roan antelope, waterbuck and kob have all shared the same fate. Until very recently the odd lion was still reported regularly from Kuntaur. But such sightings were 'outstanding faunal events' and what features in an official picture-book as 'the King of the African jungle, and particularly that of the Gambia' was a domesticated monarch called MacCal, caged at Abuko and flown in from Longleat 'courtesy of British Caledonian.

On 18 February 1977, in what came to be known as the Banjul Declaration, ex-president Jawara's Independence Day speech pledged his government's 'untiring efforts to conserve for now and posterity as wide a spectrum as pos-

sible of our remaining fauna and flora'. The enabling legislation was the Wildlife Conservation Act which, passed the same year, outlawed hunting and the trade in animal products. A first reserve had already been established at Abuko in March 1968 and, in November 1978, five of the Baboon Islands were gazetted as the 1446-acre River Gambia National Park.

Although closed to the public, the latter remains better known than the two national parks and two reserves set up since. The Niumi National Park was created in 1986 and Kiang West National Park in 1987. Opposite the latter, across the River Gambia, the local ecosystem of savanna, salt-marsh and mangrove swamp has aroused such international interest that 85 square miles have become the Bao Bolon Wetland Reserve. Newest and most visited after Abuko is the Tanji Bird Reserve established in 1993.

MacCal, caged patriarch of Abuko's lions

Nile crocodile at Katchikali

The *éminence grise* of The Gambia's ecology, the 'saviour' of its wildlife in a sense, was the late Eddie Brewer OBE. Named in 1976 the first Director of Wildlife Conservation, he masterminded the country's pioneering programme and, answerable directly to the Office of the President, maintained its momentum until his retirement in 1990. His Gambian successor has benefitted both from a well-funded German forestry mission and specialized Irish support. Keen and competent, Irish-funded volunteers provide technical assistance and training to the Department of Parks & Wildlife Management. They have published a comprehensive guide to the country's protected areas and, to defray the high cost of maintaining them, recently launched a Friends of Abuko scheme to which your contribution is welcome.

While Eddie Brewer *was* Abuko, much of his daughter Stella's early life was devoted to rehabilitating chimpanzees. Her protégés – first in Senegal's Niokolo Koba, later in the River Gambia National Park – were all first-generation immigrants, either confiscated from traders breaking the law or saved as orphans, circus-surplus or cast-off pets from overseas. They were for a while accommodated, pending transportation to the national park, in a 'rehabilitation centre' at Abuko. Nowadays the large cage there houses Patas monkeys taken from errant locals. The Gambia's last wild chimpanzees survived just into this century: so neither in the outback nor at Abuko will you see these tailless apes now. Nor indeed in the national park, where the 50-odd specimens of *Pan troglodytes* are safeguarded with justifiable scientific jealousy.

Read Stella Brewer's *Forest Dwellers* instead. The Russians paid more than for *Life on Earth* for the rights to this homely and moving account of her success in training all-too-human chimps to survive in their natural environment. Filmed by Hugo van Lawick in 1976, the book takes her story up to 1977. An American, Janis Carter, has since taken over the privately funded Chimpanzee Rehabilitation Project, living devotedly and usually alone with the 29 original survivors and their score of offspring. Though one of her retinue 'speaks' sign language, she had also to practise and not preach as the only way of teaching: building and 'sleeping' on leaf nests twenty feet up; emitting 'good food grunts' and enjoying seeds and fruit; 'fishing' with a stick for ants, to be licked off and swallowed before they sting . . . but saved by the chimpanzees' unsuspected instinct from having to show them how to catch, smash and make a Chinese meal of other monkeys.

Red colobus, mother grooming

Patas monkeys drinking

Abuko's Western red colobus have also been the object of an American girl's PhD research. This took almost four years, and in a quick trip through the forest, savanna or swamp you should hope for no more than a treetop glimpse of these thumbless, black-backed and russet-fronted primates. Of the colobus' sixteen subspecies, the *Piliocolobus badius temminckii* lives only in The Gambia and Senegal, and in troops of 20-40 in which 'female adults are the most socially mobile' and 'males go out of their way to engage females in friendly behaviours'. Which may explain why in 1999 Abuko's colobus population was found to have been a healthy 122, and stable.

Callithrix is what we should now call the common Gambian monkey which, lately thought a subspecies of the Green vervet, has been accepted as a species in its own right. The black face is framed by a spiky white halo of whiskers; the belly is silver, the back olive-green, and the whole thing frequently seen. Rare on the other hand

Callithrix aka Green vervet

are the pink-lipped Campbell's monkey, formerly thought a subspecies of the equally rare Mona monkey (the distinct booming voice of which is probably all you will perceive) and the Demidoff's galago. Because of its eyes and nocturnal habits Linnæus gave the latter the Latin name for 'ghost'. Belonging to the Slow lemurs, from which we supposedly descend, the likewise nocturnal but common Senegal Bush baby is an evolutionary relative of man.

The Patas monkey's ability to run at twenty mph and its 'home range' of twenty square miles are the reasons why it so often frustrates photographers. Researchers into its feeding habits too, since each troop's treetop sentinel prevents any close approach, and the animals shot by villagers have all too often a bellyful filched from their fields. Aids to identification are the long legs, bushy eyebrows and dull orange fur.

The Western or Guinea baboon (*gong* in Wolof) frequents open country, with a few rocks for preference. A redder version of West Africa's Olive baboon, the Gambian variety – *Papio papio* – feeds mainly on grasses, seeds and fruit, though fancies on occasions hares, birds, other monkeys and crops. It seeks safety in numbers, of up to 300 per troop.

Lounging in the track ahead or loping off over the fields, youngsters clinging to mother's undercarriage while the maned and dog-faced patriarchs bark, baboons are for visitors a regular diversion. For farmers a regular pest. Never hunted here for food, they roam fearlessly close to civilization. They steer clear however of leopards, whose natural enemy (and favourite food) they are. Though still the sporadic cause of disappearing chickens, sheep and goats, The Gambia's *Panthera pardus* is as everywhere an endangered species. Nocturnal, rare and solitary, there is little risk/hope of your encountering one.

Hippopotamuses were protected during the British protectorate, with a £100 penalty for poaching. But barely 100 are now said to survive above Elephant Island. Here they surface – piggy ears and monstrous muzzles – to delight passers-by on their boats. And, if approached too close or escorting their young, also charge, ram and try to capsize them. The hippopotamus gives birth on land, suckles underwater and lives some 30 years. Though able to wander ten miles by night and even outrun a man, it rarely

does either as in places the banks at low tide impede it and elsewhere the riverside paddies provide the daily 300-400 pounds it must eat to sustain its two tons. Hippos feature larger in village scare-talk (and travel brochures) than real life: investigating farmers' complaints of their 'ravaging' rice-fields, an Oxford University expedition found only eight offenders in seven weeks of searching.

Crocodiles occur in two species here: the 'Blunt-nosed' Nile variety and the smaller, rarer, forest-dwelling Dwarf. The Blunt-noseds are those that pretend to doze by Abuko's Bambo Pool (*bambo* being Mandinka for crocodile) or splash disappointingly, leaving ripples on the bolong, when they see you too soon in your upriver canoe. They also tend to disappoint on the 'crocodile pools'. At Katchikali, Kartung and Berending childless wives, luckless wrestlers and unsuccessful businessmen arrive from distant villages – while tourists pay admission – to see the venerated reptiles. Visitors blanch as black pilgrims descend in the hope of being blessed with a sight of the Sacred White One. If seeing is believing, I have grounds for doubting the last. The odd smallish specimens that might deign appear will sleep on oblivious, jaws ajar. Or waddle off alarmed if approached by sceptical infidels.

Its ability to generate babies and/or business is debatable, but the crocodile proves its usefulness to fishermen by eating the river's predatory catfish. These it swallows fresh and whole. Small animals are swept from the water's edge by its tail, held under and drowned in its jaws, then hidden on the bank and eaten later, very 'high'. Plovers pick parasites from backs (not *pace* Herodotus, from between teeth), new sets of teeth grow until the age of 80 and the malignly primæval appearance is not deceptive: little changed since the Mesozoic era, crocodiles are sole survivors of the archosaur family of dinosaurs. Mothers lay and incubate up to 100 eggs, help their squeaking offspring break from the shells, then safeguard them, sometimes, from mongooses and monitors.

Grimm's duiker, juvenile

The tail of the Gambian mongoose accounts for half of the animal's fourteen inches. It is also long, thick and straight, not squirrel-bushy, on the country's other self-explanatory species: Marsh, Banded, Slender, Large Grey and White-tailed. Mongooses endear themselves to man, or to readers of *The Jungle Book* at least, by engaging snakes in lone combat. But only if given no choice. Normally they prefer to hunt in packs: for mice, birds and lizards by day in the savanna, or for chickens from compounds by night. Their numbers help distinguish mongooses from squirrels which, as in Europe, are seen at most in pairs.

Duikers are the charmingly diminutive, dainty-footed antelopes of which the Maxwell's species can be seen, almost tame, at Abuko. The Western Harnessed antelopes there too are 'inscribed' with

white lines on flanks and shoulders and patterned white dots on the rump. Formerly more abundant and trusting, they could in the 1900s 'be seen running fearlessly about the streets of Bathurst . . . a common feature in the grounds of Government House'.

The Western sitatunga, a semi-aquatic curiosity, survives in Kiang West National Park and elsewhere 'in middle river'. This antelope features less aptly in the Wildlife Department's crest since Abuko grew too dry for the five originally 'imported' there. Its feet that splay in water like a camel's in sand give the sitatunga exclusive right of entry to inaccessible

Spotted hyæna at Abuko

Warthog *alias* Bush pig

Western sitatunga, male and female

swamps, and make it a 'difficult animal to meet with'. It takes its scientific name of *Tragelaphus Spekei* from the Victorian explorer who, besides discovering the source of the Nile, first found it knee-deep in East Africa. Bohor reedbuck are still reported from the north bank, oribi in the west also, but neither in any number.

Hyænas are now known to kill for themselves and not merely scavenge. They do both neatly and hygienically, devouring even carcasses and so clearing the savanna of every last bone. In a consequently well-scoured enclosure at Abuko the multiple offspring born here of Buki and Buster, the first 'imported' pair, have an air of cuddly though

cringing domesticity. From the *Crocuta crocuta*, The Gambia's Spotted variety, come sudden unnerving bursts of the whiney-cackling 'laugh'. It has, experts say, possible sexual significance. In 1902 the colonial governor sent the London Zoo a Gambian hyæna which soon became the 'best behaved and tamest in the gardens'. With Dutch and Belgian participation, a hyæna breeding programme is a current Abuko project.

The warthog (by the zoologists' curious expedient of counting toes) is related to the hippopotamus. Its raids on crops are related to the authorities who issue hunting permits. (This only to certain vetted residents and usually in the dry season when lack of food elsewhere makes north-bank plantations attractive.) Warthogs/Bush pigs swim. They also grub up roots and crops (the 'warts' protecting the face?) and, when alarmed, trot podgily off, tail erect and family following in order of importance. The warthog is here called 'bush pig' so that visitors can confuse it with the African bush pig *alias* Red hog. No confusion occurs in local minds: the latter is too rare.

Yard-long 'iguanas' (grey-green and yellow Nile monitors) you may glimpse doing press-ups in riverside clearings or fighting the current across. (The swimming sinuosity also seen is probably not a Smyth's Water snake but the 'Snake-bird', the African darter.) Odd monitors

Nile monitor, alarmed

ambling arthritically across the gardens of the Bungalow Beach and Bakotu hotels occasionally cause consternation. Agamas, at their best in irridescent yellow and blue, more often sandily drab, are the homely and ubiquitous lizards which bask in hotel gardens. Unless you move smoothly into their circular field of vision, they scuttle off jerkily up walls. Outside walls, I should add. Inside, and even upside down on ceilings, their smaller relatives are geckos. If the ceiling in question is above your bed, console yourself with the thought that without these harmless, newt-like 'house lizards' the night-time insects might be a bother.

Rarely seen creatures are responsible for the most frequent natural feature of the Gambian savanna: blind, soft-bodied termites that bind the earth with half-digested cellulose to build the astonishing peaks, pinnacles, hillocks and humps of the 'ant-hills' everywhere. In an intricate subterranean kingdom the massive queen breeds ceaselessly until, no longer fecund, she is licked to death. The 'workers' that kill her also fetch each colony's foodstuff of dead wood and straw, while 'soldier termites' with poisonous glands attempt to ward off aardvarks, and 'fishing' chimpanzees. Weaver ants 'sew' with silk spun by their larvæ the leaf nests sometimes seen at Abuko.

While civet cats 'characteristically accumulate their droppings on or inside' a termite-mound, its ventilation holes are the favourite daytime sleeping-place of snakes. Short of prodding them awake or rummaging in cemeteries, there is little chance of your ascertaining that The Gambia has 33 species. Few visitors do: the average number seen is invariably nil. What startles in the undergrowth is usually a skink and, since opening to the public 30 years ago, the Abuko Reserve has never had an 'incident'. The snakes are to blame: common Black cobras, Puff adders and Green mambas could all paralyse painfully and even kill a child, Spitting cobras hit your eyes with blinding venom, but they always hear you coming and prefer evasive action.

The non-poisonous African or Rock python has been so hunted for its twenty-foot skin that only small numbers survive, far from man. The shorter Royal python is so called because of its distinguished markings, but merits more its nicknames of 'Ball python/Shame snake'. Attacked or just approached, it betrays its stately looks and asphyxiating strength: it rolls into a ball with its head hid in the middle. Though easily found by the specialist, most snakes thus show a discreet considerate dread of the equally

timorous visitor. They add to this negative asset that of positively relishing frogs. To find your frog or Common African toad – *Bufo regularis* – one guide-book advises that you 'look around your hotel garden with a flashlight by night'. Most of us accept the other evidence and stay in bed enduring the loud collective croak.

Butterflies seem far less numerous than flower-filled gardens might lead you to expect. Only Swallowtails, their 'tailed' wings distinctive, are perennial attractions. African Migrants, green-tinged white and three inches wide, migrate obligingly near hotels and beaches. African Monarchs are recognized by orange wings tipped black, and Blue or Yellow Pansies by spots of each respective hue on black or yellow wings. Trying to identify butterflies that mimic other species' colours I find frustrating.

The Conservation Act is why even butterflies offered for sale should be declined and, ideally, reported. More durable mementos but equally taboo are tortoise- and turtleshells: the former seen on village rubbish dumps, remnants of the Bell's Hinged tortoise, the latter where fishermen beach their boats, from Marine turtles caught in the nets. The Soft-shelled River turtle does not furnish such souvenirs.

There is a wealth of seashells. On sale at the 'roadhead' south of Kartung are splendid specimens of the ten-inch *Cymbium glans*, the 'largest of the genus and the most graceful', with grains of sand trapped in its salmon-pink glaze; of spiney-whorled *Hexaplex* and *Murex senegalensis*, vermilion inside when taken alive, colourless (like all shells) when collected dead. Pied crows here are as fond as your canary of the common cuttlefish – not a fish but the skeleton of the squid. The half round, half serrated 'sand dollar' found on beaches is the skeleton of the sea-urchin. The Gambia's cockleshells even make a versatile building material: mixed like aggregate with bitumen for roads, set decoratively in concrete paths and benches, used as insulation on roofs and strewn like gravel in drives and gardens. Plaster and building-lime also come from burned

oyster-shells. The piles stacked by roadsides, not only near Oyster Creek, are destined for this: they are not evidence of aphrodisiacs or pearls. Though despised as 'mud oysters' by hotel chefs, they make thick and tasty pickings, from the mangrove roots, for villagers and fishermen on the bolongs.

The daily catch of molluscs, Ghana Town

On beaches and tidal flats, sand-crabs discern you, ogling with their 'eye-tufts', and scuttle for the nearest hole. Fiddler-crabs teem on the mud at low tide. Initially alarmed, reappearing just as promptly, they are recognized by their gigantic *chelæ*. On the males one of these claws is even fiercer, to woo females and warn off other males. The low-tide mud of the mangrove swamps is also home for the journalists' 'fish that breathe and climb trees': the African lungfish was first discovered in The Gambia, on MacCarthy Island in 1835. It hibernates during the tourist season, buried in riverside mud. The amphibious mudskipper is a biological anomaly seen by riverbanks and bolongs, moving true to its name and even scaling the stilt-roots of mangroves.

No visitor can remain oblivious to the brilliant abundance of The Gambia's birds. British tour operators feature special 'bird safaris'; travel agents on the spot offer excursions such as 'Birds & Breakfast', and at several hotels there are resident ornithologists.

Species reliably sighted to date total 560, of which over 270 in Abuko alone. Without even leaving the hotel, armchair ornithologists can birdwatch by the pool or from the terrace of their room. Common Garden bulbuls wake them at daybreak (calling 'Quick doctor quick!' so anthropomorphologists say). Red-billed Senegal Fire-finches flutter and peck under tables, Cockney sparrows of Africa but dazzlingly male-red. Pure white Cattle egrets on the lawns, Fajara's Pink-backed pelicans, African swifts dipping over swimming pools, superb Glossy starlings and some 30 wintering species enhance most hotel grounds.

Sandpipers and sanderlings, turnstones, oystercatchers, redshanks, greenshanks and godwits wade along the water-line; plovers scurry behind the beaches while Pied crows and magpies scavenge them clean. Gulls and terns perch on groynes or bob, a white flotilla, in the waves. Gorgeous Blue-cheeked bee-eaters teeter beside Long-tailed shrikes on telephone wires round Banjul. Nearby Abuko's riverine forest is the haunt of multicoloured rollers, sunbirds and barbets, parrots, parakeets and many other species. Weaver birds and lilytrotters live up to their name in nesting colonies and on ponds everywhere.

On a cruise up river or into a bolong, pelicans paddle lazily clear of your boat. Or, flying gracefully, land clumsily, to roost atop the tangled mangroves like the backdrop to a comic-grotesque opera. Perched even higher, superb River eagles look down on them and you. Immobile on a lower stump, Pied kingfishers suddenly plummet, wings folded back, on their prey. Ospreys catch the eye with a similar distant splash. Its plumage the colour of mud, the anvil-headed hammerkop refuses to move from your track, trusting in the African tradition that to kill it brings bad luck. Heavy-winged herons – Black-headed, Goliath or Grey – flap off as you approach. Cormorants perch with wings ajar to dry, while African darters wriggle underwater. Up country you flush the Double-spurred francolin: marabous and vultures near the villages may spook you.

(Row 1: Left to right) Black-headed plover, Village weaver, Purple glossy starling (Row 2) Abyssinian roller, Blue-breasted kingfisher, Red-billed hornbill (Row 3) Northern carmine bee-eater, Northern red bishop, Yellow-crowned gonolek (Row 4) Pygmy kingfisher, Crowned crane, Western reef heron

Government

The Gambia assumed its present shape, piecemeal, in the course of the 19th century

The Gambia is an independent sovereign state, the sixteenth member of the Commonwealth and 115th of the United Nations. Head of state since 1994 is President Yahya A. J. J. Jammeh, whose Alliance for Patriotic Reorientation and Construction is the majority parliamentary party. The now-banned Peoples Progressive Party formed (as the Protectorate Peoples Party) by ex-president Jawara in 1958 won the colony's second general elections in 1962 and, with internal self-government granted by Britain the following year, led The Gambia to full independence on 18 February 1965. A second referendum in 1970 succeeded (where in 1965 a first had failed) in constituting the country a republic.

The headlines that in 1982 proclaimed the creation of a new state, Senegambia, were echoes of ideas 200 years old, but untrue. A British 'province' of that name was admittedly established in 1765, when the Gambian trading stations came to be administered from the Senegalese town of St Louis. It survived, though, only until 1783 when the Treaty of Versailles returned the latter to France. The Gambia and Senegal subsequently developed into distinct political and cultural entities, and their separate independence remains unchanged. On 1 February 1982 a Senegambian confederation came into effect: beside a projected joint parliament and unified foreign policy, Senegal was to benefit from a Customs union – The Gambia's low tariffs raised to Senegal's levels would have put paid to the former's busy transit trade – and The Gambia, having never had an army, had the reassuring presence of Senegal's gendarmerie.

The latter had been brought in to quell a first uprising in October 1980 against The Gambia's first president, Sir Dawda Kairaba Jawara. A second attempted coup in July 1981 was put down after a week of fighting by 3000 Senegalese troops (and the SAS). The leader of the insurrection escaped to Libya. The bullet-scarred reception of The Atlantic Hotel required redecorating.

The Senegambian marriage of convenience broke down finally when Jawara publicly criticized the union, and Senegal's president Abdou Diouf (needing the Banjul contingent returned for his conflict with Mauritania) abandoned it as 'a waste of time and money'. A notice in the Gambia National Museum records that 'In September 1989

the Confederation split and the Union of Senegambia was discontinued'.

Despite his Economic Recovery Programme launched in 1985, despite privatisation and a much-publicized but ineffectual crack-down on corruption, Jawara's popularity and authority waned in what the *Rough Guide* describes as 'a prevailing sense of stagnation and recycled rhetoric'. 'Guest soldiers' from neighbouring states, who had saved him in 1981, were to prove his undoing thirteen years later. In 1990 a Gambian contingent went with the West African ECOMOG forces peacekeeping in Liberia. The soldiers returned unpaid and, in the consequent crisis, the Gambian commander-in-chief resigned. He was replaced by a Nigerian officer and staff, and a defence agreement with Nigeria provided the military muscle which, despite re-election for a sixth term in 1992 and an amnesty for political opponents, Jawara needed increasingly.

Banjul's massive new monument has been named the Arch 22, the central park renamed from MacCarthy to 22nd July Square. For on that date in 1994 the coup that brought the present regime to power was apparently planned, implemented and completed. Gambian soldiers at Yundum Airport – turning out to welcome Jawara home, say some; returning from serving with ECOMOG, say others – were disarmed and humiliated by their Nigerian superiors. Disgruntlement erupted (aggravated by unpaid wages) and by nightfall Jawara, his vice-president and their families were safe but stripped of power aboard the *La Moure County* (an American warship which just happened to be moored off shore).

President Jammeh's claim that the coup was spontaneous and unpremeditated is lent credence by two plain handwritten pages exhibited in the Arch 22 Museum – 'Text of the Speech announcing the takeover of government by the AFPRC on 22 July 1994' – and a rusty-legged plywood stool labelled 'Chair. This is the chair on which

Independence Day parade in Banjul's 22nd July Square

the then Chairman of AFPRC and Head of State, Captain Yahya A J J Jammeh, (now President) sat … to announce the takeover …'. Jawara, who after 24 years in power had expressed a wish to retire, left first for asylum in Dakar then (having studied young as a veterinarian in Edinburgh) to quiet retirement in Sussex.

Following the bloodless coup (which holidaymakers here at the time are said not to have noticed), the 29-year-old then-Captain Jammeh introduced a military regime under a hastily formed Armed Forces Provisional Ruling Council. Recognition came from most West African states, including Senegal, while Western governments disapproved predictably. And, on learning that the AFPRC's 'provisional' meant four years, suspended aid. With

step, to Alliance for Patriotic Reorientation and Construction which (with opposition parties competing and not wholly unsuccessful) won the second republic's first parliamentary elections in January 1997.

Our knowledge of the traditional physical divisions of the country (into 'kingdoms' or, more correctly, spheres of tribal influence) is steadily increasing. Though some correspond to modern administrative limits, they carried little weight with the Anglo-French Boundary Commissions that in the late 1880s demarcated the presentday frontier with Senegal. Abolishing African slavery by the Act of 1807, Britain announced a first 'Settlement of the Gambia' as a base from which to enforce it. In 1814 the fort on James Island was reoccupied but in ruins, so two years later the

disorder and economic collapse threatening, and a counter-coup attempted, the Foreign Office in November 1994 advised that The Gambia was 'unsafe'. With most of the country's tourists from Britain, and most of its foreign earnings from them, this served to make matters financially worse.

President Jammeh's response was *Realpolitik*: civilian rule by means of elections would be restored in not four years but two. The Foreign Office withdrew its ruinous warning and tourists returned in a 1995-96 season that has been improved upon every year since. Jammeh surprised no one by winning the presidential elections of September 1996. The AFPRC was demobbed, in an acronymic side-

Chiefs (left) and members of the Gambian bar (above)

'king' of Kombo agreed to cede by treaty the island of St Mary's for the building of Bathurst/Banjul. 'King' Kolli of Kataba in 1823 reacted similarly to the offer of British friendship (plus a small cash annuity) and surrendered Lemain/MacCarthy/Janjangbure Island, and these two administrative/military outposts constituted the original colony. Brunnay, 'king' of Barra on the north bank opposite Banjul, was persuaded to yield the rivermouth's 'Ceded Mile' in 1826. 'British Kombo' (from Oyster Creek to beyond Cape St Mary) was obtained by treaty in 1840, all of Upper Kombo in 1853. The isolated French enclave of

Albreda was handed back to Britain in 1857, and various similar acquisitions were the missing pieces in the colonial jigsaw puzzle which constituted the protectorate.

Both this and the colony were governed through Sierra Leone until separation in 1843. 'Independence', with Bathurst's own 'Governor/Commander-in-Chief/Vice-Admiral of the Port', lasted until 1866. Then the rule of Freetown's Governor-in-Chief was resumed, The Gambia reincorporated into the West African Settlements, and the governor's burden of office lightened to simply 'Administrator'. Although Bathurst's legislative council was revived in 1888, it was not until 1901 that a governor was reinstated in the 'Crown Colony and Protectorate of The Gambia' – the state's official designation until independence in 1965.

The Gambia was in 1906 administratively split into five divisions which remain much the same today. The old South Bank Division and the 'capital and colony' of Kombo-Foni have become the Western and Lower River Divisions. The North Bank and Upper River divisions have retained their name and shape, and MacCarthy Island Division (despite its convenient abbreviation MID) was recently renamed Central River Division. Banjul has a city council, and in the 'provincie' seven area councils group the 35 traditional districts which each elect an MP to the House of Representatives and is each led by a *seyfo* or chief. Unlike colonial France, which installed French nationals or trusty 'natives' to rule, Britain preferred to enlist tribal worthies as agents of the central government. The once-hereditary *seyfolu* were thus left to judge local issues, with an *alkalu* (headman) as 'law-enforcer'… and still are, although to a diminishing degree.

Five Divisional Commissioners still administer from the same five 'colonial' divisional headquarters, but appeals from the chiefs' courts are nowadays heard by five group tribunals, no longer by the DC under a tree. Subsequent right of appeal, from the Banjul and Kanifing Muslim courts too, is to the High Court of The Gambia, thence to the Supreme Court. Thereafter only the president's prerogative saves murderers and rebels from the gallows at Mile Two. A legal system compounded of English law, Native law & Custom and Common law & Equity challenges and enriches the 80-odd members of the Gambian bar.

Rather like Spike Migillan, that well-known spelling error, The Gambia's name may be a mistake. 'Gambo', 'Gambra', 'Gamboa' or 'Gambea', the term had long been known to Europeans but not, it seems, to the Gambians themselves (who referred to the river as just that: *jio, dex* or

Playing at the opening of the Law Courts, Banjul

mayo in Mandinka, Wolof or Fula). The first Portuguese explorers, according to the griots, 'landed and met a Gambian called Kambi Manneh' (or, if not that, 'Kambi Sonko'). "What is the name of this place?" they asked. "My name is Kambi", he replied. They wrote that down'. The Mandinkas' pronouncing *g* as *k* adds some credibility at least. The guide-books' version of the place-name's derivation – from *Câmbio*, the Portuguese for (money) exchange – is not endorsed even by gung-ho Portuguese.

Kambia is a town in northern Sierra Leone. Gambia, they tell you, is preceded by *The* to distinguish it from this. And/or Zambia, since 1964 and the renaming of Northern Rhodesia. No one to my knowledge confuses Rutland with Jutland or Mali with Bali. The country and the river being 'ideo-inseparables', and the latter naturally referred to as the Gambia, I prefer the explanation of straightforward mental association between the one and The other. Acknowledging the article as part of the name gives it, like The Queen's College, Oxford, the right to a capital T. The only official exception was apparently the Anglican Bishop of Gambia and the Rio Pongas. Although recently updated to Bishop of The Gambia and Guinea, the designation still results in hoteliers requesting he take a double room.

Population

The Gambia ranks fourth in Africa for the number of inhabitants per square mile

The above-average ratio of people to space is due more to lack of the latter than to over-explosive growth. The apparently high rate of demographic expansion – 4·2% per annum – is explained by immigration, mainly of refugees from wars in neighbouring states. They add 1·5% to The Gambia's natural increase of 2·7% per annum. Extrapolating from the last census total of 1,038,145 in 1993 (and by factors like 'Cumulated Current Fertility' and 'Mean Children Ever Borne' *sic*), the authorities estimate the population in the year 2000 to be 1·3 million.

The Gambia's ten-year censuses (besides enlightening elements such as 'Currently married/Ever married Economically active population Age ten years and over') enquire about Tribe/Ethnic group. 'Persons enumerated' viz. the Gambian public acknowledge themselves to be Mandinka/Jahanka, Fula/Tukulor or Wolof, Jola/Karoninka, Serahuli, Serer or Aku, Manjago, Bambara or Other Gambian.

Physical and facial traits are not so easily categorized. Travel writers talk of the 'slim athletic Mandinka with his fine and friendly traits', the 'tawny straight-haired Fula' and 'the taller Wolof, generous and intelligent, with an unnegroid nose and peaceable disposition', the 'blackest

of Gambians' in one writer's view, 'lighter' according to another. Generations of intermarriage invalidate such facile aids to identification. Appearance, blood-ties, origins and religion have all failed to provide the ethnographic missing link. While 'British Indian' or 'American Irish' indicates origins (or clan associations), 'Scot', 'Yorkshireman' or 'Cockney' general habitat (or humour), West Africa's peoples move, mix and intermarry, frustrating the experts' attempts to define. Nowadays the latter take language to be the best criterion in classifying Africa's peoples.

Only those innocent of African orthography would attempt to list them alphabetically. 'None of these peoples had any script', wrote one colonial official, or at least only the marabouts' Arabic, and the compilers of the first reports were traders, explorers, missionaries and administrators. Scholarly consistency was not their forte; their spelling, like Lawrence's in the *Seven Pillars of Wisdom*, was cheerfully erratic. Mungo Park's Feloops are thus the protectorate's Floops or Felupps, *alias* the modern Jolas, Jolahs or Diolas. The Fulas are Fulahs, Foulahs or (in Nigeria) Fulani, the Mandinkas variously Mandingas, Mungdingoes, Mangdinkas or Mandingo(e)s. As for the Wolof, I am grateful to *Enter Gambia* for all the Rabelaisian possibilities: Woloff, Wolloff, Wollof, Joloff, Jolof, Jolloff, Jollof, Djolof, Jaloff, Joluff, Galofe, Yolof, Yaloff, Yuloff, Ioloff, Ouolaf, Oloff, or Oualofe. Not forgetting the Wallofs, Oullofs and the 18th century's 'Grand Jolloiffs'.

The Gambia's most numerous are those groups that speak Mande, a dialect of the Niger-Congo family of Bantu languages. Their homeland of Manding in the Futa Jallon explains the name Mandingo, their pronunciation the alternative version of Mandinka. Although one tradition has their king Amari Sonko conquering the future Niumi and Badibu in the 7th century, Manding or Mading is known to have been founded by Sunjata Keeta 600 years later.

Mandinka villagers wait for the river ferry

Manding/Mading is better known as the empire of Mali (or Melle/Melli), which in 1329 overran the neighbouring empire of Jenne (whence *Guinea*). Escorting the traders who fetched precious salt from the coast, Mali's young hunters then coalesced into an army that went west conquering an empire from Manding on the Niger as far as the Atlantic, and south from the Sahara to modern Sierra Leone. Only the *forolu* went to war, the highest Mandinka caste of the freeborn and sons of royal clans (assisted by their *jongolu*-slaves). Their social inferiors – the *julas* (traders), *nyamalolu* (artisans), Muslims and farmers – may not have complained about their exclusion from this 'noble' occupation.

By the 1500s Mali had suffered the fate of all empires, but the Mande-speaking kingdoms that replaced it maintained

slowly engulfed by Jolas and Fulas, they were largely demolished in the Soninki-Marabout Wars. It was nevertheless with the Mandinkas, wrote one stalwart British imperialist, that 'the English and French had chiefly to fight in their "peaceful penetration" of the Gambia and Senegal'.

The Mandinka proportion of the total population (39·5%) is declining nationwide but increasing around the capital. This finding of the census was surprising, for Banjul has customarily been predominantly Wolof. Colonial Britain furthered the preponderance, recruiting Wolofs (alongside Akus) into the Civil Service. The preference was slightly unexpected, for although some Wolofs had fled the French annexation of St Louis in 1816, settling with/for the British in Bathurst, their fellows in Salum and

a piecemeal Mandinka 'commonwealth' in the Gambia, Senegal and Niger river valleys. In the first, Kaabu was foremost. Flourishing under the Nyancho clan as metropolitan Mali fell, it perpetuated ruling families from which many a Gambian still boasts his descent. Only recently, however, has this early Mandinka nation come to academic ken.

In 1623 Richard Jobson's *Golden Trade* reported the Mandinkas as 'Lords and Commaunders' here still. Travelling via the Gambia to Manding, Mungo Park wrote in 1796: 'The Mandingoes constitute in truth the bulk of the inhabitants . . . and their language . . . is universally understood, and very generally spoken'. Their fourteen Gambian states had been mapped by Le Sieur d'Anville in 1751. Each ruled by a *mansa* (king) and council of elders (*alkalis/alkalolu*), they survived unchanged for another 100 years until,

Badibu were the spearhead of the Muslim revival which Britain in the mid-19th century helped the 'pagan' Mandinkas to resist.

While some trace East Africa's Bantus back to the Niger Valley, others reverse the demographic drift to explain the facial similarities between the Wolofs and the peoples of the Nile. Arab races, the 'Libyans' of antiquity, reached the Niger in the 7th century and may have sown their seeds. The Wolofs themselves stretch collective memories only as far back as Songhoi. From this 14-16th-century empire of 'Songai', 'Sanaga' or 'Sanagha' – perhaps established by Sudanese tribes and historically demolished in 1591 – comes the modern *Senegal*. There spelt usually *N'Jay*, in The Gambia *N'Jie*, the commonest Wolof family name is further evidence in favour of their claim to descend from the *Sungai*-speaking *Songhoi* colony of Gualata. Described by Cadamosto as 'Az*anaghi* or tawny Moors', the Wolofs called this homeland Gualafa, from which *Wolof* is a short linguistic step.

The Wolofs' documented history starts with the Portuguese. Colonizing southward in the 1480s, John II of Portugal gained a foothold in Sine Salum by offering to help one Bemoi against his brother Sibetah in a struggle for this 'Moorish', Muslim kingdom. Bemoi accepted the condition that he take up Christianity, visited Lisbon to be baptized by John, sailed home escorted by a Portuguese fleet and, promptly reneguing, was stabbed by its admiral. Seventeenth-century privateers suppressed mutinies amongst the 'Jaloff slaves'; in 1730 Francis Moore located in the Ba Salum 'Kingdom of the Grand Jolloiffs' the (still-undiscovered) Gualata.

Bathurst's Methodist missionaries found the Wolofs the most easily converted. During the Soninki-Marabout Wars, the predominantly Muslim Wolofs of Badibu and Bur Salum were decimated by their co-religionist Maba: in March 1863, 2000 refugees reached Barra Point, to rather alarm the one British constable on duty. (Outram Town, alongside Oyster Creek, was built for them and those that followed.) Few Wolofs resided hitherto in The Gambia's Mandinka kingdoms, but the half of Bathurst called Melville Town was already in the 1830s better known as 'Jollof Town'. The place-name, though changed, remains symptomatic: despite a decline from 52% in 1973 to 29% in 1993, Wolofs still form Banjul's largest ethnic group.

The Fulas come numerically between the Mandinkas and Wolofs. Their 18·8% of the national total is doubled in the area of Janjangbure, but the concentration implicit misleads. For the Fulas, though increasingly sedentary, are traditionally nomads and even, in one French writer's flight of fancy, 'descendants of the Shepherd Kings of Hyskos, driven from Lower Egypt sixteen centuries before Christ'. With straight hair, fine thin lips and a negroid coloration that could be called *fula* (red), the pure Fulani are an anthropological enigma. (Most young Fula women are undisguisedly attractive, and much sought-after. Many a West African man, dutifully married young to a family friend, neighbour or relation, aspires in later life to a second, Fula wife.)

Historically we know that the Fulas' ancestral home was Massina and the Futa Jallon. In the latter they lived pastorally alongside the Mandinkas 'with whom they had no quarrel, but even some affinity'. Timbo or Toobah was the Fulas' Manding, the 'seat of the hierarchy' to which, 'when

Wolof women (opposite) and griot in traditional dress

. . . about to make war, they send . . . to invoke the prayers of its priests'. Their best-known collective and authenticated action is the 16th-century Great Trek: led by one Kolli Tengella (and guided by an oracular parrot), the 'Futa Fula' moved west en masse. They established the kingdom of *Fuladugu*, gave the Buruko Rocks the nickname of Pholey's (Fulas') Pass and disseminated the *Pholeycunda* (Fula Town) found *passim* on Francis Moore's map. Spreading north and west of the Gambia valley, they were finally contained by the Wolofs and, under the Denianke dynasty, founded the kingdom of Futa Toro which survived for 200 years more.

The 15th-century Portuguese had already found Fulas south of the river; their contemporaries are on record as purveyors of gold to Timbuktu. The warlords Maba and Musa Mollo were Muslim Fulas. Born in 1809, the son of a marabout in Badibu, 'Ma Bah' became the leader of the Muslim revival. With a Fula force of 3000 well-armed men, he broke the Mandinkas' hold on the valley and, until his death in 1867, led the British a bitty military dance.

Fula fire-eater in a tourist hotel

Fula schoolgirl, Fajara

In 1875 Musa Mollo came down from the Futa Jallon, to convert widely by the sword and found the kingdom of Fuladu.

The Fulas who in the 1850s moved down river to pillage (in a 'kind of annual outing', the *Official Handbook* says) were the Fulbe Futo from the Futa Jallon homeland ('Fulbe' being the term used by some for The Gambia's Fulas in general). The Fulbe Firdu and Torodo had gone before, the Fulbe Burure followed, and their divers offspring here now form the densest concentration of Fulas in West Africa. All that these 'Gambra Fuli' have in common is their speech (nine dialects of Fulfulde/Pulaar or Futa Fula, belonging to the West Atlantic group of Niger-Congo languages) and their cattle.

While the Fulas are multifarious the Jolas are fewer and more uniform. Their 10·6% of The Gambia's population is the tip of a demographic iceberg: the Jolas, Djollas, Djolas, Diolas, Dyolas and/or Karoninkas increase in density south through the Casamance, as far as the Ivory Coast. They are thought to be the region's aborigines but of that there is no proof: Western historians share the Jolas' ignorance as to their antecedents. The academic assumption appears to be that, as the Fulas, Wolofs and Mandinkas are known to be immigrants from elsewhere, the Jolas *faute de mieux* must have been here first.

The indigenous 'Floops' in 1447 killed the explorer Tristan Nunes, but later Portuguese relations with the Jola womenfolk were such that by 1700 their 'capital' of Bintang was 'chiefly inhabited by half-castes'. The Jolas were by then being forced west and south by the Mandinkas' advance, to be concentrated since in the district of Foni. In 1780 they housed and re-equipped a British naval force trapped by the French: '400 Jolas were mobilised to prevent the French from landing and destroying the factory of a British trader at Bintang'. 'English property, of considerable value, has frequently been left' there, noted Mungo Park, and guarded by the 'Feloops with the strictest honesty and punctuality'. Though some Jolas fought as mercenaries in the Soninki-Marabout Wars, their south-bank settlements were so ravaged by Fodi Kabba that sixteen of their 'kings' begged for British protection in 1887. And when his fellow warlord Fodi Silla was fleeing the expeditionary force in 1894, they loyally refused him asylum. The Jolas' escape route from these various marauders was from Foni into British Kombo. And even to St Mary's Island where in the 1840s they already formed a separate 'Jola Town' (and came to be called 'Banyons').

The unflattering comments of protectorate officials – that the Jolas, for example, were 'impervious to change' –

have been forgotten since 1994 when the regime was changed by a new Jola head of state. President Jammeh's attempts to mediate in conflicts in neighbouring Casamance and Guinea Bissau may have been prompted by the fact that both are predominantly fellow-Jola.

Next in numerical importance, with 8·9% of the population, come the Serahulis (*alias* the 'Serrahooli, Saruhele, Sarakole, Sera Koli, Serrekoli' or even, to Mungo Park's ear, 'Sierra-Woolly'). Speaking Mande, they are linguistic relatives of the Mandinkas but of older stock. Predating Mali and Gualata, Ghana was a 10-11th-century Serahuli empire that stretched, via The Gambia, from Mauritania to the modern state of that name. It was founded supposedly by lighter-skinned Berbers who thrived on trade with their homeland of Morocco. When their Ghana empire fell to Songhoi, many Serahulis moved south. By the 1450s they were well ensconced in the north-bank Gambian district of Wuli, where the Portuguese plied them with tobacco and strong drink. The latter may be blamed for some Afro-European interbreeding; the Mandinka kingdoms all around had a similar genetic effect and, on their Great Trek west through Wuli, the Fulas left 'the inevitable traces of their passage, in the further mixing of the already confused strain'.

West Africa's upheavals in the 19th century brought further Serahuli immigration. Itinerant and enterprising, they served as mercenaries in the north-bank kingdoms and during the Soninki-Marabout Wars. Demba Sonko, for example, left the policing of his 'kingdom' of Niumi to 700 Serahulis under his son-in-law, Ansumana Jaggi. When Demba, 'a grasping old man', welshed on their wages in 1857, the colonial governor was obliged to intervene: settling the dispute at Fort Bullen, he repatriated half the force up river in the governmental yacht. The rest were permitted to cross 'in small parties' to Bathurst, where they were 'willingly employed by the merchants and traders' and subsequently given Kombo land.

The Serahulis nowadays grow groundnuts and, on their plots by Basse, The Gambia's best cotton; their womenfolk make pots in the villages near by, but one and all they are first and foremost traders. Their dealings enriched the original Ghana. They 'carried on a great commerce with the French in gold and slaves' and, Mungo Park continues, 'derived considerable profits by the sale of salt and

Southern Gambia and the Casamance, Jola griots

55

Aku mother and contented child

cotton'. With presentday interests vested more in Liberian diamonds and Banjul hotels, the Serahulis still warrant Park's verdict of 'indefatigable in their exertions to acquire wealth'.

The Tukulors (or Tukurols) are usually not thought an ethnic entity, rather the upshot of Fula penetration amongst the Serers in Fula Torodo. The Bainunkas too, though aboriginal, have merged in The Gambia with Jolas and Mandinkas, retaining their collective identity and matriarchal society only outside our area, in the Casamance. The only other groups acknowledged by the census are the Serer(e), Manjago and Bambara. The first, according to some, are 'relics of the primitive negro race which originally occupied the coast'. They may have been pushed down to the river mouth by Mauritanian Berbers in the 10-11th centuries. The Mandinka advances that sent the Jolas south to the Casamance forced the Serers back north. They rebounded south again in the 1850s, off Maba and his horde in Sine Salum. In 1863, 2000 crossed the river, to settle in Half Die and help construct the road from Oyster Creek to Cape St Mary. Their progeny are still found fishing on the river and farming in the Kombos. And on the bank at Barra building boats.

Like the Fulas, the Bambaras (or Vangaras)(or Wangara/Guangaras) sold gold to Timbuktu. Their warrings around Fuladu delayed Mungo Park and their general bellicosity seems, obliquely, to have benefitted Britain. By repeatedly raiding Kataba for cattle and slaves, they induced its king to surrender Lemain Island in 1823. Advancing again in 1840, they were frightened off by British reinforcements: a grateful King Kolli signed a treaty of friendship and commerce, ceded land to the British government and agreed to the building of Kataba Fort. In Ansumana's 'police force' was a band of Bambaras: while the British assisted the disbanded Serahulis, they drew the line at the latter and insisted they stay well away from Bathurst.

The Akus are interesting folk. Far from being autochthonous, they date their appearance in The Gambia very precisely to the 1830s. Or rather their partial reappearance, since they are descendants of the Liberated Africans. Britain in 1772 freed her 15,000 'negro servants' and, as a new home for 351 of their number, the Sierra Leone colony of Freetown was founded in 1787 by the Society for the Abolition of Slavery. The 'Abolition of Slaves' might have been a better title, for these former domestics of the British aristocracy found themselves 'deposited in good faith on . . . that brooding forest land from whence their forefathers had come'. Gentlemen's gentlemen, they were shipped to the sticks with, as their literal companions-in-arms, 60 women 'swept from the gutters of London and Portsmouth'. The unlikely bedfellows sired a light-skinned generation which moved north to seek a semblance of Britain in Bathurst.

Meanwhile the Royal Navy, armed by the Act of 1807, was intercepting the slaving ships: French, Spanish, Portuguese and particularly Americans flying the Spanish flag. Their human cargoes were recaptured and released, for 'rehabilitation' in Sierra Leone. And whenever it was Britain's turn to control that colonial shuttlecock, Gorée, she repatriated Negro slaves from this island-entrepôt to Freetown. They had been taken originally from every coastal region, and the Yoruba-speaking Akus amongst them explain the generalized name.

The first batch of Akus, 'of English extraction', had brought with them the names of their trades or adoptive employers: Coker, Cole and Forster, Turner, Wright and Joiner-George. Later arrivals looked to the Methodist missionaries, the Señoras and the Christian Wolofs who converted and/or cared for them – whence, on Gambian gravestones, such Wesleyan wonders as Wilhelmina Monday and Shiloh Emanuel Eagleton Joiner, and Catholic conceits like Victoria St Mary Chow and Josephine Alawole Lewis.

New Year's Eve 2000, parading the traditional *fanal*

With a lingua franca of English, the Akus were soon assimilated more to the British administration than to the native population. Their better education in the missionaries' schools entitled them to senior positions: if Reform Clubs are bastions of the Establishment the preponderance, by 1912, of Akus in Bathurst's is significant. Their influence waned with the British Empire; self-government in 1963 swung the vote away from their Democratic Party and undermined much of their political power.

Generally intelligent and good-looking, the Akus soldier on as a valued 'Western' element. In their wondrous Creole or pidgin English they pray in the Anglican churches and utter unrepeatable secrets at St John's Masonic Lodge. But their numbers and distinctiveness grow less. Few presentday children play with the Akus' traditional *gesse*-masks; some fathers try to Africanize the English family name, while more and more older sisters are adopting Afro hair-styles and dress. The increasing preference of Aku girls for Muslims should mean a next generation or two just as attractive but rather less Aku.

The Portuguese deserve a mention not because they survive in any number but because they were partly responsible both for the many coffee-coloured skins and for black Gambians named Da Silva and Gomez. Trade and evangelization were *arrière-pensées* of Prince Henry's during the Age of Discovery. But The Gambia sent back little gold, its kings were less interested in baptism than rum and, for the Portuguese settlers and crews, a more fruitful discovery was the womenfolk on shore. 'They are all married', according to Jobson in the 1620s, 'or rather keepe with

them the countrey blackewomen, of whome they beget children.' The south-bank settlement of Bintang/Geregia (viz. *igreja*, the Portuguese for church) was by 1700 a half-caste town.

Intermarriage (influenced by local matriarchal tradition?) had by then also resulted in that mulatto phenomenon, the Señoras/Signares. Roman Catholic, Creole-speaking and united with once-European merchants in wedlock or in lucrative liaisons, they remained the influential better half of Senegambian society for some 300 years. Many early travellers acknowledged their hospitality; succouring the hapless Liberated Africans, Bathurst's first Methodist missionaries received much assistance from this unexpected quarter.

Senegalese Señoras accompanied the French merchants attracted to Bathurst in the 1820s, where they fast acquired a reputation for ostentatious *chic*. British officials described with admiration (and clergymen with scorn) the Señoras walking out: their finery the latest Paris creations and their jewellery so abundant on their shapely persons as to overflow on to maids alongside. The Gambia's *fanals* (big, processional paper boats lit by candles inside) are said to have originated with the Señoras of St Louis, who had scale models of their townhouses made to keep alight the candles with which servants lit their way to midnight mass.) Though their bijous and their circumstances have long since been reduced, Banjul's Wolof women still make resplendent sights.

Syrian shopkeeper in Liberation Avenue, Banjul

These fringe benefits of cohabitation came from living – on the fringes of Bathurst 'society' – with members of The Gambia's early Gallic community. After 200 years of rivalry with the French in Senegal (and despite the continuing 'intrusion' of Albreda), the British protectorate soon became the scene of a discreetly dynamic French presence. Reminders now are few – 'Le Commerce Africain' above a shack-shop at Albreda; a French grave at Fatoto; 'CFAO' still on Bakau's sold-off supermarket – but the Gallic impact was till recently important in The Gambia's mercantile history.

Joseph Maurel and Léon Prom moved here from Gorée in 1830 to set up a score of groundnut-trading stations. The firm of Maurel & Prom they founded abandoned that commodity in 1978; their Banjul base was in 1981 burned down, and in 1983 the cargo ships that bear their name made a last voyage up river. As the deeds to their original Wellington Street premises were signed by seven Maurels and two Proms, it is not surprising that the former should have gone it alone. Maurel Frères (not brothers but cousins of Joseph's) also ventured up river to buy and export groundnuts, branched into other lines around Banjul, and housed

Alex Haley in their yellow-brick depot that is now the Juffure Museum. And in 1854 one Monsieur Vermink began the *établissement* which in 1881 became the *Compagnie du Sénégal et de la Côte Occidentale d'Afrique*. The latter was simplified in 1887 to the *Compagnie française de l'Afrique Occidentale* – the 'French West Africa Company' viz. the centenarian CFAO that ran the biggest supermarkets in Banjul and Bakau.

The impression of Frenchness is enhanced by the Lebanese. The Gambia, so history books say, was 'discovered' by a Levantine. In his *Periplus* of 450 BC the Phoenician mariner Hanno reports 'an immense opening of the sea', on the shores of which he 'saw by night fires arising in all directions'. He took back to Carthage the skins of three 'gorillæ . . . of human form but shaggy and covered with hair who climbed precipices and threw stones'. Those eager to establish its historical credentials identify The Gambia from this questionable evidence of an estuary, the 'burning bush' (being cleared for cultivation) and baboons. Hanno, however, is now known to have deliberately misled: seeking new markets on behalf of a shrewd trading nation, he compiled his *Periplus* for the sake of a reputation, not to reveal commercial secrets to Carthage's competitors, the Greeks.

Whether or not these Phoenicians were here, many of their direct descendants have followed in their putative footsteps. (Until the creation of an independent Lebanon, the first to arrive were strictly Syrians.) In clothiers and grocers along Liberation Avenue fathers and sons take turns at the till. Handsome Levantines mend Mercedes and sell car parts by the main road through Jeshwang. The long-established Madis saw their oil-mill nationalized, but still do well on rents and dealerships for Nissan and Peugeot. The Milkys were pioneer hoteliers, running their properties with business-like *bonhomie* (until they were repossessed). Gambia Tours Ltd, which 'handles' Thomson Holidays clients, is the Lebanese Hobeika family's. Catholic, Muslim or Maronite, some marrying Gambians (and their numbers also swelled by kinsmen fleeing Liberia and Sierra Leone), the Syrians/Lebanese have for three or four generations been wholesaling and retailing, in three or four languages, with their famous/infamous flair.

British involvement in The Gambia has shifted in the main from governmental to individual. Independence of Britain in 1965 entailed relatively little immediate change in terms of personnel. The colony's Attorney-General became the late Chief Justice, and pre-independence administrative officers re-enlisted as contract or seconded

Civil Servants. Gambia Airways, the airport and port, the ferries, the National Trading Corporation . . . many bodies both private and parastatal benefitted in the 1970s and '80s from British management and expertise. HMG's 'technical co-operation' officers included accountants, architects, economists, engineers and entomologists. Others were appointed to lecture, survey, nurse, anæsthetize, manage projects, process seeds and teach.

Such pride of place in the expatriate community ended with the Jawara regime: in 1994 all British aid programmes stopped. (Only the independent Voluntary Service Overseas continued with a task begun in 1960. Funded partly by HMG's Small Grants Scheme, it does so currently with some 40 two-year volunteers who, living in local housing, work at local rates of pay as doctors, nurses, teachers, accountants, engineers, librarians and business and community advisers.)

A half-dozen British technical officers stayed on after the coup, 'advisory privateers'. Six training officers have since been sent to assist the Gambian government with record management, transfer of knowledge and general good governance. This under an agreement signed in 1998 whereby Britain's Department for International Development provide grants of £9 million over the next four years . . . no longer to fund new public projects – 'No money changes hands' – but, significantly now, in Poverty Alleviation programmes.

A Caledonian Society (and a popular weekly 'hash run') thrive nevertheless. For the place of official British expats has been taken to some extent by individual entrepreneurs. From Bakau to Basse, English partners (in every sense) find themselves managing guest houses and local hotels. Couples from Cumbria or Cornwall run bars and restaurants. Seafaring Brits bring down their boats to operate river- and fishing-trips. These latterday settlers number 300-400, holidaymakers some 80,000 per annum. Though Germans have re-emerged en masse on the package-holiday scene, it is still the British that The Gambia attracts most.

The Holy Ghost Fathers and associated Sisters are a vital Irish and Canadian element, while a dozen volunteers with APSO, Ireland's Agency for Personnel Services Overseas, do sterling work not only in ecotourism and wildlife management. The Gambia's other white expatriates consist of a handful of brave Scandinavians who direct the hotels they built; of Germans, in travel, fishing and most significantly forestry (establishing the Bijilo Forest Reserve and spending DM-millions on combating desertification with fenced areas of woodland countrywide) and of numerous but transient Americans. None are old hands: the Catholic Relief Services came first in 1964, the Peace Corps three years later.

Like their British counterparts, most US nationals are here to aid and advise the deprived or undernourished: not members of AID's far-reaching programmes any more, but well-organised Peace Corps volunteers some 75 in number. Equipped with libraries and 'resource centers' up river (and each with a *Peace Corps Cross-Cultural Workbook*), they teach, train teachers and help with mother & infant care and increased crop production. The excellent CRS relies more on local recruitment. Anyone reading its Annual Report will not need telling that its origins, sponsors and directors are American. It 'articulates . . . a vision statement . . . for social upliftment'. But shows for all that a remarkable commitment to women's farming, child survival, adult literacy and 'a 2nd Track, Middle-out approach to peace building'.

Though rarely recognized as such by their white contemporaries, African expatriates predominate. Among the friendly and colourful crowds in the markets of Banjul and the settlements up river you see Mauritanians in their long, loose, sleeveless robes off-white or blue. (Bearded and Arabic-speaking, these lean and hollow-cheeked *Nar* seem unlikely scions of the Berber races whose onslaughts forced the Serers and Serahulis southward.) Up from the south, also understanding Arabic, Nigerians sell shells in Banjul's Albert Market, plus strips of hide and goats' horns for mixing native medicine. The blacks that address you in excellent French are not necessarily graduates of the *Alliance Franco-Gambienne* but either 'strange farmers' or out-of-work immigrants from Senegal or Mali. (With the unemployment problem hardly any better here, is it the kinder climate, or the tourists, that attract?) Likewise more fluent in French, many stallholders and shopkeepers are immigrants from Guinea. Places like Ibo Town and Ghana Town speak for themselves: businessmen from Ghana run the biggest fishery and Serahuli smugglers grew rich on Liberian diamonds – until these were replaced by refugees. Housed at the United Nations' Kerr Elhassa camp near Basse (and in the old Atlantic Hotel), fugitives from civil war in Liberia and Sierra Leone constitute involuntary expatriate communities. With fellow-refugees from the Casamance and Guinea Bissau held in another UN camp at Arankoli, they add 1·5% to The Gambia's population growth-rate.

Religion

Lacking an establishment or articulate apologists, but indigenous-African, tribal-traditional and undoubtedly still widespread, paganism fares badly with official statisticians. In 1963, 29% of all Gambians claimed to be pagan. The census of 1973 dissected the population by Sex, Age, Tribe and twenty other attributes: 'Religious Denomination' was not one. As orthodox religion is known to have arrived here in the last 1300 years, paganism must *ipso facto* be the region's original faith. Usually euphemized as animism or fetishism, it long proved impervious to foreign persuasions and remains influential.

The Christian Portuguese made mostly opportunist converts: their churches at Bintang, Juffure and Tankular administered more to sailors and settlers than to Africans. Armed with papal bulls in favour of slavery, the Germans, Dutch, British and French that followed let drop any evangelical pretence and concentrated unashamedly on commercial exploitation. The creation of Bathurst and the British protectorate made for radical change. In 1820 The

Gambia 'was recommended to the General Wesleyan Missionary Committee as an eligible spot'. Two years later Mother Anne-Marie Javouhey, first of the Sisters of St Joseph of Cluny, visited Bathurst and planned a Catholic mission that did not however materialize till 1849. (A popular T-shirt in 1999 commemorated the mission's 150th anniversary.)

Catholicism floundered here for 50 years, most of its 'officiating Spiritans' (Holy Ghost Fathers from France) dying of disease before the age of 40. Arriving in 1905, the Irish father John Meehan gave the mission a literal new lease of life. It was detached from Dakar in 1931, promoted Apostolic Prefecture in 1951 and in 1957 made the 'Diocese of Bathurst in Gambia'. This *mutatis mutandis* is now led by five Irish priests, twelve Gambians ordained since 1985 and three Nigerian Missionaries of St Paul sent in 1992. It consists of some 15,000 souls, the fine cathedral in Daniel Goddard/Hagan Street and a network of countrywide churches and outstations that, numbering 45 in 1999, is steadily increasing.

In an intellectually admirable paper the Holy Ghost Fathers have assessed their past and present place amongst The Gambia's Muslim majority: educating, in their five 'grant-aided' senior secondary, five junior secondary and 26 primary schools; maintaining the dialogue 'Pro non-Christianis' and constituting 'the dynamic representative minority . . . spiritually responsible for all'.

Their Anglican and Methodist colleagues likewise apply themselves more to education than evangelization. The Methodists in 1821 rose to the call (above) and sent John Morgan and the ailing John Baker on a missionary reconnaissance. (They were, like a Quaker inquirer, recommended by the colonial governor to start at Tendaba, but the headman there reacted diplomatically by advising them to build near the river, 'then you can always jump into a canoe and get away'.) Bathurst's Wolofs and Akus were

Confirmation day at Banjul's Catholic cathedral

more receptive and, as the Liberated Africans Department settled batches of the latter up river, Brother Morgan's helpers followed in their wake. In 1822 Morgan opened Bathurst's first boys' high school. The girls' school founded in 1824 by the Quaker Hannah Kilham was taken over by a Methodist couple called Hawkins, and in 1835 the present Wesley Church was completed in Dobson (now Macoumba Jallow) Street. The educational cluster there still; the Bethel Nursery School beside the church in Stanley Street; the later, plainer chapels at Bakau and Serekunda, and Janjangbure's church and primary school are all tributes to the successive Wesleyans who rarely survived their tour of duty here.

Given the part of British officialdom in the early colony, the Church of England arrived surprisingly late. 'In fact it was only by accident that Anglicans came to be here at all', said the late Very Rev. J. C. Faye, one-time Gambian High Commissioner, minister of state and grand old man of pious establishment politics. The padre attached to the West Indian regiments here left when they were withdrawn, but the Bishop of Sierra Leone responded to the Bathurst merchants' offer of a stipend and accommodation by sending a permanent replacement in 1836. Only in 1901, however, was the Anglican cathedral of St Mary's completed. Its wall-plaques (many older and relocated here) show that it promptly assumed its rôle as official seat of worship. Some commemorate those who took 'decisive measures against the natives of Barra', were 'slain at Saba' or 'murdered at Sankandi'. Others are dedicated to 'Commandants of this Settlement', Colonial secretaries and Acting administrators, governors, travelling commissioners, naval captains and constables, and almost all donated by fellow officers or indebted 'directors and shareholders of the Bathurst Trading Company'.

The Anglicans duly contributed schools (St Mary's in 1939 and the Parsonage Nursery) and, remaining Aku-civic and close to the establishment, they like the Wolofs entered politics at the prospect of independence. In 1951 'Uncle' Faye founded the Democratic Party. (Merging with the Muslims as the Democratic Congress Party, this finally renounced its odd programme of confederation with Sierra Leone and bowed out in 1968.) Faye meanwhile had been headman of Kristi Kunda: its former St John's Church and Transfiguration School was the last, remotest outpost of the Anglicans' Upper River Mission. Their land at Basse was half leased off to the Standard Bank, half occupied by St Cuthbert's. The War-time hut at Bakau was in the 1970s rebuilt as St Paul's, and a mud hut thrown up in 1945 was

promoted to Christ Church, Serekunda. With St Andrew's at Lamin and Farafenni's Church of the African Martyrs, the Anglicans share with the Methodists one half of The Gambia's Christian four per cent.

That this is only one per cent lower than in 1973 is, paradoxically, the sign of a Christian revival. For in that period the country's population has risen by 49%. According to pre-independence documents, The Gambia was a predominantly Christian colony. The records, inadequate, may have reflected wishful thinking in Whitehall, but the recent rapid spread of Islam over Black Africa is incontrovertible. It was also thought by churchmen to be irreversible. Converts are born not won to Islam, they said. With large families and several wives (the two factors not unconnected) the Muslim majority in an expanding population must increase exponentially.

The Christian minority has however defied predictions and is growing in numbers too. Well funded from Rome and private donors, the active Bishop Cleary may have brought about Catholic expansion, the Education Secretariat working with the government, the Caritas development wing digging wells, helping village women and combating adult illiteracy. But like their Anglican and Methodist fellows in The Gambia Christian Council, Catholics report 'progress slow or almost imperceptible from the conversion point of view'. For it is the breakaway African Independent Churches that have fuelled the recent revival. Preachers of 'holy roller evangelism', faith healing and 'prosperity theology' have won so many converts across the continent that the proportion of Africa's to Christians worldwide has doubled from one in ten in 1970 to one in five today. Christianity, according to *Time*, is increasing by 3·5% annually in Africa compared with one per cent in Europe and North America. Focused on The Gambia, this trend translates into many a popular new place of worship, especially around Banjul: the New Covenant Worship Centre, Deeper Christian Life Mission, Celestial Church of Christ, Apostolic Faith Mission, Assemblies of God in The Gambia, Grace Independent Church, Good Seed Mission and the 'World Mission Agency Winners' Chapel'.

Organizations like WEC International – the Worldwide Evangelization for Christ – combine hot gospelling with the mainstream churches' aid: staffing a half-dozen village clinics, running rural training centres and now IT courses too. 'Multinational' is no longer just a big-business term: WEC counts fourteen nationalities amongst its 30-strong Gambian team (it not being generally known that Korea is

Church sports day on Cape Point beach

the largest provider of Christian field-workers worldwide). And combining modern evangelism with colonialism's traditional *mission civilisatrice*, the CRS is first and WEC second in teaching villagers to read in the vernacular. Their adult-literacy campaigns are not disinterested: most of the vernacular (like the President's native Jola) has little or no literature, and the missions' translations of the Bible will be their pupils' only reading matter.

There is a Seventh-day Adventist Church in Kanifing; fetishism, we may assume, is the solace of a far more sizeable minority but, whether practising or lapsed, the Gambian majority is Muslim. They are technically of the Sunni sect, and Malikite tenets are applied in the Islamic courts. This for most Gambians, though, is the *Bourgeois Gentilhomme*'s prose: at most they avow themselves members of the Senegambian Tijani or Murad communities.

The first decades of British missionary effort coincided – by chance? – with a revival of Islam. The word of the Prophet had been heard here long before, Arab armies having reached the Niger in the 7th century. The faith spread with trade, through Morocco and Mauritania to the empire of Mali: in 1324-25 one Gongo Musa performed the *Hajj* (the pilgrimage to Mecca) and resided in Cairo with so impressive a retinue as to warrant a mention in contemporary Arab chronicles. The Mandinkas' dispersal from Mali to Kaabu was no doubt a fillip to The Gambia's Islam. Except amongst the Fulas, it none the less remained the domain of a chosen few: the marabouts, 'marybuckes' or morymen, whose literacy in Arabic was useful to unschooled rulers but whose proselytes were consigned to a 'Marabout's place' or *Morykunda*. In these satellite villages they lived safe from Soninki 'contamination' but within beck and call of their Mandinka overlords.

could clearly not be countenanced by Victorian Britain in a colony and protectorate. The Royal African Corps of 'bluejackets' and marines, seconded West Indian regiments and the Bathurst Militia with enlisted English merchants received half-hearted help from Whitehall in containing the Muslim outbreaks. The problem was partly disposed of by chasing the ringleaders into French Senegal.

The failure of this Islamic revival, the British-backed success of Soninki animism is often seen as a reason for the relaxed, pragmatic tolerance shown by Gambian Muslims today. You may with impunity (and shoes removed) visit village mosques and backyard *jakas* (praying-places). Early Friday afternoon, dressed in their Friday best, the men of every hamlet start their walk to the nearest *juma*. (Prayers at the old Great Mosque on this Muslim sabbath caused Banjul's weekly traffic jam.) But devotions are affable, not fanatical: The Gambia's law is not the Shari'a; there is

Due perhaps to accumulated pique, perhaps to the appearance of more warlike marabouts, Senegambian Muslims in the 1850s commenced a series of bitty uprisings glorified with the title of Soninki-Marabout Wars. The Muslim warlords Musa Mollo, Maba, Fodi Silla and Fodi Kabba engaged bands of Jola and Serahuli mercenaries, plundered and displaced the Wolofs and Serers and destroyed the Mandinka kingdoms. Such disturbances

nothing of the blinkered and insidious Islam that taints some Middle Eastern states.

Only the lucky few can now afford the pilgrimage to Mecca. At Friday prayers the faithful are grateful to the many beggars: thanks to them another Muslim duty of almsgiving can be done. The month-long daytime fast of Ramadhan is generally observed, and the *'Ids*, here called *Koriteh* and *Tabaski*, are popular holidays (which cost

fathers new family clothes, and a sheep, and husbands new dresses and hair-dos).

Up country the *pickens* sit in the village square, learning the Arabic inscribed on wooden paddles. Older brothers, before and after school, attend the local *dala* to study the Qoran, the *Hadisi* (Hadith) and the *Sungna* (Sunna), the 'gospel according to Mohammed'. Nowadays the occasional *sering dala* even teaches Arabic as a spoken language, not simply as a vehicle of liturgy as was many Catholics' Latin. The marabouts, influential still, have reverted more to their North African rôle of soothsayers and purveyors of placebos. Famous morymen, often from Mauritania, pitch their marquees by the roadside in Banjul, to advise piously (for a price) and hold well-attended court like mediæval potentates.

Such visiting celebrities charge more than the street-corner marabout for jujus. Amulets, gris-gris, the locals' *taami matu* (and derived from *joujou*, the French for toy), they are worn round every neck, arm, waist or ankle; simple bangles, *tafu* (neck-cloths) or scraps of paper enclosed

The new Great Mosque of Banjul (above) is named in honour of its principal benefactor, King Fahd of Saudi Arabia. Friday prayers, soon after noon, are the most important. Not only men attend, but women enter separately and pray apart.

in lockets to keep the name of Allah clean. They do not appear to be sacrosanct (Gambians hand them over or open them up on request), just indispensable. When Mr Morgan in 1822 asked his parishioners to take theirs off, they burned his Wesley Church down. Church outings are popular, said one parish priest, but not for swimming: undressed, the parishioners would expose their pagan jujus. On my first drive outside Banjul, three bracelets replaced the usual one on my driver's arm: he reported late, having had to see his marabout to extend his juju-cover for up country. Childless wives, unsuccessful businessmen, the sick and soldiers off to war all apply to their marabout for the appropriate charm to wear or best *naso* to drink.

The reasons given for their use of jujus are as many as the Gambians you ask. Theologians see them as indication of the Africans' hankering for tangible tokens of the supernatural or divine, their reluctance (or inability) to indulge in purely cerebral acts of faith. Scholars point to the Old Testament parallel of Rachel's stealing *teraphim* (jujus?) from her father, and Homer's having Ulysses wear a ribbon to keep him from drowning. Frank Catholics equate them with St Christophers on dash-boards and miraculous medals of Our Lady hung round necks. There may well be a connection: the renovation of the Banjul cathedral was an opportunity for the fathers to heed Rome's admonitions on the veneration of saints and remove most of the statues. But the congregation protested, turning out to light candles to such as the 'absent St Anthony'.

Friday prayers at the King Fahd Mosque, Banjul (opposite)
Ceremonial dancing amongst Muslim Jolas (above)
Jujus and knick-knacks worn by a Lebu wife

Those whose *balandango*-roots fail to save them from bullets rarely come back and complain; but others whose jujus avail them naught appeal to the crocodile pools. Or make a pilgrimage to the holy places, idyllic spots with pagan associations like Sanneh-Mentering, Tengworo, Kenye-Kenye Jamango or Nyanitama-Dibindinto. Dressed in their best and accompanied by the alkalu, suppliant men and would-be mothers trek from even neighbouring states to offer up prayers, plus kola-nuts, money, cloth or a slave. They may stay for several days, sleeping in the flimsy thatched huts, sometimes refusing food and drink, their devotions unorthodox but their piety impressive.

Dress

So delightfully varied is the Gambians' everyday dress that jujus might seem to be the only common item of attire. Only Banjul schoolchildren are brightly and literally uniform; only green (the holy colour of Islam) is not very commonly seen. For the rest, the array of fashions and shades is amazing; except amongst Banjul's bureaucracy there is no suit-and-tie or skirt-and-blouse conformity. West African apparel is an arbitrary affair.

The lavishness and flair of what especially women wear is a revelation to first-time visitors

Circumcision To begin with what is taken off rather than put on, every Gambian boy is circumcised: in traditional tribal rituals as described in *Roots*, after lessons from a slave in manhood, morals, bushcraft and filial duty with a *kafo/lell* of contemporaries, or more often nowadays by unceremonious surgery at the local clinic. Boys coming up for 'initiation' can still be seen trekking in to the *dansukunda*, summoned by the *baringo* drum. They are fêted with gunfire and a slaughtered goat, griots' chanting and dancing at the bantaba on the actual day. They skulk in the bush for a month or two thereafter, a stick in their hand, their head in a cloth and dressed in white calico dyed from the *woloo*-tree. And finally return home, healed, with firewood and grass to reroof their neighbours' houses.

When girls undergo similar bush-surgery, feminists call it 'genital mutilation'. For most Fula, Jola, Mandinka and Serahuli girls, 'mutilation' is as accepted and normal as it is for boys throughout Islam, Judaism and much of Christendom. Mothers and aunts, not the menfolk, uphold the practice. And often ferociously so: a British mission doctor in a village up river reports the recent stoning of a government official lecturing on the undesirability (and illegality) of female circumcision. Prompted by the missions and foreign aid agencies, the authorities make sporadic efforts to discourage the practice. But Gambians of every persuasion were recently shocked to see it shown, graphically, on family TV and officially the custom is now condoned again.

For this is *Sutura*, a topic so taboo that even girls rarely discuss it amongst themselves. With prying English authors naturally less. Doctors and gynæcologists, despite rather better access, are not agreed on the procedure. 'Scar tissue confuses the issue', said one. My hope proved vain that nothing more was involved than the cosmetic labial straightening that is commonplace in eastern Africa. Most Fulas at least practise full cruel clitoridectomy, on girls as young as seven. Glimpsing village processions of pubescent candidates, their faces whitened and their dresses blue, is the closest most visitors come to evidence. Once circumcised, Fulas, Jolas and Mandinkas wear around the waist the titillating *jiljali*s that Aku and Wolof women wear willy nilly.

Besides circumcision, Muslim men share with their co-religionists everywhere the graceful and airy haftan, a practical, long-sleeved, ankle-length 'night-shirt'. Also known as *s(h)abado*, *jalabe* or *fataro*, the Wolof *haftan* is a mispronounced kaftan. Full-dress accessories are the usually matching hat that Mandinkas call *nafo* and Wolofs *kopoti*, and the heelless slippers that both name *marakisu/marakiss* (cf Marrakech). When the haftan/kaftan stops short on the calf, Gambians use its Arabic name of *abbaya*. Popular also amongst Muslim worthies is the Wolofs' three-piece suit *nyete abdu*. The sirwal-style trousers are *tubay* or *chaya*, and *dendiko* is Mandinka for any shirt or top. The *waramba* is often encountered: Wolof for 'very large', it is a male or female garment that, holed for the head, hangs loose from the shoulders.

Most Christians and young men about town are 20th-century standard. (Often their only distinctive accessories are 'tea-cosies': coloured woolly hats either knitted by Ma or bought from a stall in Albert Market which sells nothing but coloured woolly hats.) Compared with their women-folk, the men in T-shirts and jeans are sartorial non-starters. For the ladies of the capital in particular exhibit a grace and taste to which words cannot do justice. The

Older Muslim men wear the red or white *nafo/kopoti* (above)
Younger men about town prefer coloured woolly 'tea-cosies' or,
increasingly nowadays, baseball caps

Señoras and Wolofs from Senegal made a dazzling impact on 19th-century settlers. The rows of boys treadling sewing-machines in townships without a hospital or bar still say much for the demands of women's wardrobes. What amazes most is that so much feminine splendour should emerge from such humble shacks and shanties. Young women in particular now add a touch of (sometimes stumbling) stateliness with their fondness for fashionable 'platforms'.

Women also wear the waramba (above), especially up country where hard-working wives appreciate its cheap and sleeveless looseness. But most characteristic of *la Sénégambienne* is the *granbuba*. Its Mandinka alias of *buluba* – 'big sleeve' – is descriptive. Big in every respect, it drops full-length from a neck in no way décolleté, with seams down either side beneath elongated sleeve-holes. Visitors may or may not need to know that beneath the granbuba

At the 'Ids especially, women's dressmakers treadle day and night
Lengths of tie-dye and dressed dolls sold on the beach
In a *marinière*, atop the Arch 22 (below)

two metres of cloth may be wrapped into an underskirt like the lower half of a sari. This *pagne*, *sirr* or *malane* often covers a short slip or two, the *betcho*, and the latter the panties. All this is designed to enhance the African attraction that specialists call steatopyga.

Shapelier ladies prefer the *dagit/daget(o)*. Wolof for 'short', this three-quarter-length top is essentially tighter than the granbuba, with a closely fitted waist. Looser, shorter and popular, the *marinière* is likewise worn with a long matching skirt called *sepa* (a mispronounced *jupe*?). All may be topped by a matching head-dress. And are modelled by the dolls sold on the beach. About the house viz. compound, town and country women wrap a *pagne* around the waist in sarong or khanga-fashion, with or without blouse and bra.

out by the hair-pieces sold on Banjul pavements, decked out in coins, seeds, beads and knick-knacks of plastic or bone, Gambian girls construct coiffures that are often tonsorial feats.

Called in Wolof *mussor*, in Mandinka *tiko*, the head-dress is often a work of art. (Or more prosaically, to quote Mungo Park, 'a bandage . . . wrapped many times round, immediately over the forehead'.) Styling and tying are at discretion: ribbons may be added, gold thread entwined and shells inserted. Solid gold earrings, in distinctive half-moon, wheel-rim shapes, are the family savings worn by Serahuli women. The head-dress is in places a cosmetic necessity: where washing water is precious and fetched from afar, women crop their hair short or shave it hygienically off.

The ladies' hair-styles, like their attire, is just as predictable as feminine taste. Whilst 'pure' Fula women have long unnegroid hair, those in Banjul with similar inclinations must resort to *défriseurs*. The supermarkets do good business with their various brands of 'Hair Straightener for Natural Frizzy Hair'. It would in this connection be unkind to point out that Mungo Park's paragraph on local hair-dos leads straight on into thatching. It would also be wrongly unflattering to add that, boating through the mangrove swamps with certain styles in mind, you might find the pattern of the air-roots *déjà vu*. But these and many other striking styles – *berti*, *jerreh* and *dundubale/duni-bally*, *armandija* and *pess-sa-gorro* – are African delights. Helped

Simple sophistication in Banjul's city centre
Elaborate ornamentation in the villages,
Lebu (far left), Jola (right)
Muslim elder in black *haftan* and white *kopoti* (opposite)

Muslim men are typical in limp white skull-caps or embroidered 'pot-hats'; older worthies dignified by the red fez, imported complete with black tassel, and Fulas recognizable by their conical 'Chinese' straw hats sometimes patterned with coloured sticky tape.

Cross-cultural Shock, Names and Language

There are few familiar pegs to hang associations on here; little is déjà vu

Americans attending our Beirut school of Arabic were armed by their government with a paper on cross-cultural shock. This American invention, we discovered, was considered a risk not of first encounters with Arabs but with us, their British class-mates. By that token, The Gambia's cultural impact should cause not shock but trauma. Being off the beaten tourist track, beyond the scope of school geography and history, the only English-speaking country between the Channel Islands and the Gulf of Guinea has much that is 'exotic', beyond our ken.

With a slight shift of mental stance, looking analytically and not full frontal, you may feel less intellectually lost. Names are a case in point. Your driver's, guide's or waiter's, those over shops and in print seem unheard-of mumbo jumbo. Yet Arabic names like Mohammed or Abdullah are now commonplace in Europe. These the Senegambians have simply Africanized. Having the same problem as ourselves with the Arabic *h* of Mohammed, they have turned the name of the Prophet into Mamudu or Momodou. The same awkward *h* in the Arabic Fathi explains the many Gambians called Fatty (no joke). Abdullah should start with the impossible Arabic 'ain, so Abdelahi, Abdoulie or Abdu/Abdou is the Senegambian solution. Issa (the Arabic Jesus) and Othman (whence Ottoman) share this initial problem of an unpronounceable 'ain, so are simplified respectively into Issatou and Ousman. The *kh* of the Arabs' Khalifa is another built-in impediment to speech, which Gambians circumvent with their Kelefa. Abu Bakr ends up here as Baboucarr/Babukar (what Wolofs also call kingfishers!). Amongst Muslim girls the Arabic Zainab becomes the thicker-lipped Sainabou – Sy for short – while the Prophet's daughter Fatima takes on the deeper drumnote of Fatuma, Fatu or Faa, and often the rhythmic suffix Fatumata.

The *Mseu* that men are sometimes addressed by is not the *Mzee* of East Africa but *Monsieur*, imported from French-speaking Senegal and somewhat damaged in transit. A 'yard mastah' is the family head (of a compound). 'Mastah', 'massah' or 'boss' is what fellow men, Sir, call you. The children also call you, loudly and collectively, tubab. The Gambians' kindliness is an assurance that no offence is meant. The meaning is in fact not so much 'Westerner' or 'White (person)' as VIP or 'big shot'. *Tubab* is what poor blacks may call better-off neighbours.

Having wrapped your mind round your Gambian friends' names, you then find they gleefully discard and/or distort them. Nicknames and aliases are an accepted idiosyncrasy that must frustrate the CID. In the newspapers for example: 'Alhaji M.B. Njie Manager of British Petroleum … and commonly known as N'jie Dodou or N'jie B.P. has been appointed …'. Dodou along with Modu, Modi and the unlikely Lamin(e)(*Al-Amin*, one of the godhead's 99 'attributes') is short for Mohammed.

Even the terms you recognize from English may be *faux amis*, familiar but misleading. The Wolofs' *Mam*, the Mandinkas' *Mama* is obviously Mother, *Pa* naturally Father, like the un-English but more logical *Fa*. These parental abbreviations, though, are also applied to aunts and grandmothers, uncles and grandfathers respectively. And, respectfully, to you. Genealogists struggling with family-trees (*lasilos*) face problems that Berkeley Rice conveys in jocular patois: 'Karamo Fatty not Souri's propah fadda. He be small fadda. Souri's real fadda be old pa. This be his brudda'. Translated, this means that Karamo and Souri are stepbrothers. Precision in speech or spelling, nice delimitations of family or personal relations you should not expect of The Gambia's man in the street.

Vacation travel is also less confusing if you come to grips with place-names. Many are translated as they occur in the itineraries, but with these general rules in mind you can work out others for yourself. *Ba/bah* is 'big', *nding* 'little' and *tenda* the Mandinka word for wharf. *Tendaba* thus makes a good class-one example before progressing to Banjulunding. Little Banjul – *Banjul Nding* – emerges if you overlook the odd redundant vowel and split the syllables African-style, by consonant groups not in familiar English patterns.

Kunda is *chez* ('the place of') with the founder or namesake preceding. Serekunda is thus 'Sere's place', *Tubabkunda*

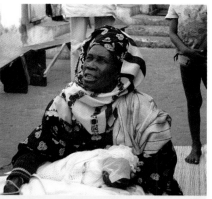

In a ceremony beside which christenings pale, eight-day-old Gambians are named. Family, friends and neighbours foregather with small gifts. Wetting a blade from a symbolic pot (containing water, soap, cotton, maize and kola), the officiating elder cuts a lock from the infant's head and says a silent prayer. Next he whispers into its ear the name its parents have chosen, then the same to the griot who proclaims it. The tuft of hair is later buried; mother, only eight days delivered, may not attend and, leaving kola-nuts and coke for his guests, father may also be hard to find, by the alms-begging griots above all. You need go no further than page 2 of *Roots* for a less cynical-realistic, more romanticized description of the Gambians' famed naming ceremony.

Alex Haley however, when not fabricating facts, based his text on Mandinka village life. With Wolof families around Banjul the ceremony nowadays, while respecting the basic ritual, is also an occasion for best dresses, fizzy drinks and sticky cakes, followed by dancing to not a kora-player but a ghetto-blaster.

or *Morykunda*, where the foreigners or marabouts live, and the north-bank Kinteh Kunda a more likely scenario for Alex Haley's story. Synonyms of *kunda* are *sare/suarra* and the lairdly *kerr, keur* or *karr*. Darsilami/Dasilami is the well-known Dar as-Salaam (Home of Peace) and Madina or Medina simply Arabic for Town. Senegambian place-names, though, are as a subject of research almost virgin. A Wolof in Fula country understands no more than you. The fact that the same name may recur throughout the country at least reduces the problem somewhat.

If in the holiday habit of learning the local language, be warned by Weil's *Linguistic Map of the Gambia*. And the official Radio Gambia which broadcasts its daily news bulletins in five different tongues. Those of the Fulas, Jolas and Serahulis are likely to be encountered less, and the lack of academic publications on them relieves me and the reader of the need to consider them here. It is however significant that the radio station's programmes, like those of Radio Syd, are not only most frequently but also equally in English, Mandinka and Wolof. For although English is the state's official language and will serve you well in hotels and around town, its teaching up river and off the beaten track does not go deep. Even in Banjul Irish priests preach to and confess their flock in Wolof, while compulsory crash courses in both this and Mandinka are inflicted on American Peace Corps volunteers.

When listening to local English, proper or pidgin, remember that, just as we cannot cope with the 'click' and other quirks of some local tongues, many Africans display an endearing inability to distinguish between *l* and *r*. Their pronunciation of both is such a liquid nondescript that you may not be able to distinguish it either. Also, as with the Biblical shibboleth, *s* and *sh* are interchanged. The Wartime airbase that was once the Jolas' *Jong Su* or *Joswa* has thus become Jeswang or Jeshwang, and Muslim boys called Sherif introduce themselves as Serif. The Mandinkas' preference of *k* to *g* we know, but *h* in place of *k* is a further complication. Are Messrs Janga, Janha, Janka and Jangka one and the same? This throaty, near-Arabic *k/h*, not a faulty typographer or ear, was why early travellers called the Serahulis Sarakole. All these jelly sounds in a dialectal hotchpot make it impossible for Gambian scholars to adopt the International Phonetic System or even agree on a unified national script. 'Mumbo jumbo', be it said without malice, may derive from the Mandinka *ma-ma-gio-mbo*, a 'magician who makes troubled ancestors' spirits go away'.

Bibliography and History

You will find very little on The Gambia in libraries and bookshops at home (although D. P. Gamble's *General Bibliography of The Gambia* is a thick and tight-typed volume; G. K. Hall, Boston, Massachusetts). Published works on traditional tribal structures are Charlotte Quinn's *Mandingo Kingdoms of the Senegambia* (Longman), Gamble's *The Wolof of Senegambia, together with notes on the Lebu and the Serer* (International African Institute, London, 1957) and Patience Sonko-Godwin's *Ethnic Groups of the Senegambia* (Book Production Unit, Banjul, 1985). The best bird book is Clive Barlow and Tim Wacher's *Birds of The Gambia* (Pica Press 1997, reprinted 1999).

Monolithic booksellers like Dillons-cum-Waterstone's sell guide-books only on The Gambia. A recent article in *The Times Weekend* pinpointed one of their problems: 'They are outdated before they are even published, as it takes on average two years from commissioning to publication. And as the shelf-life of most books is two years, there may be as much as four years between the original research and a tourist's visit'. So, with guide-books *ipso facto*, the more current details they contain, the more mistakes. While none of them receives the annual updating needed, the Directory enclosed with this *Gambia* does, and guide-books are detailed there.

For the rest, The Gambia's documentation is somewhat undistinguished. The *Commonwealth Fact Sheet* is a dated *vade mecum*; expense-account businessmen's accessories such as the Economist's *Quarterly Review* are trenchantly if ephemerally topical. There are period pieces like Richard Jobson's *The Golden Trade* (1623, but republished by E. E. Speight & R. H. Walpole, Teignmouth) and Lang's *Land of The Golden Trade* (reprinted in 1969 by the Negro University Press, New York). Mungo Park's *Travels in the Interior (Districts) of Africa* is a classic of West African exploration, first published in 1799 (and in 1984 handsomely republished by The Folio Society). The end-piece portrait of the frock-coated, top-hatted Henry Fenwick Reeve CMG, MICE, FRGS, FAS, ETC, ETC. typifies his *The Gambia*: a preened and humourless

Batik kora-player

volume, impregnated with Victorian public-school culture but dated also by its odd combination of jingoistic self-righteousness and colonial *mea culpa* (John Murray, 1912). Lady Southorn's *The Gambia* is jollier. Her style and standpoint are those expected of the wife of a colonial governor (Sir Wilfrid Thomas Southorn hangs, slightly peaky-awkward, in the National Museum) but she like many others flounders in the quagmire of Gambian history (George Allen & Unwin, 1952). Two years before the Southorns arrived, Rex Hardinge visited and wrote *Gambia and Beyond* (Blackie, 1934). It is also rather spiffing and pith-helmet but altogether lighter weight, more 'Africa and Me'. A cut above all these and a class apart is *Enter Gambia, The Birth of an Improbable Nation* (Angus & Robertson, 1968). In this the American Berkeley Rice depicts the country on the point of independence with a stylish hilarity that almost stays the course. And with a warmth and affection that Gambians tend to resent. They find that the author makes facile fun and tells home truths too flippantly – but none the less keep a copy in the National Library.

The bulk of most general books is taken up by history. It is not unfair to say that they tell half the story badly. For The Gambia's past, like affairs of state, is 'internal' and 'external'. The former, almost entirely oral, finds little place in European archives. It is the preserve of the elders and the griots, members of a hereditary caste who, accompanied by music (and according to Alex Haley), can narrate for three days without repetition their tribe's generations of families and clans, their kings, warrings, triumphs and catastrophes, their years of abundance and seasons of drought.

These *jalis/gewels/griots* are no doubt important. Attached as 'praise-singers' to each headman and king,

they traditionally preceded him on his travels (declaiming not only to scare off snakes). They continue to be popular on Gambian radio and Senegalese TV. Griots, however, misled Alex Haley to Juffure, and in her study of the Mandinka kingdoms – absolute griot domain – Charlotte Quinn found their 'tales . . . less valuable . . . than the traditions and memories of nonprofessional informants'. Oral historians regard the better griots as we would good historical novelists, and give more credence to village elders and 'tarikas', the Arabic *tarikh* (history) written by the 'Mandink-Moros' of early Muslim families like the Cissays and Tourays.

These are the sources of The Gambia's 'internal' history, which Western records ignore almost entirely. Not featuring in travellers' reports or governmental archives, the historical Gambian kingdom of Kaabu has only just been 'discovered'. 'Only in the last ten-fifteen years', wrote Winifred F. Galloway in 1981, 'have oral traditions become "respectable" in western scholarly circles'. They have been a subject of academic study for scarcely any longer, and the task that faces researchers is awesome. French *universitaires* paved the way in Senegal. In Banjul's Oral History & Antiquities Division, B. K. Sidibe and the American Dr Galloway spent months tape recording the elders and griots. They translated and, by collating, sifted the verbal grain from the chaff, academic detective work which permits the piecemeal reconstruction of the nation's past.

Meanwhile we are left with 'external' history books. It is not surprising that those used in schools tend to bypass The Gambia entirely. For outside the field of slavery, European doings in West Africa had little impact on the international scene. Here we see the tactics, not the strategy of empire: four centuries of sporadic sorties and settlement, colonial in-fighting with its *ad hoc* campaigns and expeditions. The standard histories are not best-sellers. The doyen (by default) is J. M. Gray with his *History of The Gambia* (Frank Cass, 1966). Having laboured conscientiously in official archives, this former Chief Justice of The Gambia details European relations from 1455 until 1938. You feel, though, that not having to prosecute or pass judgment, Mr Justice Gray has hardly analyzed the evidence. His 500 pages of meticulous minutiæ are presented pell-mell; in the welter of petty events it is difficult to see the historical wood for the trees.

A same-named book by Harry A. Gailey, Jr., being shorter, sins less in this direction (Routledge & Kegan Paul, 1964). It is written however in pseudo-learned Americanese that few Britons find pleasing reading. Its subtitle *An Official Handbook* sums up F. B. Archer's *The Gambia Colony and Protectorate* (Frank Cass). Reprinted in 1967, it was written in 1906, when its lists of enactments, tax returns and personnel, like its far more readable chronological narration of events, stop short. Hughes and Perfect's *Political History of The Gambia 1816-1994* is more recently relevant, and self-explanatory.

Handicrafts

A lower caste, paradoxically, provides the greatest crafts-men. Formed in 1970 and still alive if languishing, the Gambian Gold & Silversmiths Society groups 500 men of the Chem, Jobe, Mbow, Nyang and Touray families. Boys, never girls, are 'apprenticed' to their fathers at the start of adolescence. They begin with six grams of silver for a ring, progress through solid or hollow *argent massif* and graduate to filigree. With the finest rolled gold or silver webbed on a frame like the veins of a leaf, The Gambia's filigree master-pieces are models of the art (though rarer now). A rolling mill and draw-plate with holes of different sizes nowadays facilitate this fineness: older hands used a home crucible to mould their gold and silver which was then hammered and rolled even thinner. Another technique I had not met else-where was the 'rough-cast' use of *coos*: grains of this Guinea corn are set in molten ore, the whole thing fired and the coos tapped out when cold. Bijous encrusted with cow's horn, ebony or (illegal) ivory are more 'ethnic' but equally magnificent.

Silverware for sale in Banjul's Albert Market

Silver is imported as stones, not ingots, and gold like-wise from London, Dakar or Ghana but in ever decreasing quantities. Both go into pendants, earrings and brooches; letter-openers and articulated fish; exquisite miniature masks and filigree fishing-boats nine inches high. There are massive silver anklets like Beduin bangles, necklaces knotted in clove-hitches and bracelets tressed like hair. Five-dalasi armbands of copper, brass and iron (engraved on request) are cheap contrasts to silver nuggets dipped in gold.

Wood-carving is the preserve of the Janha, Lobeh, N'Jie, Sarr and Sowe clans, and their work best inspected at the Brikama Market. With the craftsmen often Bambaras or Fulas, many busts portray tribal traits: splendid pieces four feet tall and true to Fula life with three scars on each cheek, three on each temple and two in the centre of the forehead. Technically lax Muslims in this fondness for human forms, they also manufacture scale-model warriors and pipe-smoking hunters, their arrows in a quiver and an animal over their shoulders. These flank stylized silhouettes and two-dimensional faces, but most frequent are the masks which tribal rituals require to conceal them.

African masks are a study in themselves: the styles and significance of the many types are the subject of several books. Some are straightforwardly grotesque, others draped Medusa-like with snakes, or many-faced with smaller countenances beside a 'double-decker'. Small mar-vels from every neighbouring state embellish many hotels; the à la carte restaurant of the Bungalow Beach has a mural gallery of masks boned and beaded, in wood, shell and bronze.

Also carved are drums, combs, paper-knives, pestles and mortars; just-recognizable elephants and 'hear no evil' monkeys; pegmen rowing salad-bowl boats; hippos, croc-odiles and the same antelopes and sucking fawns that,

Mask at Bungalow Beach (opposite)

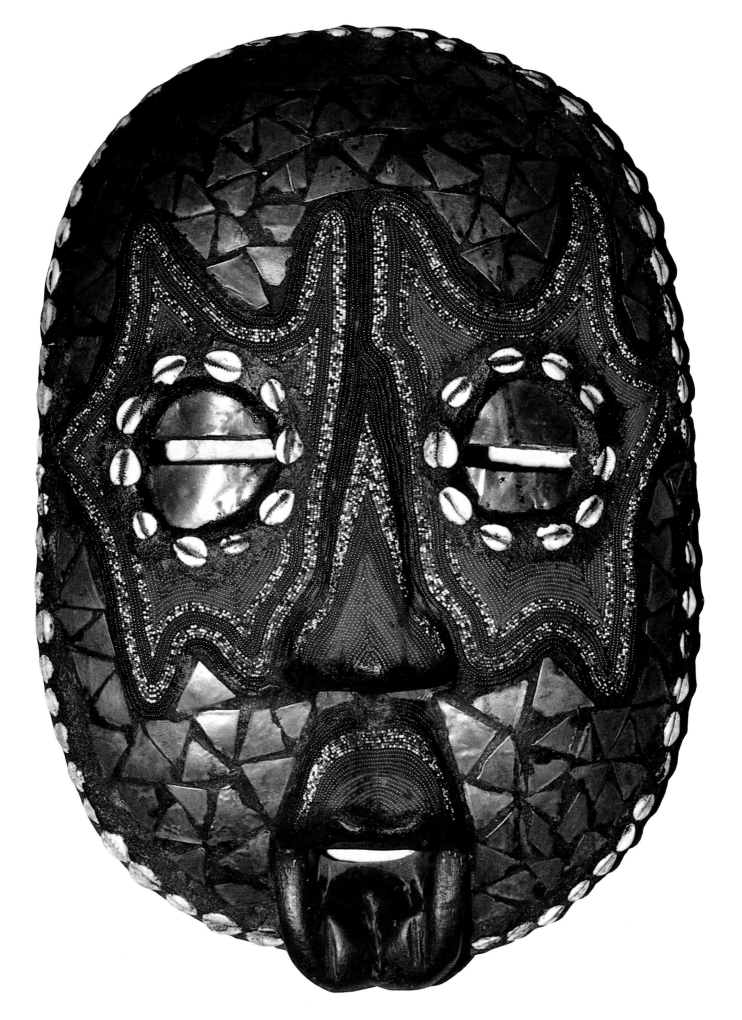

identically stylized, appear in Kenya and even North Africa, reincarnated as olive-wood gazelles. A contrast with these standard lines are the one-off abstract pieces now appearing increasingly around the tourist centres. A cross between Makonde *Ujamaa* and Hieronymus Bosch, they presumably cater for modern visitors' tastes. The reappearance of traditional African seats – two carved planks in a half-lap joint, guaranteed uncomfortable – may reflect more generous luggage allowances on flights home.

The wood used here is generally *jallo* (mahogany), the depth of its stain and shine increasing with up to five coats of brown shoe polish. (Black, they confess, is used for forging ebony.) Real ebony is distinguished by its weight and higher price: it is harder to work and imported from Senegal, Mali and Guinea Bissau. Bowls are cheap in the Wolofs' *khankhalla-*

wood; the soft 'cheese' wood of the *fromager*, bombax or silk-cotton tree is used for 'antique' statues, cracked and bleached 'with age'.

Pottery is known to have been made here for the last 6500 years. It is women's work, particularly that of low-caste blacksmiths' wives. Colanders, water containers or coolers; pots for cooking or drinking, for ablutions, medecines or burning incense; vessels for divination or *buntungo*, stor-

ing grain . . . the best are made mostly by the Jolas, Serahulis and Mandinkas. Rotund and deep-rimmed pots, two or three feet in diameter, are a speciality of Alohungari. (The most/only photogenic views of Basse show them at the riverbank market Thursday mornings.) Except on Fridays (the Islamic sabbath) the local Serahuli women work kaolin fetched from the paddies. It is sieved, crushed smooth in mortars and moistened for use the next day. Lacking both kilns and the potter's wheel, the women shape the clay by hand with a bowl as mould, scratch in a chevron or a crescent design (which they later outline with white paint) and fire each piece in a hollow, covered with kindling and wood. The villages near Basse also produce shallow platters, globular bowls and holed coos 'colanders'. In hamlets like Jifarong, laterite pots lie beside the track awaiting transport. Shaped like squat and irregular Mister Men, they have matching half-pot tops.

Nature's counterpart to these man-made shapes (or their inspiration?) are utensils from the calabash/gourd. Its inside rotted by soaking in water, its skin dried wood-hard in the sun, the *Cucurbit* provides several rural receptacles: spoons and ladles from smaller stemmed fruit split in two, and ample half-gourd bowls, often carried on heads and branded in black patterns.

Music

With captivating rhythm, Senegambian music is Indo-European mellifluous, often prototype jazz

The most spectacular Senegambian shows (apart from the bird life) are musical or muscular: the songs and traditional dances professionally performed by excellent local ensembles, and the weekly wrestling tournaments at Bundung, Serekunda or Lamin.

Fine exponents of 'choreographed ritual', Senegambian dancers are renowned for their dynamism, rhythmic flair and acrobatic finesse. Their forte is the masked or 'social' dance. The latter may represent the Cassankas' palm-wine 'harvest home'; the Balankas' 'warring' to the popular tune *Mama Manneh;* Serahuli women – in a *jembe* dance – working in paddies by moonlight or, with knives thrust symbolically and pelvises suggestively, the Jolas enacting a former forced marriage. The irrepressible Fulas that perform fakir-like in hotels are not the local circus's 'fire-eaters': bundles of flaming grass they pass casually over chest and abdomen, under their chin and down their arms, to swallow them or slowly stamp them out. These *nyamakalas'* 'musical accompaniment' – of half-gourd drum, side-blown *serndu*-flute and awful *riti/nyaanyeru*-fiddle – would be second string to anything, let alone this.

The Gambia National Troupe performing, and a kora-player (opposite)

Senegambian instruments are naturally drums and – for melody – koras, balafons and the likes of xalams and bolonbatas. You will see them all in authentic use, displayed in the National Museum and/or reproduced for tourists.

The kora is a characteristically Mandinka instrument. Entitled to 18-24 strings, this African harp-lute has generally 21, in staves of eleven and ten. Its rosewood neck and handles are held straight out, the calabash body on the performer's belly (or, if he is seated, on the ground between his knees). It is played mostly with thumbs. Whilst we beat out rhythms with brushes or sticks, using digital dexterity more for melody, these rôles are in Africa frequently reversed: drumming is a demanding five-finger exercise, while melodymakers like balafons are beaten and musical implements like thumb-pianos speak for themselves. Kora-players compromise, with six or eight fingers resting

The Jolas' *kumpo* is a startling masked dance. Preceded by a woman whose whisk and water-sprinkler cast protective spells on the circumcised and virtuous, a guide leads in the chanting exorcist. Decked in four sleeved rings of raffia, this kumpo will break the enemy's spell. In a final whirling crescendo of dust he pivots invisibly on a head-pole, his body unseen and the scene unbelievable.

Jola playing the *bugarabu*

idle under the strings, and first fingers at most helping thumbs pluck out a melody. For all that very prettily: the kora has the harp's little-bell tinkle but is less full-bodied, and the Arab qanun's polymorphic nimbleness but is more melodious. The minstrels that play this 'courtly instrument' at many hotel tables complement their 60-piece repertoire with instant lyrics in your honour. (The 'sound-holes' in the resonator-body are for notes: coins clank embarrassingly.)

The bolon or bolonbata is a lesser bent kora, with a maximum five strings tuned to the arpeggio. The neck is curved while its *keno*/rosewood is still green; the body is a smaller gourd, likewise covered tight in cowhide but with the hair left on. It is played only by Mandinkas, Fulas and the odd Guinean Susus (and not made any more tuneful by the large metal rattle round its neck).

The body itself is of rosewood not calabash on the three-, four- or five-stringed lute which Fulas call *hurde*, Mandinkas *kontingo* and Wolofs *halam*, *khalam* or *xalam*. This is the instrument you hear plucked and strummed at Wolof and/or Muslim festivals. (Musicologists consider it a prototype banjo.) Only the Serers, Fulas and Serahulis finger with the left hand and pluck with the right, as we do most stringed instruments – on their *molo* of calabash, cowhide and wood. Except for the horsehair of the *riti*/*nyaanyeru* (the one-stringed fiddle of the Fulas, Wolofs and Serers), all are stringed traditionally with twisted cowhide, gut or antelope-hide, *minau*. Or nowadays more often with nylon fishing-line. You tune by sliding the rawhide loops which attach the strings to the neck.

The balafon or bala is Africa's xylophone (a gift of the devil, Mandinka griots say, to the Kuyateh families in Sunjata's time). Its sound is admittedly not heavenly, more the hollow beauty of Japanese bells. With gourds hung in a frame beneath, its 16-19 keys are struck in resonant and skilful unison. The griots' balafon often accompanies the slightly nasal singing of lady griots, who accompany themselves with a *newo*/*karanyango*, iron bell.

The commonest wind instruments are unfortunately football whistles (which have replaced holed cow's horns). The three-holed transverse *tabiru* and the *serndu* of the Fula *gawulo*s ('musicians') are used in tribal ensembles. Or to call cows. Serahulis call *fuleh* the shorter bamboo oboe which they play with four fingers and sometimes cover with leather. The Wolofs are short of wind instruments.

Marking time for dancers, wrestlers or working parties, whistles are blown (and armlet *laala*s rattled) by players of the all-important drums. My favourite is a small drum covered in sheepskin and called *tama* which means Talk. (*Tama nding* – Little tama – is a local brand of bleeper.) You hold it under one arm and squeeze to make it change its tone. The Senegambian drum probably best known in Britain is the *jembe* (which, imported from Senegal, sells as *djembe* in music-shops).

The highest drum in pitch is the Wolofs' *sabar*, which Mandinkas call *sabaro*. The *bellengo* is their big bass drum. Also banged with the right hand, a drumstick in the left, the *kuturiba* and *kuturindingo* are the large and small *kutur*s. They are long, conical and leaned on. The Wolofs sit on the ground to beat the barrel-shaped *gorong* between their knees, while the Jolas' wood-frame of 'kettle-drums' can only be played standing up. Called *bugarabu*, they are sets of four – three differently pitched *tumba*s plus a larger *funyun-dum*. (Smaller, similar *wimpau*s sent messages to the dead.) The time-honoured beat of the *tabulo/tabala* took news from place to place; nowadays this bowl-shaped drum generally waits for prayers or funerals in each village mosque. Only when new Mandinka kings were crowned was the two-foot *junjung(o)* beaten, *en bandoulière*, with a ten-inch stick. At the other extreme is the Jolas' and Manjagos' *bombolo*, a skinless 'ideophone' from simply a split log. Fill the same with jujus and the boom of this *kumba demba* would keep Mandinka villages safe from war or fire. The Wolofs' *kheen*, the Mandinkas' *daaba* would announce kings or send special news. (Bulletins were limited to an hour or so because thereafter, like the kora's strings, the drum-skin lost its tone. Numbers performed during European tournées may last only fifteen minutes: in the colder climate skins and strings sag faster.)

Like their instrumentalists, Gambian singers harmonize simply but most effectively. Even schoolchildren sing charmingly and most melodiously: in full-throated unison, on key and in contrast to the wavering diffidence of a same-aged class at home. Senegalese cassettes and CDs record not only the 'Musical Roots of the Mandingo Tribe' but something of the origin of southern-state Blues. More professionally updated are the splendid Christian choirs: *Baati Linguere* – 'Pure (Virgin Mary) Voice' – is a group of young Catholics first formed in 1976. With consonants not in an English congregation's slithering succession, but crisp, they overpower the organist whom they do not need – they often beat him to the beat – and fill Banjul Cathedral many Sunday mornings with a moving musical experience.

Senegambian string and percussion, xalam, kora and balafon

W restling

Called *nyoboro* in Mandinka, *boreh* in Wolof, modern Senegambian wrestling derives from a deep-seated tradition that probably originated in 13th-century Mali: that of the warrior, who was accredited with powers both physical and spiritual and who ranked in the tribal caste-system directly below the ruling families. (Presentday wrestlers, like footballers in Britain, aspire to and often attain similar social status.)

This may explain why, magnificent village he-men, they strut, dance, spar and literally play to an appreciative gallery that packs the breeze-block seats most weekend afternoons at Lamin, Serekunda or Bundung. Water from the second's bucket makes fine bodies slippery and hard to grip; sand on the hands improves the hold; muscles are flexed, loincloths girded and jujus buckled on before each fight. Between the bouts a woolly-hatted retinue blows whistles and bangs drums, Fulas play flutes, Jolas mouth music and the girls chant to cheerleaders in Mandinka villages. A lap of the krinting-fenced compound in a triumphal jog-trot (and a coin collection) follows. Fingers tapped on foreheads or drawn across throats taunt or threaten. Mock biting off of genitals from a thrown opponent is less frequently seen but of deeper Black African significance: only by possessing his predecessor's penis could, for example, a Baganda claim Kampala.

There is nothing of the protracted Western business of arm-, leg- or head-locks, technical throws, faults, falls and points. The first one down loses. Full stop. One wrestler challenges another, sensibly from the same heavy-, middle- or light-weight class and usually from the same tribe, since 'mixed' fixtures are unusual. Scorning a challenge at first may lead in the end to a more ferocious clinch: round the waist, neck or knee but often first of all on the loincloth (the juju-decked *tobeh*, *ngemba* or – if given by virgins to champions

– *dala*). Pulled, twisted, tripped or lifted bodily, one of the wrestlers soon hits the dust. Punching, kicking, biting, flinging sand in eyes or poking them is permitted but not cricket: in traditional village fixtures it will be stopped by the griot or the offending *kafo*'s 'manager', by self-appointed referees elsewhere, while the crowd boos disapproval.

Banjul and Beyond

Banjul

The Gambia's capital still appears often as 'Banjul formerly Bathurst'. To be precise, 'and formerly Banjul or Banjole' should be added, since the island leased by Britain in 1816 was already known as *Banjulu* to its shifting population of foragers, criminals and runaway slaves. Explanations of the name are at variance. The Portuguese who misquoted Kambi Manneh 'found the islanders cutting raffia-palm: "What is this?" they asked. They were told *banjulu* . . . and wrote it down'. This, the griot Fabala Kanuteh's account, differs from everyone else's: that Banjul means Bamboo, once found here in profusion and first cut by one Madiba from Bakau, who consequently acquired the nickname Madiba Banjol. (The local Mandinkas circumvent the problem with their *Kunu-su-joyo*, Bird's nest Island.) In 1973 the authorities dropped the name which, like that of the town in New South Wales, had honoured Henry, 3rd Earl of Bathurst, Colonial Secretary from 1812 to 1828 and son of 'the weakest though one of the worthiest who ever sat on the woolsack'.

Though birds are still abundant, bamboos and raffia-palms soon made way for an expanding township. Having acquired the site for 100 Spanish dollars (viz. 103 iron bars) per annum, Captain Alexander Grant set his 80 men to clearing the bush and building: with timber from the mainland, rock from Dog Island and mortar from burned oyster-shells. Controlling the river mouth against slavers, attracting merchantmen with its sheltered deep-water berth, Bathurst grew

Batik seller in Banjul's Albert Market

steadily into a loose-knit conurbation. Its hamlets, separated by plots on which 'some sickly vegetation seems to be doing violence to the poverty of the soil', were mostly self-explanatory. The half-caste Portuguese Town; Soldier Town housing the 2nd West Indian Regiment seconded to Grant's Royal African Corps; the better-class 'Jollof'/Melville Town; Jola Town and the Moka/Mocamtown that became

Half Die . . . all flooded indiscriminately at spring tide and during the rains. 'The people catch fish in the middle of the streets . . . and occasionally a crocodile . . . makes its appearance.'

With the Liberated Africans came the first drainage in 1832. A dyke was commenced around Half Die and in 1846 a lock at Malfa Creek; incomplete and insufficient, they were supplemented in 1862 by the

Restored colonial corner-block, Bedford Place

Gilded kora-player at the Arch 22 (below)

officialdom was quite as much sanitary as military. Barracks built alongside MacCarthy Square grew into the governmental Quadrangle; the hospital commenced in 1853 (and ridiculed by Burton in 1863) was finally improved after 1903 with the help of the Sisters of St Joseph. Around MacCarthy Square and along Marine Parade, building proceeded in 'West African colonial' style: a nondescript (hot and unhealthy) ground floor fronted by imposing double stairways; a smarter upper storey, sometimes projecting and supported by wrought iron, and always surrounded by a colonnaded balcony; walls often whitewashed, and peaked roofs everywhere of corrugated iron. Intrinsically ugly, sheets of the last are worked ingeniously and with unusual style into spires and minarets on richer village mosques, into curving roofs and gabled dormers on Banjul's older buildings.

The latter constitute almost all of its architectural assets. On its low-lying island, the capital keeps a low profile: until the erection of the Arch 22, the Central Bank was the only skyscraper and landmark. Though the Serekunda conurbation is bigger than Banjul, and Fajara far smarter, Britons at least should have a soft spot for a capital planned around a cricket pitch.

sluice gates called Box Bar. An embankment was pushed south from Clifton Road, but only with Bund Road in place did the capital become watertight. A start was made also on the open sewerage system to be flushed by each high tide. In the mid-1950s the whole thing was reversed but, with the outflow still often merely theory, not only the sensitive welcomed the new sewage system funded by the EC in 1984. Since its

completion, the 'lattice of open drains' that sullied many visitors' thoughts on Banjul survives only in the *Rough Guide*.

Flooding, the surrounding swamp and motley immigration were the frequent cause of disease. Wesley Church plaques from 1837 result from 'the epidemic, which so awfully raged at that time'. Half Die is a numerical reminder of the cholera of 1869. The control effected by British

The Gambia National Museum
merits an early visit: not as cultural
preparation for Banjul but as an
introduction to Senegambian rites and
tribal life-styles which, on a short visit,
you would otherwise at most only
glimpse. It occupies a pleasant compound
of tamarisk and palm: the colony's British
Council Centre, which after independence
became first the National Library then in
1972 the Oral History & Antiquities
Division. Here in 1982 its Monuments &
Relics Commission installed the
collection begun by B. K. Sidibe and
officially inaugurated in 1985 on the
twentieth anniversary of The Gambia's
independence.

The first objects you encounter have
been added since: a beached groundnut
cutter and life-size *kankurang*. This is not a
dance, as one guide-book says, but a
feared pseudo-demon (from whom
women, children and the uncircumcised
must hide). Masked and covered in
baobab-bark, the potent spirit incarnate
can still be seen at ceremonies such as
circumcision, warding off evil by
threatening passers-by and kicking up
dust.

Of the three levels inside, well
captioned and with welcome ceiling fans,
the main hall has exhibits numbered in a
semblance of a circuit. The first – I make
no comment – is 'Fertility'. Jola and
Mandinka 'Symbols of Female Fertility'
feature beads and calabashes held by
'women who wish to bear children'.
(Barren village wives formed a class apart,
called *kanyalang*: for them there are dolls
to carry – including an African priapus –
and sharpened ritual sticks more
fearsome than phallic.)

Second in importance, apparently, are
'Circumcision Rituals'. Despite initiation
masks, half-calabashes and colourful
'male circumcision sticks', the display

repeats the part-refrain of 'Initiation,
Marriage & Female Fertility'. Third is a
back wall of handicrafts: basketry and
wickerwork made by men and women
from raffia, reeds or split bamboo, and
weaving, the domain of the all-male
mabos. Theirs is the museum's largest
display – 'Decorating & Dyeing Cloth' –
with cotton carders and indigo beaters,
ginning boards, shuttle-boats and
spindles. 'Agriculture' is the predictable
farm-tools (*inter alia* for planting rice and
tapping palms for 'wine'). Leatherwork –
tools, dyes, sheaths, scabbards and
handbags – is the preserve of artisans
whom the Wolofs call *ude* and the
Mandinkas *karanke*. 'Products of Smithery'
include stirrups, sickles and ceremonial
staffs, drills, guns and dinky implements
in patterned aluminium.

While smiths, leatherworkers and
weavers were low-caste *nyamalolu*, hunters
could become kings. They were
accredited with magic powers (including
kummaa, second sight by night) but for all
that needed the hunting and fishing jujus
which, with guns, slings, traps, harpoons
and bows and arrows, are exhibited here.
'Household Utensils' are mortars, pestles,
sieves and soap made by baking in the
sun a mixture of palm-oil, groundnuts
and ash. 'Traditional Kingship' was
initiated by the *junjung*, royal drum, and
maintained with the help of ceremonial
staffs. (The two *chonoo/chornos* – 200 years
old, symbolically male and female and
traditionally placed at each side of the
royal *bantaba* – have however vanished.)

The *fanals* brought by the Señoras
from St Louis evolved from model homes
to boats in the hands of Bathurst's
shipwrights. The Akus were long known
for the Christmas tradition of making and
parading these paper-covered boats lit by
candles inside. Youth clubs and political
parties nowadays undertake these
spectacular projects more. (Being for the
most part Muslim, they have done so less
since Ramadhan came to coincide with
Christmas.)

Alongside 'Ornaments' like chest
bands, waist bands, anklets, bracelets and
earrings, the heads of hair-styles are fun:
the *armandija* with up to 1000 hooks; the
Mandinkas' *duni-bally* – 'No load on head'
(because of cowrie shells plaited in

topknots) – and the Wolofs' *pess-sa-gorro*,
a cheeky, braided style meaning 'Slap
your (mother?) in law'.

Before leaving the main hall, note the
holed board-game played since
prehistoric times in Africa and Arabia.
Most widely known as *bau*, it is called
worro by Wolofs (and *mancala* by the
monthly *Geographical*). Downstairs are
drums and many of the pots and musical
instruments already described. Plus raffia
bee-hives – the Mandinkas' round, the
Jolas' square, and all made airtight with
cowdung and hung in a flowering tree –
and a chamber renovated by an Irish
volunteer to promote Alternative
Technologies viz. 'scrap art'.

The objects, if not the subjects, are
more familiar upstairs: prehistoric tools,
weapons and other flint monoliths,
stones for slings or hammers, querns and
Neolithic pottery. They resemble
Neanderthal but, as was admitted, 'it is
not possible to tell whether they were
made at some later period'. Of
unquestioned antiquity, the 'Stone Circles
ca. AD 700-1200' receive the attention
they merit but are in no way explained.
Further displays describe and/or illustrate
shell-mounds, earth-tombs and Iron Age
village middens (rubbish tips), the 'Ghana
Empire ca. AD 400-1076', 'Manding
Peoples ca. 1200-1500' and the 'Coming of
Islam ca. AD 1000s', with Qoranic texts
inscribed on laterite, paper and skin, and
misplaced 'iguana', leopard and python
skins. One corner is devoted to the
'Soninke-Marabout Wars 1850-1901',
another to the 'European Presence ca.
1450-1800' with maps and rates of
exchange, Portuguese and Holland beads,
and 'Manchester goods' traded for slaves.

'Colonial Gambia 1901-36' is a gallery
of administrators, governors and royalty
– the Prince of Wales with a Gambian
guard of honour in 1925, Queen Elizabeth
II on an official visit in 1960. The
exhibition is brought almost up to date by
'Independence and Confederation 1965-
89', in which the new regime has
generously left ex-president Jawara with
Harold Wilson and Mao Tse Tung. A final
room is frankly educational with plans
and pictures on 'Our Natural Resources'
contributed by US AID and Peace Corps
volunteers.

The Arch 22 came with the new
regime, together with gilded statues at
roundabouts and roads resurfaced and
renamed. (With Bathurst founded one
year after Waterloo, many of its streets
honoured Wellington's generals. In 1998
most were, like Bakau's, Africanized.)
Towering over the roundabout with
which modern Banjul starts, the Arch
stands astride Independence Drive (which
is now blocked off because of it). The cost
of its construction in 1994-96 – some
£720,000 – was criticized as lavish for so
poor a country. Equating it with big-city
hallmarks like Big Ben and the Eiffel
Tower, the authorities' response may have
been tongue-in-cheek but, given Banjul's
general lack of grandiosity, the need to
mark a new era was a plausible
justification.

The massive, hollow-arched pediment
on its eight fluted concrete columns was
designed by the Senegalese Pierre Kujabi
and the Gambian Amadou Samba.
Thirty-five metres (114 feet) high, it was
built by the joint Gamsen Construction
Company and inaugurated in 1996 on the
anniversary it commemorates, 22 July.

One lift having succumbed to
subsidence in the soft subsoil, the other
will help you up to the café and its
panoramic terrace. The upper level of the
central bridge is occupied by the Arch
Museum: displays of textiles including
'Modern Fashions'; agricultural
implements and traditional weapons
(home-made fire-arms, bamboo bows
and arrows, and wooden swords proof
against jujus) . . . all 'Treasures from the
National Museum' except for the
handwritten text of President Jammeh's
take-over speech and the stool that he sat
upon to make it. A shop sells Arch 22
souvenirs, and upper balconies would
offer better vistas were their doors not
usually locked. Lining the road below, in a
garden that replaced the old Government
cemetery, gilded musicians sit cross-
legged on toadstool plinths in a style best
described as African Alice.

Banjul's new portal, the Arch 22

Albert Market is a tight-packed emporium of local colour (though its claim to be a period piece – and questionable tribute to Queen Victoria's consort – now rests solely on the colonial trading places opposite: 'H. R. Carrol & Co.', 'Farage No 1 Russell Street'). On Russell Street no longer, but Liberation Avenue, the market had its façade reworked in 1983 and its original plaque removed: 'Commenced 1854 Completed May 1855'. The façade as well disappeared in a fire in 1988, and the rebuilding is sufficiently recent for boards to still acknowledge its financing by the UN Development Fund and the Peoples' Republic of China.

Behind the pavement vendors of cigarettes and suitcases, the new façade, arcaded, is two storeys of numbered and roller-shuttered shops. Upstairs tailors work in booths back to back and side by side. In the first entrance alley you run the gauntlet of money-changers; ghetto-blasters on both sides of the second make the cacophony stereophonic. In the main alleys running from here to the river, the goods on sale start familiar if pell mell: cassettes, watches, sunglasses, hair-pieces and home-made soap; powdered milk, peanuts, ginger-root and jeans; T-shirts, flipflops and the latest 'platforms'; shoe polish, locks and keys, Dutch onions, combs and perfumes; Chinese platters of yams, oranges and bananas, open sacks of nuts, seeds or sugar; toothpaste and 'Special Gunpowder' China tea.

There follows a bewilderment of unknown shapes and smells. Bowls of green *fulano* powder are mixed with water to daub on hands and feet; orange resin chunks end up as starch. Incense is burned from obnoxious black balls or a *churayi santang* mixture of seeds, and tea made from bundles of the Wolofs' *mburmbur* leaves. 'Medecines' they brew from dried shoots of *kanifingo* and the fruit of the *sito*, baobab. Leaf-covered sacks contain precious kola-nuts: yellow, pink and bitter, shaped like shelled Brazils, they are chewed as a stimulant, offered to deities and appreciated as a present, peace-offering or tip.

Built around palm-trees that survived the fire, the central hexagon houses both the counters on which village women

hawk their produce (and sleep when it is sold) and the 'tailoring department'. In a vast hive of activity like a 19th-century workhouse, rows of sewing-machines are treadled beside bolts of cloth, buttons, buckles and thread. Off left, the livestock section is cows and goats tethered to old tyres; a small mosque functions near by; local carpenters work close to the river bank. And between these and the central hexagon, three silversmiths soldier on beside the reworked *bengdula*, the tourist market of batik and tie-dye, leatherwork, woodcarvings and other handicrafts.

Beaches near Banjul

Kotu, Kololi, Sanyang and Solifor Point

Cape Point to Abuko

The Bakau-Fajara promontory constitutes most of Kombo St Mary, the colonists' 'British Kombo' and the locals' *tubab banko*. The 19th-century 'Upper' or 'Foreign Kombo' consisted of the four districts to the south, which were converted to Islam and first united (by Fodi/Kombo Silla) during the Soninki-Marabout Wars.

Bounded to the west by miles of splendid beach, the Kombos give the capital a pleasant rural hinterland, easily accessible and scenically attractive. Even the name, though typically ambiguous, adds to the milk-and-honey image: *Kom bo* ('the hatred is lifted') or, also in Mandinka, 'dew' viz. 'a land so safe that not even dew will fall on you'. Though temporarily contradicted by the marabouts' warring on both Britain and the Kombos' Soninkis, the two terms indicate how the first Mandinkas found a safe and peaceful haven here after their 14-15th-century trek west.

Cape Point received its Portuguese alias *Cabo de Santa Maria* from its 15th-century 'discoverers', and the name of St Mary's overflowed to the nearby island when Britain decided on Bathurst. Captain Grant bought a first site on this breezy Cape St Mary to build a convalescent home for the colony's fever-ridden garrison. And to hang a lantern on a lofty palm as the first of the Gambia's navigational aids. (The British High Commissioner's 19th-century residence is still called nostalgically 'Admiralty House'.) Presentday diplomats and dignitaries have their homes on the cliffs above but Cape Point itself, where sea and river meet, is now monopolized by a German-owned package hotel.

Bakau is the Mandinkas' *Ba kankungo*, Shore or Coast. It is also a long drawn-out clifftop township which, one-sidedly stately with hotels and villas, straggles along Atlantic Road. This runs on into Fajara like a Thatcherite parable, the right prosperous with sought-after houses and gardens, the left a shambles of breeze-block and corrugated iron.

The Katchikali crocodile pool requires, if not a guide, then a fair resistance to unsightliness and smells. Down the narrow Bakau alleys inland from Cape Point the close-packed locals make signposts superfluous. One of the pool's Bojang owners should be at the entrance with his transistor and your ticket. A couple of crocodiles dozing on the banks, cattle egrets on a circle of water lettuce, often there is little else to see.

Associations may be of more interest than appearances. Accredited with supernatural powers, the site was revealed to the Mandinka Bojang family by a ruler's sister called Katchikali. She first tested the worthiness of one Nkooping and his sons Jaali and Tambasi by begging them to help retrieve her child, supposedly lost down a well. For showing willing, they were rewarded with the well itself, where 'any woman washed will, providing she sleeps with no other . . . before the same time next year bear a child'. Jaali and Tambasi in return rewarded Katchikali with the first thing they caught in their nets: two crocodiles, which their mother put into the well. Eight generations of Bojangs ago, these reptiles (and the *pakanju*-water lettuce which soon overgrew the site) were the prelude to the presentday scene.

When the water is too little for the crocodiles to submerge, the women to bathe ritually or the Bojangs to make *naso*-potions, there is no lack of helpers to dig deeper. The first were from Madibakunda, 'Bamboo' Madiba's place; for the re-excavation of 1981 volunteers came from all around, an impressive collective effort. In 1985 a bulldozer was borrowed.

Few tourists have difficulty heeding the warnings: 'Please for safety reasons don't touch any of the crocodiles . . . without the advise of the pool guide'. The cohabitation of 70-odd carnivores so close to Katchikali's compounds you may find surprising. I have a theory that, having always been fed fish, the reptiles here have never developed a taste for humans . . . but keep my distance just in case I have it wrong.

The promontory of Cape Point (above)

The 'Afro-colonial' Department of Agriculture

Bakau beach (below)

Saturnis moth

Abuko is synonymous here with wildlife conservation and means, for visitors, the Nature Reserve beside the Lamin Stream. In 1916 its source was fenced to form the Abuko Water Catchment Area; the density of its riverine forest increased in consequence and this attracted game. The attention of the locals, too, who holed the fence and poked in their pigs to feed, illegally tapped the protected palms for toddy and, worse, took to poaching. When in 1967 a leopard made these misdemeanours dangerous, one wily Kalilu called on the Wildlife Conservation Officer to shoot it for 'killing domestic pigs'. The latter, Eddie Brewer, was led through a hole in the fence to the scene of the crime, accompanied by his daughter Stella who continues the story: 'I compare that hole . . . with Alice's Looking-Glass, for beyond we discovered an incredible world we had not known existed. With each step, we became more enchanted by what we saw. We were walking from the familiar savannah into the cool, damp atmosphere of a tropical rain forest'. Their immediate desire to preserve this 'glimpse of what The Gambia must once have looked like' was realized in March 1968 when a 'receptive and sympathetic government' agreed to establish the reserve. Its area was extended from 188 to 259 acres in 1978 and enclosed in an eight-foot wire fence with the help of the then World Wildlife Fund. A further barrier to encroaching locals is the 2000 *malina*-softwoods planted since.

Botanists make their way by the numbered trunks of the *50 Trees of Abuko Nature Reserve* usually on sale with your ticket. In the first loose forest of drier Guinea savanna, trunks are caked with mud by tree-ants and treetops decked with their 'nests'. The path soon drops to the main Bambo Pool, pretty with White water-lilies and statuesque with palms. Planks take you across a swampy side-stream and steps past the first hide to the Education Centre, a cool green 'colonial' structure fronted by a defunct fountain and planned in 1970 as the reserve's rest house. This in 1976 made way for a rather more demanding display of ecological documentation. The upstairs 'observation galleries' have earned their laurels, not

because of the occasionally functioning telescope, but as the camera platform for a fight to the death, on the Bambo Pool below, between a python and a crocodile (who won). Here, or on the two other pools dammed in the Lamin Stream, you are most likely to sight Nile crocodiles, Nile monitors and any number of the reserve's 270 bird species.

Tight, eerie jungle follows – gallery forest, evergreen and fed by surface water (as opposed to tropical rain forest which depends on precipitation). Off left (reassurance for the claustrophobic) there are at first snatches of the open bright savanna, but soon you are engulfed by a wondrous lush dark world. Stepping over massive roots, edging round mighty trunks, you hear or glimpse the many monkeys; some, like the squirrels, may scamper over the path, snakes rustle safely away, butterflies and birds flutter in brilliant contrast to the chiaroscuro.

Abyssinian roller

Then a turn in the track and you face a hyæna. It is safely caged, though, in a compound its kin share with vultures. The wardens at the kiosk here are as welcome for their cool drinks as their friendly information. They will show you round the Animal Orphanage. In the largest, 'London Zoo' construction are no longer chimpanzees but Patas monkeys, parrots and parakeets confiscated from illicit traders. When the birds' clipped wing-feathers have regrown and the primates been rehabilitated, they are released. The adjacent enclosure of almost tame bushbuck is shared with irascible Crowned cranes and caged baboons. Alongside, behind wire, are The Gambia's immigrant lions. The first here was Whisky, imported from the Casamance and killed in 1981 by a puff adder bite to the head. In replacement (and in exchange for two hyænas) the Rabat Zoo sent Dyllis, who was due to have a mate. In February 1982, flown and 'donated to the people of The Gambia' by British Caledonian Airways, MacCal arrived from Longleat. And eight days later Dyllis died – of a virus imported by her consort to be? A second mate, Dylise, came in 1984 to provide MacCal with offspring before dying in 1999.

Purple glossy starling

Cattle egrets in nuptial plumage

Around the Kombos

Brikama's rôle in the visitor's Gambia seems doubly disproportionate. Tour firms include it in trips to Abuko, advertising it as a typical up-country township (and The Gambia's third largest). Divisional headquarters and chief town of Kombo Central, it has however little of interest save for the woodcarvers' market. Its history, too, is more remarkable than the presentday place.

Brikama in Bainunka means Women's Town, the governmental quarter established here for the matriarchal locals' former female rulers. Soninki animists, Brikama's Mandinkas stood long and firm against the Muslim marabouts. By 1873 these henchmen of Fodi Kabba's controlled every Foreign Kombo settlement save Brikama and Busumbala. Tomani Bojang, ruler of the former, even offered *in extremis* to cede his lands in return for British protection, but this – with his troops embarked in 1870 and only a 100-man constabulary left – Administrator Callaghan was unable to provide. In mid-1874 Brikama fell to the Muslims, in June 1875 Busumbala also. Chief Bojang and his Soninki subjects sought refuge in British Kombo. Though disarmed, they built a stockade at Lamin, whereupon Fodi Silla sent a threat to 'pursue them to Cape St Mary and destroy them'. The rains saved the colony: they broke and so stopped play. As a diplomatic alternative to certain military defeat, Callaghan's successor, Sir Samuel Rowe, presented Tomani with an ultimatum: on 29 September 1875, rather than evacuate the Kombos, he 'agreed to shave his head, become a marabout, adopt a Muslim name, lay down his arms and destroy his stockade'. With Fodi Silla thus assuaged and the British colony reprieved, the Kombos' two centuries of unbroken Bojang rule came to an end. Fodi Silla's counter-undertaking to let the Soninkis cultivate in peace (and his good-behaviour bonus of £50 per annum) was forgotten by the 1890s. Now however the stronger protectorate was able to take the retaliatory action that led to Fodi Silla's capture, exile and death, and to the reinstatement of a local Bojang chief.

Ghana Town is self-explanatory, but a grandiose name for a fairly minor place. (It has, like Bijilo, been bypassed by the new Kombo coast road being built with Kuwaiti aid.) The hamlet, inland, is little more than a malodorous acre in which sundry fish dry on palm-frond platforms and, dried, are then stacked flat. On the beach, however, is the unexpected sight of thousand upon thousand of superb orange-pink shells smashed and dumped. The living molluscs are fetched in here by the boatload, brought ashore in buckets on the women's heads, piled on the sand and then sorted, shelled and sold. Given what visitors pay for these *cymbium glans*, the locals are discarding a small fortune.

Sanneh-Mentering is Brufut's sacred place, an altogether prettier and more evocative spot. A short walk from Ghana Town (preferably accompanied by the alkalu of Brufut) brings you to the clifftop clearing with its simple hut and massive baobab. Graffiti are carved in the trunk, by Allied soldiers who were warned of Sanneh's sanctity and 'punished for their impiety'. While those who left their initials 'suffered indescribably all night' (from mosquitos?), the patriot who put 'Scotland for Ever' was killed soon thereafter, self-righteous locals say (war-time safely increasing the odds on such divine retribution).

The stone at the foot of the tree is for alms: a few bututs from tourists, and kola-nuts, cloth or a slave from the pilgrims who come in the hope of a baby or more profitable business. A fertility-bringing wash costs a few dalasis; a week-long vigil in the mud hut, in abstinence until the alkalu returns with a sacrificial sheep, rather more.

I had the luck to arrive once at the same time as a group of young wives from Gunjur. Beautifully dressed, all gold on silk and satin, they came with a biddy carrying her knick-knacks in a halved gourd. They first prayed and placed their coins beside the baobab, then filed down steeply for the ritual washing in seawater – a solemn, impressive procession between the lofty lines of palms.

Woodcarver, Brikama

Offloading the fishing-boats, Ghana Town

Sanneh-Mentering (opposite)

Tanji you often noticed from afar, the stench wafting as far as the smoke from its 'fish-curing site'. Since most of the old sheds were replaced by modern shelters, the approach to the village along the Kombo coast road is rather more savoury, and given interest by a new reserve. Signposted variously as 'Tanje/ Tanji-Karinti/ Tanji & Bijol Island' Bird Reserve, its 1512 acres encompass the Bijol Islands and the low-forested coastal flats north and south of the Tanji River estuary. Established in 1993, the reserve is supported by the Tanji Birders, a group of UK fundraisers some 200 strong.

The reserve has eclipsed (and the roadwork almost effaced) what little remained of a short-lived ilmenite 'industry'. Along the embankment parallel with the road ran a railway built by the Gambia Minerals Company to transport ore from its mines at Batukunku and Fantatinting to a 'wet mill' near Brufut. Abandoned because of unprofitability, the post-War project survives only in these stretches of line and equipment lying rusting in the bush.

Tanji begins with a pretty lagoon, a bridge and the civilized compound where the Spanish captain of the *Joven Antonio* breeds camels for rides on the beach. The fish-curing sheds are neither sightly nor fragrant. If not averse to smoke or kipper-smells, you can enter and see the procedure – once your eyes have grown accustomed to the gloom. Piles of firewood stand outside the older wooden sheds (which sometimes made it redundant by catching fire themselves).

The beach is liveliest when the fishing-crews come home. Children play, girls gut fish and, beneath the twisted baobabs, the Serers repair their long bright boats and stretch their nets on wooden frames to dry. The self-styled 'sipriters' (shipwrights!) nail the long mahogany planks and caulk them with *tuppa*, a rope-and-cotton

filler. The sides are painted gay with names, dates and/or Arabic imprecations, a crescent moon (the Cross of Islam) or a random geometry of triangles and squares with a face just discernible somewhere.

Driving on blithely past the police post's 'Stop Immigration & Custom' sign, you reach the Tanji/Tanje Village Museum. This was conceived and created in 1995 by a former curator of the National Museum and Juffure's (and author of *Traditional Crafts in The Gambia*): Abdoulie Bayo. It is very much a collector's home-from-home, lovingly assembled with visitors in mind (and, with its owner living in, open every day of

the year). The need for firewood for local fish-curing has for years caused deforestation here (despite the signs 'No tree felling'): Mr Bayo began his one-man counter-attack in 1994, and by '99 was planting 1700 trees per annum. Sixty species are labelled and annotated on his museum's Nature Trail.

A 'Natural History Gallery' of fish and bird prints; nets, horns, dyes and Gambia maps; turtleshells, seashells, snakeskins and a case of bugs may, like the instruments to play and/or buy, be standardly documentary. But the open-air display in the adjoining three acres gives an excellent insight into tribal life-styles, techniques and superstitions. One local tea helps cure head-aches (if poured in your pillow, not drunk); another beverage from *combretum* supposedly saved The Gambia from plague in the 1950s. Village weavers seemed particularly vulnerable: if their *pagne*

of cloth was stolen, they would suffer from pains in the joints; if hung up, it would not sell well or, if approached by a menstruating woman, bring bad luck. Teenagers are traditionally escorted to their cirumcision by the village blacksmith, whose forge is taboo to women (as are eggs to virgins because they make them barren). Village family planning consists of a ban on wives' having sex whilst breast-feeding viz. for two years after giving birth. Bringing shame on the couple if breached, the method is no doubt an even better prophylactic than the much-publicized *Fankanta*, contraception (which Banjul's Imam Fatty has denounced as 'a Western idea and a threat to Islam').

Gunjur is best reached from Brikama, via Kiti and Sifoe on a broad and generally passable laterite 'highway'. South from Tanji, by Tujering and Sanyang, the beaches grow more beautiful as the tracks deteriorate. Stumbling in and out of hamlets as their main street, the 'coast road' finally straightens and widens into Gunjur. A long approach between citrus gardens and low compounds softens the transition from blissful beach to urban bustle. Which the town centre does not lack: bush-buses parked pell mell, two mosques and two markets, police and hand-pumped petrol, a cinema and even a 'travel agent for rural development'. Populous, Gunjur is a relative metropolis.

To clear the site, the locals say, the first settlers had to raze a termite-mound, and *tungo/guru* viz. 'anthill/demolish' became the *Tunjuru* from which *Gunjur* derives. In the second half of the 19th century Gunjur was a marabout base and thus, for British officialdom, a 'hotbed of insurrection'. Fodi Kabba originated here, starting his long inglorious career a lieutenant in Maba's army, and being first mentioned in (British) dispatches by Governor O'Connor in 1855. Fodi Silla was finally routed here, too, in the expeditionary force's successful second attack. If all this is ephemeral and past, marabout religiosity survives in the nearby holy places, which for visitors form the principal interest of this chief town of Kombo South.

Kenye-Kenye Jamango ('Mosque soil') is the most important and easily accessible. Made holy by the sojourn here of one Shaikh Omar Futiu in the late 1830s, it overlooks a magnificent sweep of beach, with (relative) home comforts for the many pilgrims who spend up to a year here: praying in the palm-frond mosque, sleeping in the breeze-block shack, drawing fresh water from cement-rimmed wells and relaxing at the ritual bantaba.

You need stamina and a local guide for Tengworo ('Six Palm-trees') where, a half-mile south of Kenye-Kenye, the newly circumcised are washed. Barren women offer bread in the hope of a baby at Nyanitama-Dibindinto, north of Kenye-

Kenye behind the beach – which, under guidance again, is your best means of approach.

Kartung's claim to sacrosanctity is the Folonko crocodile pool. (Its notoriety derives from the track from Gunjur, which I rarely have the heart to use even a hired car on. Lorries loaded with sand for Banjul have pummelled it into deep ruts.)

The pool 'functions' like Katchikali's, is likewise often covered with *pakanju*-water lettuce and has resident reptiles equally unpredictable. But its site is fractionally more dramatic and, being remoter, less frequented. The authorities have enclosed Folonko's enclave with a high wire fence, and in 1980 half encircled the pool itself with a breeze-block wall. Steps down enable 'people to perform the ritual bath, wash their hair and drink a bit of the water. These people are mainly barren women or people with stomach trouble'. On the camp-fire crescent of cement blocks and logs, shady beneath the *kobo*-figs and palms, you can sit and wait for a sight of the white crocodile.

Gunjur beach, late afternoon (above) and at midday with the fishing-boats beached

Kartung crocodiles

Boatyard at Kartung (opposite, upper)

Kenye-Kenye Jamango, a holy place (lower)

The North Bank to Juffure and Niumi

The Banjul-Barra ferry was once again modernized in 1998. In May of that year the Dutch-built *Barra* was inaugurated to supplement and eventually replace the German *Banjul* and *Niumi* commissioned in 1978 and '79. (Custom-built to connect with the then-new terminals, they could not be used elsewhere – and, because of a technical oversight, could on occasions not even be used here. Ferry and terminal were incompatible at certain states of the tide: then all fell back on the old wooden *Barra*, *Bakau* and *Bulok* they theoretically replaced.)

Boarding the Banjul-Barra ferry

Embarking at the Wellington Street/Liberation Avenue terminal, you are piped off by a siren and whistle ensemble – to a half-hour of dolphins plunging their way up river; boys with cinema-usher trays of cigarettes, kola-nuts, hard-boiled eggs, Juicy Fruit chewing-gum and gumdrops called 'Cough'; blind beggars not tapping but intoning, and vendors hawking watches, radios, flipflops and plastic dolls strung like a Playboy lifebelt round their waist.

Barra at first sight is all decrepit relics of the groundnut trade: the broken-down 'evacuation belt' high on its lengthy jetty, beached lighters and the wire-fenced compound of 'bins'. But buses and taxis also clamour for fares on to Dakar; you hear as much French as English in the open-air and the equally busy covered market; Serers build boats on the bank and, a half-mile seaward, Fort Bullen is unmistakable. (The very local hotel is the price you pay for missing the last ferry back to Banjul.)

This odd assemblage is all that remains of the 'kingdom' that featured so prominently in The Gambia's pre-independence history. Christened *Barra* by the Portuguese, Niumi ('the Coast') controlled the lower river: European well-being, first at James Fort and later in Bathurst, depended to a large extent on the (proffered or enforced) goodwill of its rulers.

Fort Bullen The colonial joke that The Gambia's borders were dictated by the range of Britain's gunboats on the river was an evident nonsense already in 1816 when Bathurst was built: its Six Gun Battery and other pieces could not cover even the river mouth and extra fire-power was required on Barra Point against the slavers still trading with Albreda. This the rulers of Niumi had refused, fearing that such guns could be used against their stronghold of Essau. But in 1823 Brunnay/Burungai Sonko came to power; in 1826 HMS *Maidstone* showed the flag together with the *African*, the first steam vessel seen on the river; the governor proposed an annual £100 subsidy and – frightened, enticed and habitually drunk – Burungai agreed to the north bank's 'Ceded Mile' and the fortification of Barra Point. Two cannons were brought across from Bathurst and installed; discharged soldiers and liberated slaves soon settled alongside in the mud-hut Berwick Town. Named after the commander of the intimidating *Maidstone*, Fort Bullen saw action for the first and last time during the so-called Barra War.

Receiving missionaries 'drinking rum from . . . a tea-kettle', chasing the French Resident at Albreda back to Bathurst, Burungai so mistreated British traders in

Fort Bullen and Barra beach

The sacred crocodile pool, Berending

the Ceded Mile that his subsidy was suspended in 1830. The following August a drunken brawl at Barra led, by mistake, to the sounding of the alarm. Soldiers, ships' crews and civilians hurried across from Bathurst and misguidedly marched on Essau. Burungai's Mandinkas, forewarned, forced them back to their boats at Fort Bullen, killing, even decapitating over 30 Britons. Panic rallied the colony's inhabitants; the French moved in from Albreda for protection; 'all, who could carry arms, were drilled and enrolled in a militia; a strong stockade was erected across the island'.

Coming to the rescue from French Gorée, Commandant Louvel of the *Bordelaise* first co-ordinated this defence effort and in September, with men of the West Indian Regiment, sailed for Barra. But despite the traders' formation of the 'River Fencibles' and the despatch by Governor St Germain of more troops from Senegal, the Anglo-French force was still too small. Only on 5 November 1831 – when one British commander had been dismissed, another suffered a nervous breakdown and most of the French been recalled – did Freetown's *Plumper* and *Panchita* arrive with sufficient troops to retake Barra Point. Repeated bombardment and (when the ammunition ran low) hand-to-hand fighting finally induced Burungai to surrender. On 5 January 1832 his subjects 'publicly declared their sorrow for the outrages . . . committed in an unjust and cruel war'.

Transit camp in the 1860s for the Muslim refugees from Maba (and its twenty-strong garrison increased to 230 when the marabouts attacked in 1862), Fort Bullen is not on record as having been manned after 1870. Except during World War II, when the 1st Coast Battery took up positions against the (never fulfilled) menace from Vichy-held Senegal. The fort was in the early 1970s proclaimed a national monument.

While these various actions are well documented, no one seems to know when the building was actually completed: 64 paces by 46, circular bastions on each corner and embrasures twelve by 24 on the firing-step of its brick or laterite-block walls. Standardly inscribed with the royal 'GR' and gunmaker William Carron's 'WC°' hall-mark, cannons litter the fort. World War II counterparts rust on the beach, their emplacements on the bastions. Fort Bullen is embellished neither by the lighthouse atop another bastion nor its refurbishment in 1996 for the first Roots Homecoming Festival. This brought with it an *ad hoc* rest house and 'modern shower and toilet facilities' so that now, its brochure boasts, Fort Bullen is 'one of The Gambia's big historical tourist attractions'.

Berending Beyond the Serer 'boatyards' and their *jaka* on Barra beach, the road forks round the magnificent baobab of Essau. This rust-red/dust-red hamlet was once the Mandinkas' capital of *Yesseu* and means 'Throw yourself' (into the river?). A new north-bank road financed by the European Development Fund takes you round the Jiffet Bolong and on to Berending. Just before the village a track to the right stumbles down to the crocodile pool. The attraction of the hollow is not so much its namesake *bere n'ding* (small stone) as the riverine greenery of the small pool and the lattice of air-roots that edge it. Someone soon materializes to show the way to the burrows of the tight-palm coppice in which the sacred crocodiles repose. He

Mandinka mother at Berending

should be one of the Sonko family, descendants of Burungai and owners of the area. It was discovered, so they say, by Sumar Bakary and Fodi Brama, Sonko brothers who lie buried where the women now wash. Berending's supernatural properties, and its pilgrims' wash-and-drink rituals, are like Katchikali's and Kartung's, the only difference being that, if anyone in Berending is due to die by night, the crocodiles all cry the day before.

Dog Island, when you sail out from Banjul, is the first perceptible feature as the river narrows. So named because of the barking, dog-faced baboons that

greeted early sailors, it had in 1661 been first baptised Charles Island in honour of the third Stuart monarch. Within a year Major Holmes' soldiers numbered 119 and James Island (then manned by only 29) still took second place in the empire-builders' thinking. Its vulnerability to the mainland at low tide induced Britain to abandon Dog Island in 1666. One year later Duke Jacob of Courland disregarded the danger and established a garrison, whereupon the 'natives made a surprise attack and cut all the Courlanders' throats'. The same fate befell the Frenchmen whom one Captain Ducasse sent ashore to found a trading station in 1678. Eclipsed by James Island, the place served thereafter only as quarry and sanctuary: the British, by the king of Barra's leave, built Bathurst with Dog Island rock and, during the Soninki-Marabout Wars, 200 women and children fled from Maba to be evacuated from here in the Liberated Africans' canoes.

Niumi National Park was gazetted in 1986: nineteen square miles of coastal wetland and mangrove swamp which, rather like the Mara/Serengeti, constitute with the adjacent Salum Delta park in Senegal a single ecological unit. The Masarinko Bolong dissects The Gambia's part of the park and in it survive two rare, endangered species: the African clawless otter and West African manatee. Leopard, Spotted hyæna, kob, oribi, duiker and crocodile are species more easily seen, especially by those with time to spend on the park's Jinack Island.

That an international boundary runs plumb through the last does not bother visitors to the Madiyana Safari Lodge, and seems to go unnoticed by the Serer inhabitants of its four villages, two Gambian, two Senegalese. The visitors arrive either by boat from Banjul (sometimes escorted by Bottle-nosed dolphins, but rarely the Hump-backed variety) or by road on from Barra, then boat: up the Karenti Bolong to the sea and slow over the sandbanks of Buniada Point to the island's seven-mile beach. 'Jinack' is of course the 'Djinakh' of the Survey Department's map and the 'Ginack/Ginak/Gineck/Ginek/Jinak/Jineck/Jinek' you see advertised also.

James Island, in the language of the brochures, is the Sentinel of the Gambia River. Winifred Galloway's monograph on it is subtitled *A Nutshell History*: the history of James Island is in fact that of the whole pre-colonial country in an albeit complex nutshell.

Though the presentday patch of baobabs and crumbling walls gives little indication of its past importance, James Island with Albreda and Juffure constitute The Gambia's most popular river excursion.

After Tristan Nunes (the Portuguese Nuno Tristão) had in 1447 seen the Gambia and died, the Venetian Luiz de Cadamosto was sent south by Portugal's Prince Henry the Navigator (whose mother, most English historians hasten to add, was daughter of 'our John of Gaunt'). Joining forces with Antoniotto Usodimare, Cadamosto entered the river mouth in 1455, but the crews of their three caravels mutinied at the sight of the natives' canoes. They returned in 1456 and, sailing up to Badibu, passed a small island 'shaped like a smoothing iron'. Here they buried a sailor named Andrew, whence the original 'St Andrew's Island'. The two explorers failed in their quest for the riches of Timbuktu and/or the source of the Nile, but they did make friendly contact with the rulers of Badibu and Niumi. Diego Gomez in 1458 continued the search for the kingdom of Prester John, accompanied by an abbot of Soto de Cassa who made the first conversions. But with Philip II of Spain's seizure of the Portuguese throne in 1580, the 'Portingales' in Africa became increasingly detached. Convicts and refugees from the Inquisition, Moors and Jews expelled in 1609, they proved better traders than evangelists and, sowing their seeds with useful ambiguity, left to The Gambia both cash crops from the Americas and the mulatto Señoras.

Dispossessed by Philip II, the Portuguese pretender (one Antonio, prior of Crato) fled from Lisbon to the English court, where he survived by selling the Portuguese crown jewels and 'exclusive trading rights'. In 1588 Elizabeth I confirmed his ten-year grant of the last to a group of London and Devonshire merchants, whereas James I in 1619 preferred 'English gentlemen' for the 'exclusive right of trade to Guinea and Binney' (Benin). These odd early monopolies on speculative trade in unknown parts were often unexpectedly effective. Edward IV had in 1483 prevented two English ships sailing to 'Guinea'. Still in deference to Portuguese rights, Francis I restricted Frenchmen likewise in 1529 and, prior to Antonio's arrival, Elizabeth limited English ships to waters in which the king of Portugal 'hath not presentlie domaine, obedience and tribute'.

The various English 'patentees' did not enjoy such guarantees. The Guinea

Tobago from his godfather, England/Scotland's king James I/VI. And needing slaves for his plantations there, he sent to the king of Niumi for a plot of land at Juffure. With this source of water and firewood on shore, Courlanders under one Major Fock built the first fort on St Andrew's Island in 1651. Another was reportedly constructed on St Mary's Island (likewise leased from the king of Niumi). During The Gambia's Baltic decade, a stalwart commandant called Otto Stiel maintained such relations with the local populace that they helped him see off French and Dutch intruders (speciously entitled to Courland

ensure the safety of his garrison on Dog Island. Having ousted Otto Stiel and his seven remaining men and women, he established Britain's first West African outpost on St Andrew's Island. Which he renamed after James, the then Duke of York and Charles II's future successor.

By 1672 the Royal Adventurers were bankrupt, and replaced by the Royal African Company. The Company of Merchants Trading to Africa took over in 1752, and all maintained on James Island a poorly supplied and sporadic garrison of soldiers, artisans, clerks, gardeners, 'linguister'-interpreters and 'factors' in charge of the trading-post 'factory'.

James Island, fort and jetty

Company is less known for its mercantile success than for *The Golden Trade*, written by one of its ships' supercargoes, Richard Jobson. The subsequent Royal Adventurers, to whom Cromwell and Charles II gave patents, had to contend increasingly with European freebooters. Dutchmen independent since the Spanish War of Succession; Spanish captains redundant from the same and turned privateer; merchant-sailors from Rouen, all traded along the 'Guinea coast' with little respect for exclusive rights.

Germans even appeared on the scene in an odd teutonic interlude. Since 1640 ruler of Courland (the later Baltic states of Latvia/Lithuania), Duke Jacob had received as a christening gift the island of

possessions by the dukedom's metropolitan involvement in such unlikely developments as Sweden's annexation of Poland!).

German-Gambian friendship was cemented even by a visit to the Baltic of Niumi's black ambassadors. Then rudely interrupted by Britain, who in 1661 seized the island in what the Courlanders considered a flagrant breach of international law. The 'Royal Adventurers of England Trading into Africa' justified their acquisition by the pretext that the island was Dutch and thus at the time an enemy possession. Their envoy, Major Robert Holmes (whom Pepys describes as 'a rash, proud coxcombe'), first 'caressed and entertained' the natives of Niumi to

France meanwhile was the scene of similar politico-mercantile, state-run speculation. With Gorée seized in 1677, the Senegalese town of St Louis became the base and the *Compagnie Sénégalaise* the agent of increased French activity along the River Gambia. The ruler of Niumi in 1681 relinquished Albreda to the French (for a monthly rental of four iron bars) and Britain was, during the few periods of peace, obliged to recognise this enclave until it was negotiated out of existence in 1857. A twenty-minute boat ride from James Island, by the on-shore wells which supplied the fort's water, it epitomized The Gambia's live-and-let-live extension of Franco-British rivalry at home. When relations there worsened into war, as in 1689, the British would land and dutifully take Albreda. When in 1695 Monsieur de la Roque sailed from Albreda to James Island to demand a British surrender, he was 'regaled magnificently and the health of each party's respective king was drunk'. The British 'resolved to wait . . . and fight until death': the French fired two shots, the garrison surrendered.

The French destroyed James Fort, confiscated its sparse stores and arms and spiked the guns that their ships could not remove. The Treaty of Ryswick having ended King William's War in 1697, The Gambia reverted to the *status quo*. The Royal African Company rebuilt the fort but in 1698 lost its monopoly of Britain's 'Guinea' trade and thereby the means to maintain it. The scenario is repeated in the Spanish War of Succession, the island's ransom being the only variation. Monsieur de la Roque returned in 1702: James Fort again surrendered. His colleague however, one Captain St Vaudrille, this time offered to spare it if paid £6000. The Royal African Company agreed, but would the French accept delayed payment in three £2000 instalments? The fort, by then derelict, was rebuilt in 1703. Its garrison ('the dregs of London's taverns') mutinied in 1708 but, finding nothing worth plundering, spiked the guns and left. With the Treaty of Utrecht in 1713 the Franco-British situation once again returned to *status quo*.

The Company reconstructed and reoccupied James Fort, to see it seized in 1719 by a Welsh pirate, Howel Davis. 'While he was looting the island's stores, half the fever-ridden fourteen-man garrison decided to join him.' In 1725, on not 5 but 1 November, the powder-house exploded, removing part of the fortifications and eleven of the Europeans. The unedifying sequence of armed Anglo-French bickering, between Albreda and James Island, continued until 1763 when the Seven Years' War ended in the Treaty of Paris and the surrender to Britain of, not only Canada and Florida, but also all of Senegal except Gorée. The governor of the new Crown Colony of Senegambia resided at St Louis but,

James Fort, ravaged more by time and climate than by 18th-century 18-pounders

because of his 'overmastering aversion to correspondence', his lieutenant-governor on James Island was left do deal as best he could with the felons sent to man the garrison. Too weak to prevent continued French slaving at Albreda, he did just manage in 1768 to hold the island against 500 natives of Niumi who, attacking in twenty canoes, were bent on avenging one of their interpreters who had died unnaturally there.

The province of Senegambia ended with the American War of Independence.

Siding with the Thirteen States, the French recaptured Gorée and St Louis, retaking and razing James Fort once again in 1779. Senegal's official return to France by the Treaty of Versailles in 1783, sporadic raids by French privateers, a brief reoccupation by a sergeant's guard after Waterloo, then in 1829 James Island's final abandonment.

The French in 1779 had, with the bastions, blown up the piles which kept the then three-acre island from erosion. Not only its political rôle has gone: its physical area continues to decline as the globe warms and the Gambia's waters rise. For some time yet, though, this will not prevent your taking the outboard to the pontoon and wandering up to the roofless walls. The many generations and calibres of cannon – '1753 24 pr', 'Anno 1777', some repositioned, one off shore underwater – are tokens of the fort's vicissitudes. Its patched and hotchpotch architecture – crude mortared masonry, courses of red brick, some windows' lintels and smooth plaster still intact – results from its repeated reconstruction. Their roots undermining the twenty-foot walls, their bare boughs reaching up to the eleven slits for roof-beams, the baobabs tower as vertical counterparts to the recumbent cannons. Below the silver 'lighthouse' the eagle-eyed find in the sand blue Trade beads and broken green glass from the garrisons' bottled solace: rum.

Albreda *alias* Albadarr (from the Arabic for the full moon?) was the island garrison's on-shore sparring partner during the Franco-British altercations described above. From the first mud hut permitted by the ruler of Niumi's lease of 1681 (and destroyed by fire in 1686) grew a French trading station that was 'destroyed, rebuilt, burned, rebuilt, overrun and rebuilt again'. At one time the French presence consisted of 'two black butlers . . . to hoist their colours every Sunday'; at another, of 'only one Frenchwoman, all the men except her husband being dead' (and she having survived five spouses in three years). Until its resident slavers were ruined by the Act of 1807, Albreda (*pace* Alex Haley) must have been a busy entrepôt. And, according to the authorities, a colonial R&R centre at which 'those who were sick or jaded on James Island could come for recuperation'.

The atmosphere nowadays is more one-hut reminiscent. Weaver birds nest noisily in season by the uprooted tree trunks where the locals sun-dry fish; '*Le Commerce Africain*' is still the sign over one shack-shop. Posing in its frame of baobabs, the derelict, two-storey hulk was not a slave-house, as guides and guide-books say, but the CFAO's 'factory'. The French sold it to the authorities for one symbolic dalasi but it has clearly given up waiting for them to make of it a museum. In lieu of this (since installed at Juffure) the National Council for Arts & Culture has contributed a visitors' map-plan, and the 'Ceded Mile' was in 1995 declared a National Monument Area.

By the kapok-tree on the sandy 'village square' stood the flagstaff that, so the guides say, guaranteed the freedom of any slave that touched it. The Carron eighteen-pounder that recently replaced it, inscribed '*GR*' and made in 1810, is an apter historical feature than the gawdy gilt couple alongside

Juffure, to visitors, is a two-faced place. A fascinating object of fact and fiction, it offers, like a play on a revolving stage, two totally different scenarios. Programmed by *Roots*, most pilgrim-spectators enjoy the evocative if primitive Mandinka-village scene. They dutifully suspend disbelief and wonder at the sight of 'Kunta's bantaba tree', the 'Kinteh Kunda compound' and the widow of griot Fofana who, perched on the ancestral canopied bed and clutching her framed and faded cover-feature magazine, poses as a flesh-and-blood link with our misplaced hero.

But Alex Haley devotees will search in vain for any nearby 'village bolong . . . which took' the Kinte womenfolk 'around a turn into a wider tributary… twisting inland from the Gambia River'. They must also turn a blind eye to the 'Portuguese chapel' and, similarly a stone's throw away, the long-established French outpost at Albreda. These are part of Juffure's other décor, that of historical reality. Three hundred years before Kunta Kinte's time the Portuguese founded the first Juffure, north-east of the present site and named San Domingo. This in local parlance soon became *San Dimonko*, further corrupted into *Sandi Munko Joyo* as the later local alias for James Island. The two-floored 'Portuguese chapel' was probably a shop, store or home. Visible from the track a half-kilometre on from the Albreda-Juffure crossing, it is one of The Gambia's better ruins: small (ten paces square) but unexpectedly tall, with neat courses of mortar between its laterite blocks, patches of plaster still intact and a yellow-brick arch over one lower window.

The Juffure ceded to the Courlanders was probably closer to the presentday site. The Dutchmen captured whilst trying to evict them in 1660; Major Holmes' soldiers disembarking one year later; the African Company's agents that acquired a plot at 'Gilliflee'; the British garrison of the fort erected here in 1721; the French and English 'factors' who, well into Kunta Kinte's time, 'traded side by side in the village' of 'Gilliflee', 'Jithrey' or 'Jillifrey'… none lent credibility to the Haley theory that Juffure – 'four days up-river from the coast' – was the authentic birthplace of his historical Gambian ancestor.

In the early 1980s I realised that *Roots* did not tally with the facts and debunked

Juffure – American *Roots* pilgrims, griot Fofana's widow and Alex Haley's photo

it in a *Gambia Holiday Guide* published in 1983. I later learned that a Swedish journalist had come to the same conclusion earlier. His exposé prompted Haley to sue – but then pay out handsomely to have the article suppressed. I had no such luck. Just a tingle of gratification in 1993 when, one year after the author died rich and famous from the fraud, his archives revealed that the Kunta Kinte 'legend' had in fact been bunkum.

None of which detracts from the impact Haley's novel and TV series had in making the horrors of the slave-trade better known. (The Gambians' response has been to shift the emphasis from the American author to a generalized remembrance that they galvanize into an International Roots Homecoming Festival each June.) The history of the iniquitous commerce in 'black ivory' is documented well in the Juffure Museum. To the right of the track from Albreda, it was opened in 1996 in the Maurel Frères' entrepôt built by the British in the late 1840s. Help with the initial display came from as far afield as Ireland and Ghana, the exhibits and information from Gorée, Hull, Maryland, Wisbech and one ex-assistant manager of The Atlantic Hotel. The academic presentation was in 1998 made more graphic-attractive with painted wooden cut-outs of the slavers and their victims: slaves in shackles, plantation ladies with parasols, and a black child on a barrel-head, for auction.

There are a few relics on show – footlocks, necklocks and the double neck-yokes called *coffles*; buttons, beads, sherds, 'Bronze Manillas' (bracelets) and 'Kissi pennies' (iron bars) – but the museum's strength is its posted history. Taken from Hugh Thomas' *The Slave Trade*, the statistics are awesome: 4·65 million Africans deported by the Portuguese, mostly to Brazil; 2·6 million enslaved by the British, 1·6 million by the Spanish and 1·25 million by the French. Two thirds of all slaves traded were female; ten per cent of those caught died during capture or the 'Voyage of no Return' to the Americas.

There is however no 'Eurocentric' condemnation: the exhibition acknowledges that slavery in Africa and Arabia predated the arrival of the likes of

Sir John Hawkins. Senegambian society consisted traditionally of one third slaves. These *jongolu* could be born into servitude, prisoners of war, convicted criminals or debtors. Though universally outlawed since 1888, when Brazil finally accepted abolition, slavery is far from suppressed. In early 2000 *Time* published the distressing number of slaves still

Juffure Museum mural (above)

Roots memorabilia (below)

taken annually in Arabia and eastern Africa. Both there and further west, voluntary and temporary slavery continues: African villagers faced with famine sell themselves, simply to survive, to landowners able to sustain them.

The interest of the south-bank road on
from Brikama is initially, as compensation for the pot-holes, a series of minor
historical sites and several very worth-
while 'ecological lodges' and camps. The
maps on pages 8-9 should help locate
them.

Maka Sutu A first, fascinating
ecotouristic project is found on the
Mandina Bolong (or rather not found
without a guide, there being five overland
and three creek-approaches). If *Maka*
really is Mecca mispronounced, the
Mandinkas' *Maka Sutu* should mean Holy
Forest. Local reverence may explain the
survival of the botanical delight that two
Londoners discovered after several years
of searching: a pristine expanse of
riverine, hardwood and palm-forest, salt-
flat and mangrove creek. They bought
four acres in 1992 whereupon the locals
(the spot's sanctity being broken?) took to
felling trees. By enlisting the help of the
Forestry Department; ecologically
converting the villagers around; by
planting trees and flowers and building,
the two unusual Englishmen had by 1996
developed their 1000-acre 'Maka Sutu
culture forest'.

Brefet For another short sortie into the
outback follow the main road on past
Tumani Tenda ('the first community-
owned ecotourist camp in The Gambia')
and turn north at Bessi. The alkalu of
Brefet will escort you out from the tidy,
Jola-Mandinka compounds and down to
a beautiful bolong. A copse of ancient
baobabs, their massive corpses lying
supine on the shore, marks the site of a
former 'factory'. Established by the Royal
Adventurers in 1664, plundered by the
French in 1724, intermittently settled by
private British traders and raided by
Albreda's slavers as late as 1820,
'Barrowfat' is now a square yard of
reddish rock, grey shells embedded in its
whitened mortar.

Bintang is reached by a laterite side
'road' signposted at a hamlet called
Killing (which official maps euphemize as
Killy). Tourist maps still mention
Bintang's alias of (I)Gereja. But of this, the
Portuguese for Church; of the base built
here by Cromwell's patentees in the 1650s;
the 'Vintan/Vintang' of the Portuguese
mulattos; the factory permitted to the
French by the Jola king of Foni in 1717
(and retaken by Britain in 1724); of Mungo
Park's 'Vintain' of 1795, the presentday
inhabitants know nothing. In the absence

Toniataba, the round house

Hacking a dug-out, Tankular (upper left)

Bwiam, Wolof girl and iron pot

of local guides, one looks for historical
spoor: a site near the bolong, any trading
station's lifeline; ideally on an eminence,
for coolness and ease of defence; perhaps
surrounded by baobabs (from seeds
placed in Portuguese tombs) . . . and sure
enough, left of the jetty, the small hill was
strewn with graves and masonry, until
they were obliterated by a recent Italian
project. Unless an incurable antiquarian,
you may think the journey better justified
by the Bintang Bolong Lodge, built on
stilts above the tidal flats and mangroves.

Bwiam is named after its original
owner, one Bwiamu Sambu, and famed
(all things being relative) for its enigmatic

commissioners' and six of their Gambian escort. The chieftain responsible was hanged instanter and his village of Dumbutu destroyed. Rebuilt, it now bestrides the junction to the national park headquarters.

The reserve was set up in 1987 at Eddie Brewer's prompting and with funds from US AID but, after both disappeared, its development became spasmodic. Tourism improving and revenue increasing, Kiang West is now back in business as the most accessible and rewarding reserve up river, with a visitors' centre and self-catering accommodation at the Dumbutu headquarters and, more importantly, the greatest range of species and most varied habitats. Forty-four square miles of deciduous and riverine woodland, Guinea savanna, tidal flats and mangrove creeks, it also boasts the Gambian singularity of cliffs all of 70 feet high.

The attractions are not only birds (some 300 recorded species, and 21 birds of prey) and animals (every species resident in The Gambia being represented here). There is history, too, the Warden hastens to point out: in a patch of paving from a Portuguese trading station and vestiges of a *kollon* (well) which, situated near the clifftop viewing shelter, gave its name to this Tubab Kollon Point.

iron pot. It protrudes like the conning-tower of a buried submarine, three stumps (inverted legs?) rising from its bird-limed surface. Mention 'Dogon' to passers-by and they will show you along the track to the T-junction close by the pot. They may also recount its supernatural properties. Some *tubab* (foreigners) once dug all day without working it free. 'And when they returned to dig next day, the soil was back in place around the pot.' (After heavy rain, though, it becomes disprovingly wobbly and could, I suspect, be dislodged by anyone willing to risk offending local feelings.) In time of war the rusting pot is said to turn so that its aperture indicates the quarter of the enemy's attack.

Tankular's baobabs shade the men making bricks and hacking dug-outs with

their hoes. On the muddy beach new boats 'soak', filled with water. Shrimp-traps are slung to dry in the stunted mango and in the lowly waterfront compound (where women sit smoking pipes with babies on their backs) hangs the hamlet's only curiosity: a nondescript ship's bell, dating from 1711 and endowed with the power of ringing itself whenever an enemy or shipwreck threatens. A scrap of compensation for the track from Sankandi is the better-founded information that near by stood a Portuguese trading station.

Kiang West National Park is best visited by road via Dumbutu or Tendaba, after the highway has crossed the Brumen Bridge and swung north past Sankandi. At the last, in 1900, the marabouts shot dead two British 'travelling

Tendaba, or the remoter Kemoto, is the best base for exploring Kiang West. It is served by a signposted laterite 'highway' from Kwinella, a hamlet on the south-bank road now known more for its colourful Thursday-morning market than as the site, in 1863, of the only set battle in the Soninki-Marabout Wars. Attacking with an army of 5000 marabouts, Maba was routed here by the Soninkis, leaving 500 dead. (Relics of British intervention – four unmounted, uninscribed cannon – can still be seen en route for the park beneath Batelling's massive kapok-tree.)

A whimsical signboard to 'Tendaba Airport'; signposts to the national park; a school, fish-market and jetty with lovely river-vistas . . . Tendaba (which means Big Jetty) is little more than its visitors' camp. A Swedish sea-captain developed the two-acre site in 1972, selling out in 1976 to a second Swede long renowned as The

Gambia's only white game warden. An unusual item of décor is a World War I naval mine. 'It just floated up one day. We assume it's been defused.'

Toniataba is the last place of interest to visitors before the south-bank road is crossed by the Trans-Gambia Highway. A well-marked mile north of the road on from Kwinella, Toniataba's village centre is dominated by a remarkable round house. Its owner, Hajji Fudali Fatty, is a fine nonagenarian, white-robed and habitually telling his 'rosary' of beads in strikingly long-fingered hands. He is the last son of Shaikh Othman, a famous Mandinka marabout and alleged purveyor of jujus to Fodi Kabba and Musa Mollo. They would visit him, so the story goes, in this very house: a vast cone of thatch on six-foot walls 60 paces in circumference, supported inside by split bamboos, cement-floored and divided by once-whitewashed mud partitions.

With an interpreter, and shoes removed, you are welcomed in to hear its history: 'When Shaikh Othman *alias* Jimbiti Fatty *alias* Wuli Musa Fatty died, his son Lamin Fatty moved in. He died 120 years old and the next son, Kemu Fatty, inherited. He died at 130 and the house passed to Hajji Fudali' . . . I trusted he would live to at least 140 and was reminded of Dr Galloway's remark that 'Chronology is perhaps the weakest aspect of oral history, which tends to "telescope" lists, while genealogy tends to "expand" it again'. The place-name should at least bear out the Hajji: *Tonia*, Mandinka for Truth, which one pledged oneself to tell beneath its *taba*, kola-tree.

Kataba Fort is seasonally visible close to the north-bank road east of Farafenni. Now fighting off only the undergrowth, its ruined walls and arches survive as a reminder of Britain's colonial confrontations in both Salum and Badibu. After king Kolli had ceded MacCarthy Island, his hostile neighbour Kementeng/Kemintang proved increasingly troublesome. Faced in 1841 with a joint attack by Kementeng, the Fulas and Bambara raiders, the king of Kataba welcomed the British force, signed a treaty of friendship and commerce and gave land for the building of the fort.

Janjangbure was built, a mud-brick township, when king Kolli in 1823 ceded to Britain the island of the same name (which means Refuge). First christened Lemain(e), the island was later renamed in honour of Sir Charles MacCarthy, the African administrator so opposed to slavery that, by pressurizing a reluctant Earl of Bathurst, he succeeded in having Grant sent from Gorée and Bathurst built. Whether the late name of Georgetown commemorated Britain's third Hanoverian, who had recently died after ten years of well-documented 'madness', or his heir George IV, 'an undutiful son, bad husband and callous father, least regretted by those who knew him best', really does not matter.

Tendaba

As headquarters of the Central River (ex-MacCarthy Island) Division, The Gambia's unofficial 'up-country capital' still has much of an old-time trading outpost. The post office might have been an English chapel with its now-disused doorway Gothic-arched. Beside it, the old government rest house has the customary corrugated iron distinguished by unusual whirls and frills. The Home Government of the 1820s may have boggled at permanent building, resting content with the island's mud-brick Fort George and Fort Fatota, but the DC's headquarters is a splendid colonial pile.

From the post office, police post and a new and very narrative memorial, you can walk up the desultory main street (which is even more desultory since the south-bank road was surfaced and the river steamer sank). The long, orange-shuttered frontage of the Methodist Church and primary school seems a disappointing upshot to the years and endeavours that the Wesleyans spent here. Permitted by the king of Kataba to quarry mainland rock after 1827, merchants from Bathurst built the first stores and John Morgan the first mission station. Its congregation was swelled by the Liberated Africans and discharged soldiers settled up river. Its educational mission grew into the famous Chiefs' School reserved for the *seyfolu*'s sons (and rebuilt by the government in 1927). Then renamed the Armitage High School, it remains The Gambia's only secondary boarding establishment.

The roofless hulk of the so-called 'slave market' is unmistakable on the island's north bank. Not only self-appointed guides, even knowledgeable elders point out the wall-rings for the 'shackled and manacled slaves' inside. They are more likely to have served, I think, for bolting the doors or hitching horses. Apart from East Africa's crudely walled pens, physical vestiges of the slave-trade are few. The reason is simple: as a non-perishable commodity, human beings did not need expensive entrepôts. Gables here indicate a once-ridged roof, to keep rain off precious trading goods, not slaves; a slave-pen would not have been, as this is, floored with tiles; the regular arched doorways, neatly rimmed in brick, and generous windows subsequently blocked are scarcely compatible with a prison.

The problem is compounded, prominently, by new signs near by: 'Attention Attention! . . . Visit the Horrors of Slavery . . . Slaves underground room . . . Tip box available for any offer'. Given the township's obvious poverty, it might have been charitable not to let the truth intrude. That Janjangbure was established by the British in the 1820s is nowhere denied. There is no suggestion of sub-stantial construction prior to 1827, when the first building rock was imported. And Britain abolished slavery in 1807.

Mungo Park Memorial Only those who brave the north-bank ferry and either a hired boat or the track through Karantaba have a chance or making out the plaque on the plain cement obelisk that honours Britain's greatest West African explorer. 'Near this spot Mungo Park set out on the 2nd December 1795 and the 4th May 1805 on his travels to explore the course of the Niger.' The spot was Pisania, a then-prosperous, long-vanished trading station. In December 1795 the 24-year-old Scottish doctor commenced the lonely and epic trek recounted modestly yet with polished detail by his *Travels in the Interior of Africa*. The second departure in 1805 was again under the auspices of the African Association, but this *Mission to the Interior of Africa* had military and political objectives also. Park was given a commission and an escort of 250 soldiers 'for the purpose of dislodging the French from Albreda . . . of re-establishing English factories in the River Gambia, and of extending the relations of commerce with that and the neighbouring countries'. Frequently at loggerheads with the African Corps' Lieutenant Martyn and encumbered by his retinue (a clumsy contrast to the first journey's black boy, two donkeys and one horse), Park reached the Niger with only Martyn and three half-crazed soldiers still alive. His journal stops short on 16 November 1805 when, near Bussa, all were waylaid and killed.

Janjangbure/Georgetown, the 'slave market'

Ferry at Fatoto

Home by boat with pots bought
at Basse market (opposite)

Basse is headquarters of the Upper River Division and a largely Fula and Serahuli centre. (Its parish church is dedicated to St Cuthbert, a cowherd like many a Fula.) It is also a lively place of trade, made livelier of late, if not lovelier, by increased *trafic* with nearby Senegal, by refugees and, inversely, by Georgetown's decline. There is, seasonally, much local-crop activity. From December to March, tugs may be moored waiting for their lighters to be filled from the groundnut depot. Its eight bins, each for 700 tons, were built in 1974 when the late Gambia Produce Marketing Board took over here from private buyers.

Kapok is collected here too in February and March: lorries loaded with the white floss you see ferried from the north bank in the Dutch-built *Sandugu Bolong*. The ginnery also constructed in 1974 was in 1992 entrusted to GAMCOT, and this joint Franco-Gambian venture has made of cotton Basse's most remunerative product.

Attractions for visitors are the Thursday-morning market (held then because that was when the weekly steamer docked) and Tradition. The market's *pièce de résistance* is its array of earthenware: platters, bowls, colanders and African amphoræ, delivered by donkey-cart from Alohungari and carried away on the ladies' heads. 'Tradition' is the name of an impressive private initiative to encourage (and market) local arts and crafts. With dancers, drummers, Fula fire-eaters and a café/restaurant serving local dishes, its spinners, dyers, weavers, potters and woodworkers occupy the last surviving riverside trading depot. It was built for Maurel Frères in 1906 and leased in 1994 by a Canadian lady-volunteer as base for the splendid enterprise.

All this in Basse Duma Su, *Basse/Bassa* being a mat (on which the town's founder, one General Tiramakang, reportedly first rested). *Duma Su* (Lower Home) is literally the quarter that ventured down to the river's edge in the dry season. The rains used to flood it and then Basse shrank to the *Santu Su* (Upper Home) where it is now concentrated.

Fatoto After 1934 the mail brought up by the Travelling Post Office aboard the weekly steamer was carried on from Basse by a 'travelling postman' who, if he cycled fast enough, reached Fatoto twelve hours later. Modern visitors to Basse need only an hour or two's sortie for this 'roadhead' in The Gambia's eastern reaches. A Mandinka-Fula-Serahuli village, Fatoto in Mandinka means 'spread out', which it is, between the mast-topped hill and the baobabs along the swamp. The market has signs of life; on the dramatic banks where the deep-cleft track ends, women wash, cattle wallow and a tiny ferry shuttles when it must. But in between there are only derelict vestiges of this once-flourishing trading station. Of the six colonnaded premises standing in the 1980s only two brick hulks survive. They were impressively built, but on their walls of brick or mortared stone even the graffiti have eroded away. The crumbling white-tiled or red-brick floors are littered and overgrown; concrete lintels top doorways and windows long removed. With the air of a Western ghost-town, this easternmost administrative centre has now more cows than humans.

The Stone Circles

The Stone Circles are a Senegambian enigma. Though similar, isolated structures are found in the Sahara and as far south as Guinea, the largest known concentration lies scattered north of the Gambia in its mid-river region: clusters of laterite columns, numbering from ten to 24 and many still standing up to nine feet high. Their total, never verified, may reach three figures, but the lack of inscriptions and associated objects has frustrated all attempts to define them historically or ethnographically.

Speculation as to their age ('pre-Islamic viz. 15th-century but post-neolithic'/'as old as 100 years BC') was cut short by recent carbon-14 tests which dated some megaliths to approximately AD 750. Skeletons found in the central graves make them unquestionably burial sites. But these, the only facts we have, themselves pose further problems. The graves are older than the circles; the average height of their negroid incumbents (an impressive 5' 9") suggests a Bantu origin from the south, while all analogous megalithic cultures are found to the north: in Mesopotamia 3000 years BC, in the Egypt of the pyramids, at Stonehenge and Avebury, on Malta and even the Canary Islands as late as the 14th century.

Few accept that a tall black race originated here, evolved the Circles without outside influence and developed the iron implements buried in the graves

and used to shape the stones. The region, apart from a few modern mosques, has no other monuments. What lofty southern immigrants buried their dead here with copper and iron artifacts (the trappings of kingship) and evidence of human sacrifice; later returned to mark the sites with designs derived north of the Sahara and, leaving no clue as to the significance, moved on?

Oral history viz. local tradition has it that the builders were of Egyptian origin. Travelling with an intelligent driver taught me that the comments of visiting specialists can become local lore. The Circles have been the subject of some 30 excavations since the 1880s (all inconclusive). Anglo-Gambian, British, French and Canadian teams have all explored the area with Gambian diggers and guides, and conversational speculation may well be already part of

Stone Circles at Wassu and Lamin Koto

the gospel according to the griots. (Their 'curse' on those who disturb these tombs of the 'ancient gods/giants' was vindicated, or inspired, by the prompt death in 1931 of a certain Captain Doke and two other excavators.)

Apart from the carbon-14 dating and the physical finds, expedition reports contain little more than intelligent topographical guesswork. That relatively few workers could have quickly chiselled even the largest ten-ton columns because freshly quarried laterite is soft (hardening only after exposure to the air). That the iron tools none the less required would have been available locally because laterite contains ore-quality iron (which is known to have been smelted here since circa 500 BC). That taller stones were slid into upright position by means of an encircling trench (because the same stones have fallen back outwards into the trenches' soft refill). What is more challenging and as yet unknown is why designs and sizes vary, with stones from two to nine feet high and from one to four feet in diameter, with circles of ten to 24 stones measuring twelve-twenty feet across; why Ker Bach has a monolithic V-shape, why others are topped by a cup-shaped depression, this fitted in some cases with a neat stone ball. Artistic licence is an unsatisfactory answer: the Circles are so similar over so large an area that they must have been the work of a single society.

127